D0874013

Northwestern University

STUDIES IN *Phenomenology &*

Existential Philosophy

GENERAL EDITOR
John Wild

ASSOCIATE EDITOR
James M. Edie

CONSULTING EDITORS
Herbert Spiegelberg
William Earle
George A. Schrader
Maurice Natanson
Paul Ricoeur
Aron Gurwitsch

Sense and Non-Sense

Maurice Merleau-Ponty

Translated, with a Preface, by

Sense and Non-Sense

HUBERT L. DREYFUS &
PATRICIA ALLEN DREYFUS

NORTHWESTERN UNIVERSITY PRESS

1 9 6 4

This translation of Maurice Merleau-Ponty's *Sens et non-sens*
(Paris: © Les Éditions Nagel, 1948) is based upon the
third edition, issued by Nagel in 1961.

Translation copyright © 1964 by Northwestern University Press

Library of Congress Catalog Card Number: 64–23443

Printed in the United States of America

Introduction

ON THE EVE of the Liberation, Jean-Paul Sartre and Maurice Merleau-Ponty decided to found a journal. Sartre's *Being and Nothingness* had appeared two years before, and Merleau-Ponty was just completing his major philosophical work, *Phenomenology of Perception.* Now they were eager to test their opposed versions of existential phenomenology in all areas of experience. Sartre recalls their attitude: "We would be stalkers of meaning. If there is a truth, then one must hunt it everywhere. Every social product and every attitude—the most public and the most private—are its illusive incarnation." [1] They would use their systematic philosophies to interpret current cultural and political phenomena without resorting to technical vocabularies and without presupposing a familiarity with the history of philosophy—yet making their readers aware of the philosophical implications of events. Full of enthusiasm they founded *Les Temps Modernes.* The essays collected in *Sense and Non-Sense* appeared as articles in this and other periodicals between 1945 and 1947 when Merleau-Ponty was in effect editor-in-chief and political director of the journal. [2] Together with Sartre's articles collected in *Situations,* they display a combination of metaphysics, specificity, and lucidity unique in philosophical literature.

1. Cf. "Merleau-Ponty Vivant," Sartre's moving account of his association with his fellow philosopher which was published in the issue of *Les Temps Modernes* dedicated to Merleau-Ponty (Nos. 184–85, p. 316) and was reprinted in *Situations IV.* Throughout the Introduction we have supplied the translations of quotations from Sartre.

2. For reasons he kept to himself, Merleau-Ponty never let his name appear with Sartre's on the masthead of *Les Temps Modernes.* Sartre conjectures that this was an escape-hatch kept ready by Merleau-Ponty in case Sartre's political enthusiasm or incompetence led him to take an embarrassing stand. And, indeed, in 1952, this anonymity allowed a break over Sartre's support of the politics of the French Communist Party, without a public scandal.

Written when Merleau-Ponty's interest had just broadened from epistemology and the behavioral sciences to include aesthetics, ethics, political theory, and politics, *Sense and Non-Sense* is the best introduction to Merleau-Ponty's thought, for it both summarizes his previous insights and gives them their widest range of application. Each essay opens a new perspective on the fundamental insight that "the experience of chaos prompts us to see rationalism in historical perspective . . . , to seek a philosophy which explains the upsurge of reason in a world not of its making . . ." and elaborates this insight in a concrete context. The first part of the book, called "Arts," harks back to *Phenomenology of Perception*. The analyses of that work are focused and enriched in descriptions of the primordial perceptual world which Cézanne was trying to paint, the encounter with the Other as expressed in the novel, and the *gestalt* quality of experience brought out by the technique of the film. "Ideas," the second part of the book, introduces what Merleau-Ponty has elsewhere called his "ontology of sense" and sets this ontology in its context in the history of thought. The third part, "Politics," makes use of these ideas to clarify the political dilemmas facing intellectuals in postwar France—dilemmas which still face anyone not uncritically committed to the ideology of one of the two major powers.

Although each article in *Sense and Non-Sense* can be understood in its own terms, each can also be understood as an application of Merleau-Ponty's phenomenology of perception. Approached in this way the collection reveals its unifying theme. In *Phenomenology of Perception*, Merleau-Ponty draws on the most recent developments in philosophy and the behavioral sciences—the phenomenology of Husserl, the existential philosophy of Heidegger and Marcel, and the results of gestalt psychology—to produce an original and complex analysis of the source and status of order in the perceptual world. From Husserl, Merleau-Ponty learned a technique for describing experience without reducing it to what we think it must be on the basis of science or the demands of an epistemological theory. He also learned from the late Husserl that rationality or order is not given beforehand—either in the world of ideas, in God's mind, or in our own categories—but that order is continually made out of disorder by our ability to *give* meaning to our experience.

From the Gestaltists, on the other hand, Merleau-Ponty learned that we *discover* meanings by responding to solicitations already in our experience. Thus we are not the absolute source of meaning. We do not *give* ready-made sense *to* our experience from a transcendental position outside the world as in Husserl, but rather we make sense *out of* our experience from within it. In Heidegger—particularly the Heidegger after *Being and Time* whom Merleau-Ponty seems intuitively to understand just as Sartre understood the Heidegger of the first period —Merleau-Ponty found a philosophical version of the view that meanings are not *given to* experience but *received from* it. Merleau-Ponty, following Heidegger, calls the activity of organizing the world by responding to it from within "being-in-the-world" or "ex-istence."

Merleau-Ponty starts his analysis from the Gestaltist principle that whenever I perceive, I perceive a figure on a ground. A spot on a page appears to be *on* the page, i.e., the paper is perceived as present behind the spot. Whatever appears suggests in its very appearance something more which does not appear, which is concealed. For this reason the figure can be said to have meaning since—unlike a brute datum, and like a linguistic expression or a work of art—it refers beyond what is immediately given. For example, when I perceive an object, such as a house from the front, the back is involved in this perception not merely as a *possible* perception which I judge could be produced if I walked around the house, nor as a *necessary* implication of the concept "house." Instead, the back is experienced as *actually* co-present— concealed but suggested by the appearance of the front. Philosophers of ordinary language such as Gilbert Ryle have made a similar point by noting that under ordinary conditions we do not say that we see the front of a house but say that we see a house from the front. Both Merleau-Ponty and the Oxford philosophers would go on from such considerations to suggest there is something wrong with the traditional view that we experience "sense data"—isolated units of experience, which must then be organized by the mind.

Another way to see this same point is to notice that the referential character of perception, unlike an interpretation I give to experience, cannot be changed at will. If I have good reason to believe I am confronting a façade, then I cannot see it as a house; nor can sheer will power, or even philosophical arguments about what I can "really" see, get me to perceive a façade when I am convinced I am confronting a house. My experience organizes itself according to its own laws. Sometimes it even leads me to see what I intellectually judge *not* to be the case, as when the moon appears larger at the horizon than at the zenith.

Husserl recognized that this passivity of perception represents a difficulty for his view that we freely *give* sense to our experience. He concluded that the transcendental ego which gives the meaning must develop habitual ways of sense-giving over which it has no control. Sartre rightly objects that the notion of a pure spontaneous transcendental consciousness being bound by habits is absurd. He suggests that pure consciousness does not really form habits but deceives itself into thinking it has done so in order to limit its awareness of its agonizing freedom. This only displaces the problem. It is unclear in Sartre's theory why a pure consciousness is afraid and how it can delude itself. In the 1920's Gabriel Marcel pointed out that "I am my body." Merleau-Ponty takes up this suggestion and is the first to argue—and herein lies his originality in the phenomenological movement—that the perceptual habits are formed by the embodied person.

Like Marcel, Merleau-Ponty means by "body" neither an object known from without nor a pure subject completely transparent to itself. For Merleau-Ponty the body is just the capacity to experience perceptual solicitations and to make them more determinate by moving to reveal what is concealed. Instead of *judging* that there may be more to objects than is revealed, our body is ineluctably *set to see* more, and this anticipation—which we cannot arbitrarily alter—explains our experience of the other sides of objects as co-*present*, not just as co-*meant*. This bodily set-to-explore—the correlate on the side of the subject of the figure-ground structure of experience—thus turns out to be precisely that organizing activity which has been called "ex-istence." Merleau-Ponty alludes to this fundamental role of the body in his *Sense and Non-Sense* essay "The Film and the New Psychology" when he concludes: "We must rediscover a commerce with the world and a presence to the world which is older than intelligence."

Our body, then, is our way of being-at-the-world-from-within-it. In order to perceive, we must be involved in the world we are perceiving. As Merleau-Ponty puts it in his posthumously published book *Le visible et l'invisible* (Paris, 1964), "Our body is both an object among objects and that which sees and touches them." This philosophy of incarnation has two revolutionary consequences.

First, we must have an "outside" and thus be exposed to things and to others if we are to have a world at all. For Merleau-Ponty the problem of our relation to others does not begin with the question: How could I as a mind ever get to know other minds? Rather, he gives us a description of the way I, as an embodied person, am related to other embodied persons. Phenomenologists and linguistic analysts agree in calling into question the classical Cartesian separation of mind and body and the related claim that we know our own feelings by introspection and the feelings of others by deductions from their behavior. As Merleau-Ponty says in his discussion of the new psychology, "Introspection gives me almost nothing." On the other hand, everyday experience shows the body to be expressive. Therefore, "We must reject that prejudice which makes 'inner realities' out of love, hate, or anger, leaving them accessible to one single witness: the person who feels them. Anger, shame, hate, and love are not psychic facts hidden at the bottom of another's consciousness: they are types of behavior or styles of conduct which are visible from the outside. They exist *on* this face or *in* those gestures, not hidden behind them."

Second, since it is from within the world that we perceive, our experience is always perspectival, i.e., incomplete. For although we can be practically certain for example that we see a house, there is always more to the object than we can ever perceive. The reference of the figure which leads us into the ground may always be misleading, and upon further investigation we may discover aspects of the object which bring about a re-organization of our experience so that we see the object in a different way or even see a different object. True, we do not often notice this feature of experience; and when we do, we discount it as a change in our perception of the object rather than a change in the object itself. The object, we assume, is completely determinate and independent of our investigation of it. This is an inevitable prejudice, according to Merleau-Ponty. The basic task of phenomenology is to overcome this *"préjugé du monde"* by describing the way experience *develops*, uncovering the steps by which perception hides its activity of organization and thus leads us to see the object as an independent entity. Phenomenology, then, is not simply the study of how objects appear to common sense but is a description of the way objects *arise*. This shakes our perceptual faith in the independent solidity of objects—or rather, it calls our attention to the fact that it is indeed a *faith*. A study of the genealogy of objects reveals the fact that perceptual meanings can become stabilized but are never absolutely secure. It makes us aware that our experience is always meaningful yet always menaced by disorder and non-sense.

If concepts could in turn be shown to grow out of perception and therefore to reflect its irreducible contingency, reason and order would be neither prior to experience nor guaranteed. This would be the final step in developing what Merleau-Ponty calls an "ontology of sense." *All* experience would be construed on the model of perceptual experience, which is never totally without meaning and whose meaning is never definitive. Man would move between chaos and the absolute.

At the time he was writing the articles in *Sense and Non-Sense*, Merleau-Ponty was already planning a volume to be called *The Origin of Truth*. This book was to "give a precise description of the passage of perceptual faith into explicit truth" (as a footnote in "The Metaphysical in Man" in *Sense and Non-Sense* attests). He was still at work on this project when he died 15 years later. Lacking this final link in his argument, we will have to judge the value of his ontology of sense pragmatically, by seeing whether it casts new light on diverse areas of our experience. Merleau-Ponty would have welcomed this challenge;

the success of *Les Temps Modernes* and the diversity and originality of the essays which follow are the most persuasive justification of his ontology.

I

The phenomenologist is not alone in investigating how rationality is achieved. The painter and the writer are engaged in the same enterprise. According to Merleau-Ponty, "the joy of art lies in showing how something takes on meaning." Cézanne, for example, was not interested in the naturalistic painting inherited from the Renaissance which assimilated objects to pre-existent rational forms and placed them in geometrical perspective. Nor was he satisfied with the attempts of the Impressionists to dissolve this objective order into its original elements of light and atmosphere. He was engaged in what he felt was the futile but fascinating task of painting a landscape or a still life *as it takes form*. He tried to paint the genealogy of solidity.

Similarly, with the breakdown of rationalism the novel and philosophy have converged in their concern with man's experience of the world prior to all thought about it. In their novels Sartre and Simone de Beauvoir try to express the struggle involved in *becoming* rational and *developing* a morality. In "A Scandalous Author" Merleau-Ponty defends Sartre's obsession with the chaotic and disgusting as an attempt to dig beneath the perceptual and social order to discover its roots in a more savage experience. "Metaphysics and the Novel" takes up this point in more detail. It argues that Simone de Beauvoir's novels are not immoral but deal with people who cannot accept the finished and eternal norms of their society and must return to contradictory and menacing human interactions in an attempt to work out their own moral order through honesty and generosity. No matter what its subject, the technique of the film is pre-objective *par excellence*. Although the traditional painter may present a finished object and the novelist can break in to say exactly what he means, the essence of the motion picture is that it conveys the meaning of a scene through the rhythm (the duration and sequence) of its shots. Thus it reproduces the way meaning emerges through the organization of experience.

Merleau-Ponty claims that in the 20th century "the novel and the theater will become thoroughly metaphysical." If he has grasped the central concern of contemporary consciousness, we would expect to find his approach illuminating outside France and in areas other than those he explicitly treated. A test case might be the theater of the absurd, about which a great deal has been written but which still seems to leave both critics and audiences groping for the right words. Can the theater of the absurd be understood as a study of the achievement of rationality? Not in its early phases, to be sure. Ionesco's plays begin normally enough, but once irrationality erupts, we witness the accelerating disintegration of order. Even here, however, Merleau-Ponty's theory is helpful. He recognizes that "since there is no longer any human nature on which to rely . . . , in every one of man's actions the invasion of metaphysics causes what was only an 'old habit' to explode." But Merleau-Ponty would say of Ionesco what he says of Camus' *The Stranger*. "It is easy to strip language and action of all meaning and to make them seem absurd. . . . But that other miracle, the fact that in an absurd world language and behavior do have meaning for those who speak and act, remains to be understood."

Recently, however, a new form of the theater of the absurd—which Merleau-Ponty would undoubtedly have recognized as "thoroughly metaphysical"—has appeared in England. These are the plays of Harold Pinter. The Aristotelian convention that a drama has to have a beginning, middle, and end expresses a conception of order in which each event has intelligible antecedents and therefore intelligible consequences. As rationality becomes a problem, transitional dramatists like Ionesco reject this view. They study disintegration. Their plays may have a beginning but no end (Ionesco), or neither a beginning nor an end (Beckett). A metaphysical drama in Merleau-Ponty's special sense of the term however, would have a middle and a (relative) end—but no beginning. "The germ of universality . . . is to be found ahead of us in the dialogue into which our experience of other people throws us by means of a movement not all of whose sources are known to us."

Pinter's plays focus on disorder: abrupt and absurd events which are never explained. This can be an intrusion of disorder from above, as in *The Dumbwaiter*, where a dumbwaiter descends with a clatter into the hideout of two waiting gunmen; the eruption of disorder from below as in *The Room*, where a blind Negro taps his way up from the dank cellar to intrude into Rose's room; or a kind of horizontal intrusion as in *The Collection*, when two ménages find themselves involved in an incomprehensible triangle. An analysis of any one of these plays leads critics to conclude that Pinter is concerned with religion, the unconscious, or social interaction respectively; but this misses the common theme of all three works: something savage intrudes into an island of order, suddenly revealing this island's vulnerability and demanding a response. The response may be either an attempt to answer the old questions—to find reasons for the uncanny event and place it in a conventional context (e.g., Gus' questions in *The Dumbwaiter*)— or it may be an unquestioning acceptance of authority, as when Ben tries to supply the exotic dishes the dumbwaiter demands. Or one can incorporate the threat, as when Rose gives up anxiously trying to see everything in a (rosy) light and, with shock and perhaps relief, finds herself plunged into blindness. Whatever the response—and there is always some character who takes up the challenge forced upon him— Pinter's plays, unlike Ionesco's, do not continually re-enact an acceleration into chaos. They move toward the re-establishment of order. One is left with the uneasy feeling that it is a menaced and precarious order which may at any moment disintegrate and have to be achieved again; but, as Merleau-Ponty remarks in his discussion of politics, man is "thrown with other men into a drama which will not necessarily end well but which at all events is moving toward some end." There are constant upsurges of spontaneity and contingency, but the miracle is that with the aid of language, society, convention, and creativity we always take them over and make sense of them—for a while. Merleau-Ponty dwells on the theme that absurdity is not accelerating but is constantly being tamed. Sartre is not wrong to insist that we deceive ourselves when we assume that our meanings are securely anchored in being: life requires risk and creative effort. But it is another kind of self-deception to suppose that, just because there is contingency, no order can be achieved. While Sartre and Ionesco try to show that man is condemned to absurdity, Pinter dramatizes Merleau-Ponty's contention that "we are condemned to meaning."

At the end of a Pinter play a member of the audience has "understood" when he has given up expecting an explanation of the abrupt intrusion. Like the characters, the audience can make sense of events only in terms of their effects; the onlookers are forced to participate in the generation of sense from non-sense. We are forced to stop asking the Aristotelian questions. Then we discover along with the characters that, as Merleau-Ponty puts it, "existence is the very process whereby the hitherto meaningless takes on meaning."

II

It should not be surprising that Merleau-Ponty is able to throw into relief certain unique features of contemporary art by taking perception as a model for artistic activity. As he suggests in his Preface, his interest in perception is itself an expression of the contemporary concern with the basis of rationality. In "Ideas" Merleau-Ponty situates this concern with respect to other thinkers. He shows how the categories of the phenomenology of perception can be understood as an outgrowth of, and contribution to, the behavioral sciences, how a model of existence based on perception sensitizes us to the insights and limitations of previous philosophers, and how it suggests constructive criticisms of contemporary philosophy.

In his discussion of painting and the film, Merleau-Ponty makes constant use of the findings of the gestalt psychologists. The discoveries of the "new psychology" also turn out to be essential to the behavioral sciences. In their study of perception, the Gestaltists found structures of experience whose organizing principles are independent of our explicit awareness and conscious control, yet which have to be understood as if controlled by an idea, i.e., a function or goal in respect to which the parts in the structure are assigned their role. In "The Metaphysical in Man," Merleau-Ponty tries to show that this notion of a meaning which no one need be reflectively aware of must be carried over to the other sciences of man if one is to make sense of phenomena in the fields of linguistics, sociology, and history. Each of these disciplines has become stultified by trying to understand its subject matter either in terms of mechanical causation or in terms of the working out of a conscious idea. They have oscillated between empiricism and idealism. Since in these areas there are no isolated elements unaffected by the wholes of which they are a part, to be linked by cause and effect, "We must learn to recognize a totality where phenomena give mutual expression to each other and reveal the same basic theme." In the disciplines under discussion, this amounts to recognizing the "sublinguistic structure" or "the spirit of a society." *Sense and Non-Sense* as a whole illustrates this technique. In seeking to reveal the underlying theme of our age, Merleau-Ponty takes up various aspects of our culture and calls attention to their typical features. The theme which emerges can be formulated as a concern with the status of reason, but this idea is empty apart from the paradigm cases which embody it, just as a list of the common traits of the members of the Jones family may not capture their family resemblance as well as a perspicuous arrangement of the family around one of its typical members.

Since the ultimate "miracle" which confronts Merleau-Ponty in his study of perception is the advent of sense from non-sense, the classical philosopher most attractive to him is Hegel. This may seem strange at first, since Hegel was Kierkegaard's favorite whipping-boy. But Hegel was introduced into France only one generation ago, after idealism had run its course in Germany, England, and America. Merleau-Ponty, therefore, has a fresh understanding of Hegel's significance. Hegel is the philosopher "who started the attempt to explore the irrational and integrate it into an expanded reason." The dialectical philosopher was the first to reject the traditional opposition of matter and form shared by empiricists and idealists alike (the view that experience can be analyzed into meaningless data to which the mind gives form or meaning) and the first to affirm that experience itself is pregnant with meaning. Hegel contended that it was precisely the duty of the philosopher to "reveal the immanent logic of human experience." He was the first to show that meaning had to be achieved, that time and tragic sacrifices are required for reason to become manifest in history. But Hegel was still a classical philosopher—albeit the last. He held that the triumph of reason was assured from the start, that the final resolution of the contradictions in history was implicit in each stage of the historical process. In the language of Hegel's *Logic,* the Absolute is prior to history.

In Merleau-Ponty's view, Hegel failed to take seriously the contingency of experience evident in the perspectivity and incompletability of perception. If there is a meaning implicit in all experience which will eventually be made explicit, then in the end the perspectivity of perceptual experience will be overcome; everything will be clear, there will be no figure concealed in the ground, no chance of error, and perception will have turned into science. For embodied knowers this can never be the case. Once we recognize the irreducible contingency of perceptual experience and the fact that moral, cultural, and political phenomena are founded on perception, we are no longer able to claim any guaranty for the ultimate achievement of order. This is Merleau-Ponty's way of stating the Kierkegaardian critique of Hegel without appealing to moral and religious experience. Hegel attempts to overcome the incompleteness and contradictions in individual experience by absorbing the individual in a universal harmony, thus eliminating the incarnate perceiver (the epistemological equivalent of Kierkegaard's moral individual) who raised the original difficulties.

Kierkegaard opposes his philosophy of existence to Hegel's absolute idealism; Merleau-Ponty existentializes Hegel. Emphasizing the dialectic while playing down the Absolute, he proposes basing Hegel's *Logic* on his *Phenomenology of Mind* rather than the reverse. The result is a pruned Hegelianism modeled on perception—a true genealogy of meaning in which the later stages are not contained in the earlier ones.

This recasting of Hegel's view of the Absolute necessitates recasting Hegel's theory of the great man. According to Hegel, the Absolute actualizes itself by using men unaware of the ultimate meaning of the needs of their age or the significance of their action. This is the famous "cunning of reason." Merleau-Ponty agrees that meaning comes into the world through the thought and action of men—this is the "metaphysical in man"—but since there is no Absolute, men must be aware of the forces of history in order to help them to expression.

The introduction of conscious activity, or praxis, transforms Merleau-Ponty's already existentialized Hegel into Marx. Marx's answer to Hegel's Absolute idealism, as Merleau-Ponty understands it, is not materialism but a philosophy of human action. Man, as a creature of needs caught in the non-sense, the frustrations, of a given society, must force these contradictions into the light until they become unbearable and must then transcend them in some new, temporary resolution. The greatness of Marxism lies not in its having treated economics as the principle or unique cause of history but in its treating "cultural history and economic history as two abstract aspects of a single process."

Marxism thus understood illustrates and justifies Merleau-Ponty's conception of the sciences of man. An aspect of a culture or a personality cannot be understood in isolation. An ideology may function differently—as right or left, bourgeois or proletarian—depending on the total historical situation. And just as, in the understanding of a person, all factors—although interdependent—are not equally important (bodily behavior being more reliable than fleeting feelings), so in the understanding of history the economic perspective, the way men set up their relation with nature and with each other, is of fundamental importance. "Not that this explains everything in the cultural order, but no progress can be made in the cultural order, no historical step can be taken unless the economy, which is like its schema and material symbol, is organized in a certain way." A view of man cannot be divorced from man's needs and social situation without becoming abstract, i.e., merely another ideology.

This is the weakness Merleau-Ponty finds in Sartre's *Being and Nothingness*, which in general he wholeheartedly defends for its emphasis on the contingency of experience. Sartre's philosophy is still a philosophy of consciousness in spite of its concern with involvement, and consciousness as pure nothing is *at* the world but not *in* it. Consciousness in Sartre lacks the opacity necessary to account for the figureground character of perception and the content necessary to account for its involvement in a certain society and history. Merleau-Ponty "expects the author to develop a theory of passivity."

Merleau-Ponty finds his critique of Sartre, as well as his own theory of how to overcome Sartre's difficulties, already anticipated in Marx's notion of praxis. "Once man is defined as consciousness, he becomes cut off from all things, from his body and his effective existence. He must therefore be defined as a relation to instruments and objects—a relation which is not simply one of thought but which involves him in the world in such a way as to give him an external aspect, an outside, to make him 'objective' at the same time that he is 'subjective.' " Lacking a theory of passivity and involvement, Sartre has no place in *Being and Nothingness* for an account of society and history. He has lost Hegel's and Marx's insight into the dialectical relation of man and his world. "The book remains too exclusively antithetical: the antithesis of my view of myself and the other's view of me, the antithesis of the *for itself* and the *in itself* often seem to be alternatives instead of being described as the living bond and communication between one term and the other."

Sartre accepted this criticism. As he remarks in his memorial article, "It was Merleau who converted me. . . . He taught me [concerning] that . . . action which since Hegel and Marx has been called praxis." Sartre's *Critique of Dialectical Reason* shows he learned his lesson well. He echoes Merleau-Ponty in referring to his former existentialism as an "ideology," and he accepts (without acknowledgment) all of Merleau-Ponty's specific suggestions.

Just as in "Marxism and Philosophy" Merleau-Ponty anticipated by some 15 years the combination of Marxism and Existentialism which Sartre has just produced, so in "Concerning Marxism" he anticipated its dangers. Sartre accepts the Marxist view without reservation. For him it provides Knowledge with a capital "K." He quotes with approval a Marxist claim that "Marxism forms today the system of co-ordinates which alone permits it to situate and to define a thought in any domain whatsoever—from political economy to physics, from history to ethics."

Even in 1948, when he was nearest to Marxism, Merleau-Ponty was more cautious. He drew a firm line between his position and what he considered the erroneous view of the Marxists. Marx had indeed brought philosophy down to earth and given a central place to man in the achievement of rationality. *Marx,* himself, even realized the contingency of history: that chaos and absurdity were one of the possible ways for history to end. But *Marxists* still share the traditional assumption that the achievement of order is guaranteed. The revolution will occur; the proletarian class will triumph and put an end to the contradictions of history. It is this assurance that the end of history is implicit in each of its stages which Merleau-Ponty rejects along with Hegel's Absolute. Even if history has been rational up to now, we have no guaranty that it will continue to be so, since we no longer believe in God or the Absolute. "The date of the revolution is written on no wall and in no metaphysical heaven." All action is open and therefore menaced. There is not even a guaranty that the supposed progress up to a point may not turn into chaos and have to be retroactively crossed off, just as the concordant developing perspectives of a perceptual object can, by its later breakdown, show the object to have been an illusion. If we cannot be sure that *in the end* history will produce a classless society in which all needs are satisfied, we cannot be sure *now* that the Marxist perspective is the best way to understand contemporary events.

This might seem to contradict Merleau-Ponty's argument that when events are "put in perspective" economic analyses provide the "principal condition" for understanding society. But Merleau-Ponty is certain only that our relations with nature are *fundamental*, i.e., that other cultural relations presuppose them just as the personality requires the body; their explanatory power is not assured. In "Concerning Marxism" he holds that "we retain the right to give [economic conditions] a privileged place in our analysis of phenomena, if it has been established that they give a more faithful indication of the course of things when one is considering a sufficiently broad segment of history." But this does not mean that a Marxist analysis is helpful in the short run of day-to-day politics or that it will continue to be useful even in the long run. We can only test the hypothesis on events and must not force events into our "explanatory" mold. We have no assurance that we have discovered the secret of history.

If Merleau-Ponty were to review the recent work of his self-avowed pupil, he would certainly criticize him severely for having forgotten the contingency of perception and for propounding the Marxist version of the recurrent philosopher's illusion—the illusion of absolute clarity—which Merleau-Ponty seeks to reject so as to see clearly (or, better, to sense truly) the obscure order in actual events. We must indeed try to understand events, but history, like perception, is perspectival. Man can act only from within a situation, this being understood in terms of his own background (from which he can never be completely emancipated) and in terms of the anticipated meaning of his action (never fully realized by the action itself).

Man does not *give* sense to history, i.e., apply categories to senseless events; nor does he simply *read off* the meaning of a process inevitably working itself out. He must be ready to articulate and amplify whatever meaning he finds, make what sense he can of events. We are simply "invited to make the logic of history triumph over its contingency without being offered any metaphysical guaranties." History leaves man free to have greater or less understanding of his situation and thus to act effectively or ineffectively in the world. It is with this subtle and sobering sense of history that in 1945 Merleau-Ponty took the last step from the ambiguities of perception to the risks of political action.

III

During the Occupation Merleau-Ponty learned how men are used by history. Each person has a social role; and, in an occupied country, anything he does, any public pronouncement he makes, is an action he performs as a citizen rather than as an individual, affecting everyone— victor and vanquished alike. Not a person's intentions but the outcome of his acts are judged; no one's hands are clean. As soon as the war was over, Merleau-Ponty recorded these discoveries in the first issue of *Les Temps Modernes:* "We were no longer permitted to be neutral in the combat. For the first time we were led not only to awareness but to acceptance of the life of society."

The combat, moreover, did not end with the war. Merleau-Ponty and many other intellectuals returned from the Resistance with the realization that the Occupation had brought to light what the illusory rationality of the prewar period had masked: the fact that society is torn by conflicts and that no act is without complicity. In "The War Has Taken Place," Merleau-Ponty expressed the general mood. Outside the university, freedom is inseparable from power, and values must be made to participate in existence. Freedom, individuality, and rationality have to be won in interaction with others. True, the contradictions in a society distort everyone and everything within that society, but men's actions can be efficacious in overcoming these contradictions. Merleau-Ponty emerged from the war as a spokesman for Leftist French politics.

His first inclination, again like most other French intellectuals at the time, was to see the social conflict as a class struggle and to embrace revolution as the only hope of resolution. The political analyses collected in *Sense and Non-Sense* (written during his first two years as political director of *Les Temps Modernes*) reveal the farthest limit of his swing to the Left. At a time when Sartre admits that he "stuttered in the language Merleau-Ponty already spoke," Merleau-Ponty surveyed the political situation of postwar France. He concluded that "reformism was in point of fact impossible," that the choice was therefore "socialism or chaos," and he recommended that one "pursue what is, in effect, the politics of the Communist Party."

Even in this first period of enthusiasm however, he was by no means naïve; he accepted the policy but not the philosophy of the Party. His discussion of Marxism as a political movement remained true to his philosophical critique. The burden of his essays is that there is no absolute point of view on history, no guaranty that Marxism will finally triumph. He verges on writing off the categories of Marxism as so general as to be useless for understanding contemporary events or determining political action. The coming of the revolution is not a fact but a "vow." His commitment to the Communist Party is not based on the conviction that it *will* win but follows from his judgment that it should, for "the world will not become organized, will not stop rending itself . . . unless the men who are least involved with the special interests of imperialisms regain possession of the economic apparatus."

This total change in the means of production, moreover, cannot be brought about by liberal reforms. "If one's goal is to liberate the proletariat, it is *historically* ridiculous to try to attain that goal by non-proletarian means, and choosing such means clearly indicates that one is renouncing one's pretended goal." Since revolution was impossible at the moment, the only alternative was to align oneself with the party which spoke for the workers—and then wait. This was what it meant at that time to pursue the politics of the Party. As for the outcome, "We will play this waiting game without illusions about the result to be hoped from it and without honoring it with the name of dialectic."

This is Merleau-Ponty's consistent view throughout *Sense and Non-Sense*. But a note added to "For the Sake of Truth," presumably in 1947, indicates a change. The U.S.S.R., Merleau-Ponty discovered, had lost faith in the world revolution and was representing the interest not of *all* workers but only of those in Russia. This made it necessary for the non-Communist Left to state clearly why it was not Communist. Merleau-Ponty's subsequent writing reflects this change. He emphasizes the goal rather than the Party.

He had written in his article on faith that "man's value does not lie in . . . an unquestioned faith. Instead, it consists of a higher awareness of . . . when it is reasonable to take things on trust and the moment when questioning is in order." When word reached him in 1950 that there were Russian concentration camps, he felt the time for questioning had come. He still affirmed that "we have the same values as the Communists" but declared, "We may also think they are compromised in being incarnated in today's Communism." He was no longer willing to "further their politics."

Merleau-Ponty lost his Communist friends but for a time still remained political director of *Les Temps Modernes*. This was the first stage of Merleau-Ponty's changing relation to Sartre. As Sartre was at last "learning there was history," Merleau-Ponty was becoming increasingly aware of its complexity. The last straw was the evidence that the North Koreans had started the war in Korea. Merleau-Ponty discovered that Stalin too could be imperialistic. Although he remained on the board of *Les Temps Modernes* for two more years, he refused to write any more articles about politics. The final break, as recounted by Sartre, came in 1952. It did not express a new realization; it simply expressed the fact that Merleau-Ponty and Sartre were temporally and temperamentally out of phase with each other. Merleau-Ponty was always a step beyond Sartre. Moreover, as Sartre himself put it, "I was more dogmatic; he was more *nuancé*." At a time when Merleau-Ponty had become disillusioned with Communism, Sartre chose increasing activism and Communist sympathy—simply as an absurd act of will. Or so it seemed to Merleau-Ponty, who found just the opposite meaning in day-to-day political events.

In *Les Aventures de la Dialectique* Merleau-Ponty publicly attacked the politics of Sartre and *Les Temps Modernes* for being confused, credulous, and arbitrary. "What we see [of the U.S.S.R.] is not sufficient to prove that the interest of the proletariat is in that system," he wrote. In 1945 he thought the only alternative to revolution was chaos. Now the time had come "to know whether there isn't more of a future in a regime which does not claim to remake history from the bottom up but only to change it."

To Sartre and the Communists this change seemed shockingly inconsistent. Hadn't Merleau-Ponty rejected reformism as a bourgeois mystification? They could recall his vow in "Faith and Good Faith": "If the individual goes along with Party . . . , it is because the Party has proven its worth, because it has a mission in history, and because it represents the proletariat." But such a reversal was consistent with the deeper theme of Merleau-Ponty's ontology of sense. His approach to politics had always been empirical. He had tried from the start to free himself from the French intellectual's tendency to live in abstractions. Now he had another ideology to combat: the idea that there was "true history" carried by "a revolutionary class." "Once we have conjured away the nostalgia of Communism," he wrote, "we awaken from daydreams and everything becomes new and interesting." The question whether Communism would serve the interests of the proletariat had to be decided on the basis of the available evidence, and the evidence showed neither that the Party had a mission in history nor that it had the proletariat's interest at heart. Merleau-Ponty continued to learn the lessons of history, whereas Sartre remained loyal to his master's cast-off discovery.

In "Metaphysics in Man" Merleau-Ponty had warned against the danger of an Absolute Knowledge. "If I believe that I can rejoin the absolute principle of all thought and all evaluation . . . , the suffering I create turns into happiness, ruse becomes reason, and I piously cause my adversaries to perish." Still, at that time he did not doubt that the

Communist Party in some mysterious way allowed for individual criticism—"an exchange between private judgments and Party decisions." Now Merleau-Ponty read the signs differently. Without retracting his earlier criticism of the parliamentary system (that it can be controlled by the powerful by means of the press, etc.), he concluded that one must work within a parliamentary regime, "for the parliament is the only known institution which guarantees a minimum of opposition and at least some truth." This reluctant defence of democracy is not an optimistic affirmation. Rather, it results from rejecting the pessimistic conviction of the Right (that social order is so precarious that it must be preserved at all costs) and the optimism of the Left (which affirms that the perfect life to come after the revolution justifies all sacrifices). He bases his toleration of parliamentary democracy on a sense that, in history as in perception, disorder may always erupt but order and stability generally prevail. "Methodical optimism," as Merleau-Ponty calls it, suggests that—since there can be no definitive solution and need be no forcibly imposed order—democracy is the least possible political evil. This conclusion strikingly resembles the view of Reinhold Niebuhr and the American intellectual Left.

IV

The last two essays in the collection are not strictly political. Merleau-Ponty takes up questions of faith and commitment, first in a discussion of Christianity and then in an examination of the moral situation of modern man.

The essay on "Faith and Good Faith" is interesting because it brings Merleau-Ponty's agnosticism so close to the existential Christianity of Kierkegaard that the distance which separates them is sharpened by contrast. Like Kierkegaard, Merleau-Ponty sees the Incarnation as the central experience of Christianity. This seems plausible enough; but, as Merleau-Ponty points out, Augustine's religion was still a religion of the Father, of direct communion with a God beyond the world, and Christianity has remained marked by this beginning. Kierkegaard makes the same point when he protests that Christianity is in danger of understanding itself as a religion of immanence, and he sees in the Incarnation the proof that salvation is not already within us but resides in *our relation to Another*. Merleau-Ponty shifts the emphasis from Christ by regarding Christianity as the religion of the Spirit. Thus Merleau-Ponty gives the Incarnation a social interpretation. For him, it shows that "God is no longer in Heaven but in human society and communication." His faith is "not in a doctrine or a party but in the relations among men." There is no mention of the fact that the individual Christian is supposed to achieve his salvation through his relation to Christ or, as in early Kierkegaard, to some other specific human being who is a Saviour for him.

According to Kierkegaard, faith is an irrevocable commitment to someone or something which so defines the self that to deny this commitment is to destroy the self and the world. Such a faith creates an involved sense of certainty or assurance. Merleau-Ponty, on the contrary, understands all faith on the model of our perceptual experience. "Each of our perceptions is an act of faith in that it affirms more than we strictly know, since objects are inexhaustible and our information limited." This leads to an understanding of an unreserved commitment but not of an irrevocable one. At one point, quoting St.-Exupéry, Merleau-Ponty seems to countenance such an absolute commitment— the hero goes into battle "because he would be nothing if he were to back out"—but such a commitment would be an absolute risk, and for Merleau-Ponty taking such a risk is absurd. For Kierkegaard, too, it is absurd, and for that very reason he calls it faith. Perceptual faith, however, is more cautious. "If commitment goes beyond reason, it should never run counter to reason itself." Thus Merleau-Ponty holds on to a modicum of traditional reason and consequently can only conceive of eternity as a retreat from time, not as total involvement in it. "One cannot get beyond history and time, all one can do is manufacture a private eternity in their midst, as artificial as the eternity of a madman who believes he is God." Order and sense, which arise in the world like the figure on the ground in perception, are always subject to retroactive change. Nothing is guaranteed against loss *for* the individual because nothing is definitive *of* him. For Merleau-Ponty, man and mankind are always in the process of creating themselves, but they never arrive at an irrevocable commitment where the only alternatives are to work out the consequences of this commitment or suffer total loss.

In morality, this humanistic existentialism disabused of certainty and sainthood rediscovers the pagan possibility of heroism. But this is not a Greek heroism, guaranteed by a set of social values for which the hero can sacrifice himself with the assurance that his sacrifice will be sanctioned and approved. Nor is it a Hegelian heroism in which the hero has a sense that, although he is not understood, he is nevertheless doing the work of the World Spirit. "Man the Hero," written expressly to conclude *Sense and Non-Sense,* introduces an existential hero. This hero is condemned to being-at-the-world-from-within-it, and this means he is condemned to follow out fragile meanings without either the triumph of an absolute or the relief of despair.

At first this may seem to echo Pascal's cry that "seeing too much to

deny and too little to be sure, I am in a state greatly to be pitied"—
which leads Pascal, by way of the Wager, to an irrevocable commitment to Christianity. But Merleau-Ponty's diagnosis of the pitiable
state is that it arises only because we seek an absolute. Kierkegaard
and Pascal demand such an absolute and obtain it at the price of an
irrevocable commitment. Merleau-Ponty proposes to reduce the risk by
renouncing the demand for absolute certainty. "If I have understood
that truth and value can be for us nothing but the result of the verifications or evaluations which we make in contact with the world, before
other people, and in given situations of knowledge and action, then
. . . the world recovers its texture . . . , and knowledge and action,
true and false, good and evil have something unquestionable about
them, precisely because I do not claim to find in them absolute evidence." "Metaphysical and moral consciousness dies upon contact with
the absolute."

If one does not seek absolute evidence, Merleau-Ponty assures us,
individual and social commitments can result in a moment of meaning
which is its own reward. This is inspiring, to be sure, but in the rush of
his last cadenza Merleau-Ponty neglects to mention one difficulty: it
would follow from his sense of the "contingency of all that exists and
all that has value" that, even though a *"gloria"* may be experienced as
unquestionable, it may still turn out to be illusory. There is no guaranty that we may not later be forced to repudiate the commitment and
to view the sacrifices made for it as wasted effort. How then can we
ever trust these "moments of victory"?

To demand such certainty, however, is to miss Merleau-Ponty's
point. We cannot expect the assurance promised by Kierkegaard and
Pascal, but neither must we suppose, like Sartre, that in the face of
death all victory will be seen as vain. *There is meaning.* The perpetual
possibility of error does not exclude the "miracle" of veridical perception; nor do the dangers of infatuation and enthusiasm exclude the
"miracle" of a commitment which is maintained. Preserving the validity of a moment of victory even after the excitement dies away
depends in part upon us—on our ability to make sufficient sacrifices
"out of loyalty to what we have become"; the rest is out of our hands.
Although we have no guaranty against disillusionment, we must trust
such a moment and live by it as long as it seems significant to us.
Injustice and non-sense are not eliminated, but the hero is all the more
heroic for not being a saint but only a man.

Acknowledgments

THE TRANSLATORS would like to thank Rudy and Alice Binion for their heroism in resolving the ambiguities of the original text, Bob Erwin for his editorial probing of the penultimate manuscript, Sam Todes for his helpful suggestions for the Introduction, and M.I.T. for supporting the work with a summer grant.

Contents

Sense and Non-Sense

Preface

SINCE THE BEGINNING of the century many great books have expressed the revolt of life's immediacy against reason. Each in its own way has said that the rational arrangement of a system of morals or politics, or even of art, is valueless in the face of the fervor of the moment, the explosive brilliance of an individual life, the "premeditation of the unknown."

It would seem that the communion between a man and his power to choose cannot long be endured. Among the rebels, some have unconditionally surrendered to the Communist discipline, others to a revealed religion, while others—those most loyal to their youth—have split their lives in two: in their roles as citizens, husbands, lovers, or fathers, they follow the rule of a fairly conservative reason, localizing their revolt in literature or poetry, which thereby become a religion.

It is true enough that sheer rebellion is insincere. As soon as we desire something or call others to witness, that is, as soon as we live, we imply that the world is, in principle, in harmony with itself and others with ourselves. We are born into reason as into language. But the reason at which we arrive must not be the same reason we abandoned with such a flourish. The experience of unreason cannot simply be forgotten: we must form a new idea of reason.

When we confront a genuine novel, poem, painting, or film, we know that a contact has been established with something, that something has been gained for men; and the work of art begins to transmit an uninterrupted message. But the meaning of the work for the artist or for the public cannot be stated except by the work itself: neither the thought which created it nor the thought which receives it is completely its own master. Cézanne is an example of how precariously expression and communication are achieved. Expression is like a step taken in the fog—no one can say where, if anywhere, it will lead. Even

[3]

our mathematics no longer resembles a long chain of reasoning. Mathematical entities can only be grasped by oblique procedures, improvised methods as opaque as an unknown mineral. Instead of an intelligible world there are radiant nebulae separated by expanses of darkness. The world of culture is as discontinuous as the other world, and it too has its secret mutations. There is a cultural time which wears down works of art and science, although this time operates more slowly than that of history or the physical world. The meaning of a work of art or of a theory is as inseparable from its embodiment as the meaning of a tangible thing—which is why the meaning can never be fully expressed. The highest form of reason borders on unreason.

Likewise, if we are to rediscover a system of morals, we must find it through contact with the conflicts revealed by immoralism. As Simone de Beauvoir's book *L'Invitée* points out, it is a question of knowing whether there is indeed a certain line of conduct which can justify each man in the eyes of his fellows or whether, on the contrary, our condition does not make all ways of behaving mutually unforgivable and whether, in such a situation, all moral principles are not merely a way to reassure rather than to save ourselves, a way to wave questions aside instead of answering them.[1] In morality as in art there is no solution for the man who will not make a move without knowing where he is going and who wants to be accurate and in control at every moment. Our only resort is the spontaneous movement which binds us to others for good or ill, out of selfishness or generosity.

Last of all, the political experiences of the past thirty years oblige us to evoke the background of non-sense against which every universal undertaking is silhouetted and by which it is threatened with failure. Marxism was the hope of generations of intellectuals; for proletarians, and through them men of every nation, were to find in it the way to respect and join each other. Prehistory was going to end; a word had been spoken which looked for an answer from that vast latent humanity, always silent until now. We were about to witness the birth of that absolute novelty, a world where every man counts. But Marxism lost confidence in its own daring when it was successful in only one country; it abandoned its own proletarian methods and resumed the classical ones of history: hierarchy, obedience, myth, inequality, diplomacy, and police. Just after the war one again had reason to hope that the spirit of Marxism would reappear, that the movement of the American masses would take up the banner. This expectation is ex-

1. Mlle de Beauvoir's novel *L'Invitée* has been translated into English under the title *She Came to Stay* (Cleveland and New York, 1954).—Trans.

pressed in several of these essays.[2] We know that it was a mistaken hope, and we are now witnessing the opposition of an America almost unanimously preoccupied with "Red-hunting" (an America displaying all the hypocrisies that Marxist criticism unveiled in the liberal consciousness) and a Soviet Union which considers the division of the world into two camps a *fait accompli,* accepts the military solution as inevitable, and does not count on any awakening of proletarian freedom, especially when it risks national proletariats in sacrificial missions.

Just as Cézanne wondered whether what came from his hands had any meaning and would be understood, just as a man of good will comes to doubt that lives are compatible with each other when he considers the conflicts of his own particular life, so today's citizen is not sure whether the human world is possible.

But failure is not absolute. Cézanne won out against chance, and men, too, can win provided they will measure the dangers and the task.

2. Cf. "Concerning Marxism," p. 123, and "For the Sake of Truth," p. 170.

PART I

Arts

1 / Cézanne's Doubt

HE NEEDED ONE HUNDRED working sessions for a still life, five hundred sittings for a portrait. What we call his work was, for him, only an essay, an approach to painting. In September, 1906, at the age of 67—one month before his death—he wrote: "I was in such a state of mental agitation, in such great confusion that for a time I feared my weak reason would not survive. . . . Now it seems I am better and that I see more clearly the direction my studies are taking. Will I ever arrive at the goal, so intensely sought and so long pursued? I am still learning from nature, and it seems to me I am making slow progress." Painting was his world and his way of life. He worked alone, without students, without admiration from his family, without encouragement from the critics. He painted on the afternoon of the day his mother died. In 1870 he was painting at l'Estaque while the police were after him for dodging the draft. And still he had moments of doubt about this vocation. As he grew old, he wondered whether the novelty of his painting might not come from trouble with his eyes, whether his whole life had not been based upon an accident of his body. The uncertainty or stupidity of his contemporaries correspond to this effort and this doubt. "The painting of a drunken privy cleaner," said a critic in 1905. Even today, C. Mauclair finds Cézanne's admissions of powerlessness an argument against him. Meanwhile, Cézanne's paintings have spread throughout the world. Why so much uncertainty, so much labor, so many failures, and, suddenly, the greatest success?

Zola, Cézanne's friend from childhood, was the first to find genius in him and the first to speak of him as a "genius gone wrong." An observer of Cézanne's life such as Zola, more concerned with his character than with the meaning of his painting, might well consider it a manifestation of ill-health.

For as far back as 1852, upon entering the Collège Bourbon at Aix,

Cézanne worried his friends with his fits of temper and depression. Seven years later, having decided to become an artist, he doubted his talent and did not dare to ask his father—a hatter and later a banker—to send him to Paris. Zola's letters reproach him for his instability, his weakness, and his indecision. When finally he came to Paris, he wrote: "The only thing I have changed is my location: my ennui has followed me." He could not tolerate discussions, because they wore him out and because he could never give arguments. His nature was basically anxious. Thinking that he would die young, he made his will at the age of 42; at 46 he was for six months the victim of a violent, tormented, overwhelming passion of which no one knows the outcome and to which he would never refer. At 51 he withdrew to Aix, where he found landscape best suited to his genius but where also he returned to the world of his childhood, his mother and his sister. After the death of his mother, Cézanne turned to his son for support. "Life is terrifying," he would often say. Religion, which he then set about practicing for the first time, began for him in the fear of life and the fear of death. "It is fear," he explained to a friend; "I feel I will be on earth for another four days—what then? I believe in life after death, and I don't want to risk roasting *in aeternum*." Although his religion later deepened, its original motivation was the need to put his life in order and to be relieved of it. He became more and more timid, mistrustful, and sensitive: on his occasional visits to Paris he motioned his friends, when still far away, not to approach him. In 1903, after his pictures had begun to sell in Paris at twice the price of Monet's and when young men like Joachim Gasquet and Emile Bernard came to see him and ask him questions, he unbent a little. But his fits of anger continued. (In Aix a child once hit him as he passed by; after that he could not bear any contact.) One day when Cézanne was quite old, Emile Bernard supported him as he stumbled. Cézanne flew into a rage. He could be heard striding around his studio and shouting that he wouldn't let anybody "get his hooks into me." Because of these "hooks" he pushed women who could have modeled for him out of his studio, priests, whom he called "sticky," out of his life, and Emile Bernard's theories out of his mind, when they became too insistent.

This loss of flexible human contact; this inability to master new situations; this flight into established habits, in an atmosphere which presented no problems; this rigid opposition in theory and practice of the "hook" versus the freedom of a recluse—all these symptoms permit one to speak of a morbid constitution and more precisely, as, for example, in the case of El Greco, of schizophrenia. The notion of painting "from nature" could be said to arise from the same weakness. His extremely close attention to nature and to color, the inhuman character of his paintings (he said that a face should be painted as an object), his devotion to the visible world: all of these would then only represent a flight from the human world, the alienation of his humanity.

These conjectures nevertheless do not give any idea of the positive side of his work; one cannot thereby conclude that his painting is a phenomenon of decadence and what Nietzsche called "impoverished" life or that it has nothing to say to the educated man. Zola's and Emile Bernard's belief in Cézanne's failure probably arises from their having put too much emphasis on psychology and their personal knowledge of Cézanne. It is quite possible that, on the basis of his nervous weaknesses, Cézanne conceived a form of art which is valid for everyone. Left to himself, he could look at nature as only a human being can. The meaning of his work cannot be determined from his life.

This meaning will not become any clearer in the light of art history —that is, by bringing in the influences on Cézanne's methods (the Italian school and Tintoretto, Delacroix, Courbet and the Impressionists)—or even by drawing on his own judgment of his work.

His first pictures—up to about 1870—are painted fantasies: a rape, a murder. They are therefore almost always executed in broad strokes and present the moral physiognomy of the actions rather than their visible aspect. It is thanks to the Impressionists, and particularly to Pissarro, that Cézanne later conceived painting not as the incarnation of imagined scenes, the projection of dreams outward, but as the exact study of appearances: less a work of the studio than a working from nature. Thanks to the Impressionists, he abandoned the baroque technique, whose primary aim is to capture movement, for small dabs placed close together and for patient hatchings.

He quickly parted ways with the Impressionists, however. Impressionism tries to capture, in the painting, the very way in which objects strike our eyes and attack our senses. Objects are depicted as they appear to instantaneous perception, without fixed contours, bound together by light and air. To capture this envelope of light, one had to exclude siennas, ochres, and black and use only the seven colors of the spectrum. The color of objects could not be represented simply by putting on the canvas their local tone, that is, the color they take on isolated from their surroundings; one also had to pay attention to the phenomena of contrast which modify local colors in nature. Furthermore, by a sort of reversal, every color we perceive in nature elicits the appearance of its complement; and these complementaries heighten one another. To achieve sunlit colors in a picture which will be seen in the dim light of apartments, not only must there be a green—if you are painting grass—but also the complementary red which will make it vibrate. Finally, the Impressionists break down the local tone itself. One can generally obtain any color by juxtaposing rather than mixing the colors which make it up, thereby achieving a more vibrant hue. The result of these procedures is that the canvas—which no longer corresponds point by point to nature—affords a generally true impression through the action of the separate parts upon one another. But at the same time, depicting the atmosphere and breaking up the tones submerges the object and causes it to lose its proper weight. The composition of Cézanne's palette leads one to suppose that he had another aim. Instead of the seven colors of the spectrum, one finds eighteen colors—six reds, five yellows, three blues, three greens, and black. The use of warm colors and black shows that Cézanne wants to represent the object, to find it again behind the atmosphere. Likewise, he does not break up the tone; rather, he replaces this technique with graduated colors, a progression of chromatic nuances across the object, a modulation of colors which stays close to the object's form and to the light it receives. Doing away with exact contours in certain cases, giving color priority over the outline—these obviously mean different things for Cézanne and for the Impressionists. The object is no longer covered by reflections and lost in its relationships to the atmosphere and to other objects: it seems subtly illuminated from within, light emanates from it, and the result is an impression of solidity and material substance. Moreover, Cézanne does not give up making the warm colors vibrate but achieves this chromatic sensation through the use of blue.

One must therefore say that Cézanne wished to return to the object without abandoning the Impressionist aesthetic which takes nature as its model. Emile Bernard reminded him that, for the classical artists, painting demanded outline, composition, and distribution of light. Cézanne replied: "They created pictures; we are attempting a piece of nature." He said of the old masters that they "replaced reality by imagination and by the abstraction which accompanies it." Of nature, he said that "the artist must conform to this perfect work of art. Everything comes to us from nature; we exist through it; nothing else is worth remembering." He stated that he wanted to make of Impressionism "something solid, like the art in the museums." His painting was paradoxical: he was pursuing reality without giving up the sensuous surface, with no other guide than the immediate impression of nature, without following the contours, with no outline to enclose the color, with no perspectival or pictorial arrangement. This is what Bernard called Cézanne's suicide: aiming for reality while denying himself the means to attain it. This is the reason for his difficulties and for the distortions one finds in his pictures between 1870 and 1890. Cups and saucers on a table seen from the side should be elliptical, but Cézanne paints the two ends of the ellipse swollen and expanded. The work table in his portrait of Gustave Geoffrey stretches, contrary to the laws of perspective, into the lower part of the picture. In giving up the outline Cézanne was abandoning himself to the chaos of sensations, which would upset the objects and constantly suggest illusions, as, for example, the illusion we have when we move our head that objects themselves are moving—if our judgment did not constantly set these appearances straight. According to Bernard, Cézanne "submerged his painting in ignorance and his mind in shadows." But one cannot really judge his painting in this way except by closing one's mind to half of what he said and one's eyes to what he painted.

It is clear from his conversations with Emile Bernard that Cézanne was always seeking to avoid the ready-made alternatives suggested to him: sensation versus judgment; the painter who sees against the painter who thinks; nature versus composition; primitivism as opposed to tradition. "We have to develop an optics," said Cézanne, "by which I mean a logical vision—that is, one with no element of the absurd." "Are you speaking of our nature?" asked Bernard. Cézanne: "It has to do with both." "But aren't nature and art different?" "I want to make them the same. Art is a personal apperception, which I embody in sensations and which I ask the understanding to organize into a painting." [1] But even these formulas put too much emphasis on the ordinary notions of "sensitivity" or "sensations" and "understanding"—which is why Cézanne could not convince by his arguments and preferred to paint instead. Rather than apply to his work dichotomies more appropriate to those who sustain traditions than to those men, philosophers or painters, who initiate these traditions, he preferred to search for the true meaning of painting, which is continually to question tradition. Cézanne did not think he had to choose between feeling and thought, between order and chaos. He did not want to separate the stable things which we see and the shifting way in which they appear; he wanted to depict matter as it takes on form, the birth of order through spontaneous organization. He makes a basic distinction not between "the senses" and "the understanding" but rather between the spontaneous organization of the things we perceive and the human organization of ideas and sciences. We see things; we agree about them; we are anchored in them; and it is with "nature" as our base that we construct our sciences. Cézanne wanted to paint this primordial world, and his pictures therefore seem to show nature pure, while photo-

1. Cézanne's conversations with Bernard are recorded in *Souvenirs sur Paul Cézanne* (Paris, 1912).—Trans.

graphs of the same landscapes suggest man's works, conveniences, and imminent presence. Cézanne never wished to "paint like a savage." He wanted to put intelligence, ideas, sciences, perspective, and tradition back in touch with the world of nature which they must comprehend. He wished, as he said, to confront the sciences with the nature "from which they came."

By remaining faithful to the phenomena in his investigations of perspective, Cézanne discovered what recent psychologists have come to formulate: the lived perspective, that which we actually perceive, is not a geometric or photographic one. The objects we see close at hand appear smaller, those far away seem larger than they do in a photograph. (This can be seen in a movie, where a train approaches and gets bigger much faster than a real train would under the same circumstances.) To say that a circle seen obliquely is seen as an ellipse is to substitute for our actual perception what we would see if we were cameras: in reality we see a form which oscillates around the ellipse without being an ellipse. In a portrait of Mme Cézanne, the border of the wallpaper on one side of her body does not form a straight line with that on the other: and indeed it is known that if a line passes beneath a wide strip of paper, the two visible segments appear dislocated. Gustave Geoffrey's table stretches into the bottom of the picture, and indeed, when our eye runs over a large surface, the images it successively receives are taken from different points of view, and the whole surface is warped. It is true that I freeze these distortions in repainting them on the canvas; I stop the spontaneous movement in which they pile up in perception and in which they tend toward the geometric perspective. This is also what happens with colors. Pink upon gray paper colors the background green. Academic painting shows the background as gray, assuming that the picture will produce the same effect of contrast as the real object. Impressionist painting uses green in the background in order to achieve a contrast as brilliant as that of objects in nature. Doesn't this falsify the color relationship? It would if it stopped there, but the painter's task is to modify all the other colors in the picture so that they take away from the green background its characteristics of a real color. Similarly, it is Cézanne's genius that when the over-all composition of the picture is seen globally, perspectival distortions are no longer visible in their own right but rather contribute, as they do in natural vision, to the impression of an emerging order, of an object in the act of appearing, organizing itself before our eyes. In the same way, the contour of an object conceived as a line encircling the object belongs not to the visible world but to geometry. If one outlines the shape of an apple with a continuous line, one makes an object of the shape, whereas the contour is rather the ideal limit toward which the sides of the apple recede in depth. Not to indicate any shape would be to deprive the objects of their identity. To trace just a single outline sacrifices depth—that is, the dimension in which the thing is presented not as spread out before us but as an inexhaustible reality full of reserves. That is why Cézanne follows the swelling of the object in modulated colors and indicates *several* outlines in blue. Rebounding among these, one's glance captures a shape that emerges from among them all, just as it does in perception. Nothing could be less arbitrary than these famous distortions which, moreover, Cézanne abandoned in his last period, after 1890, when he no longer filled his canvases with colors and when he gave up the closely-woven texture of his still lifes.

The outline should therefore be a result of the colors if the world is to be given in its true density. For the world is a mass without gaps, a system of colors across which the receding perspective, the outlines, angles, and curves are inscribed like lines of force; the spatial structure vibrates as it is formed. "The outline and the colors are no longer distinct from each other. To the extent that one paints, one outlines; the more the colors harmonize, the more the outline becomes precise. . . . When the color is at its richest, the form has reached plenitude." Cézanne does not try to use color to *suggest* the tactile sensations which would give shape and depth. These distinctions between touch and sight are unknown in primordial perception. It is only as a result of a science of the human body that we finally learn to distinguish between our senses. The lived object is not rediscovered or constructed on the basis of the contributions of the senses; rather, it presents itself to us from the start as the center from which these contributions radiate. We *see* the depth, the smoothness, the softness, the hardness of objects; Cézanne even claimed that we see their odor. If the painter is to express the world, the arrangement of his colors must carry with it this indivisible whole, or else his picture will only hint at things and will not give them in the imperious unity, the presence, the insurpassable plenitude which is for us the definition of the real. That is why each brushstroke must satisfy an infinite number of conditions. Cézanne sometimes pondered hours at a time before putting down a certain stroke, for, as Bernard said, each stroke must "contain the air, the light, the object, the composition, the character, the outline, and the style." Expressing what *exists* is an endless task.

Nor did Cézanne neglect the physiognomy of objects and faces: he simply wanted to capture it emerging from the color. Painting a face "as an object" is not to strip it of its "thought." "I realize that the painter interprets it," said Cézanne. "The painter is not an imbecile." But this interpretation should not be a reflection distinct from the act of seeing.

"If I paint all the little blues and all the little maroons, I capture and convey his glance. Who gives a damn if they want to dispute how one can sadden a mouth or make a cheek smile by wedding a shaded green to a red." One's personality is seen and grasped in one's glance, which is, however, no more than a combination of colors. Other minds are given to us only as incarnate, as belonging to faces and gestures. Countering with the distinctions of soul and body, thought and vision is of no use here, for Cézanne returns to just that primordial experience from which these notions are derived and in which they are inseparable. The painter who conceptualizes and seeks the expression first misses the mystery—renewed every time we look at someone—of a person's appearing in nature. In *La Peau de chagrin* Balzac describes a "tablecloth white as a layer of newly fallen snow, upon which the place-settings rise symmetrically, crowned with blond rolls." "All through youth," said Cézanne, "I wanted to paint that, that tablecloth of new snow. . . . Now I know that one must will only to paint the place-settings rising symmetrically and the blond rolls. If I paint 'crowned' I've had it, you understand? But if I really balance and shade my place-settings and rolls as they are in nature, then you can be sure that the crowns, the snow, and all the excitement will be there too."

We live in the midst of man-made objects, among tools, in houses, streets, cities, and most of the time we see them only through the human actions which put them to use. We become used to thinking that all of this exists necessarily and unshakeably. Cézanne's painting suspends these habits of thought and reveals the base of inhuman nature upon which man has installed himself. This is why Cézanne's people are strange, as if viewed by a creature of another species. Nature itself is stripped of the attributes which make it ready for animistic communions: there is no wind in the landscape, no movement on the Lac d'Annecy; the frozen objects hesitate as at the beginning of the world. It is an unfamiliar world in which one is uncomfortable and which forbids all human effusiveness. If one looks at the work of other painters after seeing Cézanne's paintings, one feels somehow relaxed, just as conversations resumed after a period of mourning mask the absolute change and give back to the survivors their solidity. But indeed only a human being is capable of such a vision which penetrates right to the root of things beneath the imposed order of humanity. Everything indicates that animals cannot *look at* things, cannot penetrate them in expectation of nothing but the truth. Emile Bernard's statement that a realistic painter is only an ape is therefore precisely the opposite of the truth, and one sees how Cézanne was able to revive the classical definition of art: man added to nature.

Cézanne's painting denies neither science nor tradition. He went to the Louvre every day when he was in Paris. He believed that one must learn how to paint and that the geometric study of planes and forms is a necessary part of this learning process. He inquired about the geological structure of his landscapes, convinced that these abstract relationships, expressed, however, in terms of the visible world, should affect the act of painting. The rules of anatomy and design are present in each stroke of his brush just as the rules of the game underlie each stroke of a tennis match. But what motivates the painter's movement can never be simply perspective or geometry or the laws governing color, or, for that matter, particular knowledge. Motivating all the movements from which a picture gradually emerges there can be only one thing: the landscape in its totality and in its absolute fullness, precisely what Cézanne called a "motif." He would start by discovering the geological foundations of the landscape; then, according to Mme Cézanne, he would halt and look at everything with widened eyes, "germinating" with the countryside. The task before him was, first to forget all he had ever learned from science and, second *through* these sciences to recapture the structure of the landscape as an emerging organism. To do this, all the partial views one catches sight of must be welded together; all that the eye's versatility disperses must be reunited; one must, as Gasquet put it, "join the wandering hands of nature." "A minute of the world is going by which must be painted in its full reality." His meditation would suddenly be consummated: "I have my *motif*," Cézanne would say, and he would explain that the landscape had to be centered neither too high nor too low, caught alive in a net which would let nothing escape. Then he began to paint all parts of the painting at the same time, using patches of color to surround his original charcoal sketch of the geological skeleton. The picture took on fullness and density; it grew in structure and balance; it came to maturity all at once. "The landscape thinks itself in me," he said, "and I am its consciousness." Nothing could be farther from naturalism than this intuitive science. Art is not imitation, nor is it something manufactured according to the wishes of instinct or good taste. It is a process of expressing. Just as the function of words is to name—that is, to grasp the nature of what appears to us in a confused way and to place it before us as a recognizable object—so it is up to the painter, said Gasquet, to "objectify," "project," and "arrest." Words do not *look like* the things they designate; and a picture is not a *trompe-l'oeil*. Cézanne, in his own words, "wrote in painting what had never yet been painted, and turned it into painting once and for all." Forgetting the viscous, equivocal appearances, we go through them straight to the things they present. The painter recaptures and converts into visible objects what would, without him, remain walled up in the separate life of each consciousness: the vibration of appearances which is the cradle of things. Only one emotion is possible for this painter—the feeling of strangeness—and only one lyricism—that of the continual rebirth of existence.

Leonardo da Vinci's motto was persistent rigor, and all the classical works on the art of poetry tell us that the creation of art is no easy matter. Cézanne's difficulties—like those of Balzac or Mallarmé—are of a different nature. Balzac (probably taking Delacroix for his model) imagined a painter who wants to express life through the use of color alone and who keeps his masterpiece hidden. When Frenhofer dies, his friends find nothing but a chaos of colors and elusive lines, a wall of painting. Cézanne was moved to tears when he read *Le Chef-d'oeuvre inconnu* and declared that he himself was Frenhofer. The effort made by Balzac, himself obsessed with "realization," sheds light on Cézanne's. In *La Peau de chagrin* Balzac speaks of "a thought to be expressed," "a system to be built," "a science to be explained." He makes Louis Lambert, one of the abortive geniuses of the Comédie Humaine, say: "I am heading toward certain discoveries . . . , but how shall I describe the power which binds my hands, stops my mouth, and drags me in the opposite direction from my vocation?" To say that Balzac set himself to understand the society of his time is not sufficient. It is no superhuman task to describe the typical traveling salesman, to "dissect the teaching profession," or even to lay the foundations of a sociology. Once he had named the visible forces such as money and passion, once he had described the way they evidently work, Balzac wondered where it all led, what was the impetus behind it, what was the *meaning* of, for example, a Europe "whose efforts tend toward some unknown mystery of civilization." In short, he wanted to understand what interior force holds the world together and causes the proliferation of visible forms. Frenhofer had the same idea about the meaning of painting: "A hand is not simply part of the body, but the expression and continuation of a thought which must be captured and conveyed. . . . That is the real struggle! Many painters triumph instinctively, unaware of this theme of art. You draw a woman, but you do not see her." The artist is the one who arrests the spectacle in which most men take part without really seeing it and who makes it visible to the most "human" among them.

There is thus no art for pleasure's sake alone. One can invent pleasurable objects by linking old ideas in a new way and by presenting forms that have been seen before. This way of painting or speaking at second hand is what is generally meant by culture. Cézanne's or Balzac's artist is not satisfied to be a cultured animal but assimilates the culture down to its very foundations and gives it a new structure: he speaks as the first man spoke and paints as if no one had ever painted before. What he expresses cannot, therefore, be the translation of a clearly defined thought, since such clear thoughts are those which have already been uttered by ourselves or by others. "Conception" cannot precede "execution." There is nothing but a vague fever before the act of artistic expression, and only the work itself, completed and understood, is proof that there was *something* rather than *nothing* to be said. Because he returns to the source of silent and solitary experience on which culture and the exchange of ideas have been built in order to know it, the artist launches his work just as a man once launched the first word, not knowing whether it will be anything more than a shout, whether it can detach itself from the flow of individual life in which it originates and give the independent existence of an identifiable *meaning* either to the future of that same individual life or to the monads coexisting with it or to the open community of future monads. The meaning of what the artist is going to say *does not exist* anywhere—not in things, which as yet have no meaning, nor in the artist himself, in his unformulated life. It summons one away from the already constituted reason in which "cultured men" are content to shut themselves, toward a reason which contains its own origins.

To Bernard's attempt to bring him back to human intelligence, Cézanne replied: "I am oriented toward the intelligence of the *Pater Omnipotens*." He was, in any case, oriented toward the idea or the project of an infinite Logos. Cézanne's uncertainty and solitude are not essentially explained by his nervous temperament but by the purpose of his work. Heredity may well have given him rich sensations, strong emotions, and a vague feeling of anguish or mystery which upset the life he might have wished for himself and which cut him off from men; but these qualities cannot create a work of art without the expressive act, and they can no more account for the difficulties than for the virtues of that act. Cézanne's difficulties are those of the first word. He considered himself powerless because he was not omnipotent, because he was not God and wanted nevertheless to portray the world, to change it completely into a spectacle, to make *visible* how the world *touches* us. A new theory of physics can be proven because calculations connect the idea or meaning of it with standards of measurement already common to all men. It is not enough for a painter like Cézanne, an artist, or a philosopher, to create and express an idea; they must also awaken the experiences which will make their idea take root in the consciousness of others. A successful work has the strange power to teach its own lesson. The reader or spectator who follows the clues of the book or painting, by setting up stepping stones and rebounding from side to side guided by the obscure clarity of a particular style, will end by discovering what the artist wanted to communicate. The painter can do no more than construct an image; he must wait for this image to come to life for other people. When it does, the work of art will have united these separate lives; it will no longer exist in only one of them like a stubborn dream or a persistent delirium, nor will it exist only in space as a colored piece of canvas. It will dwell undivided in several minds, with a claim on every possible mind like a perennial acquisition.

Thus, the "hereditary traits," the "influences"—the accidents in Cézanne's life—are the text which nature and history gave him to decipher. They give only the literal meaning of his work. But an artist's creations, like a man's free decisions, impose on this given a figurative sense which did not pre-exist them. If Cézanne's life seems to us to carry the seeds of his work within it, it is because we get to know his work first and see the circumstances of his life through it, charging them with a meaning borrowed from that work. If the givens for Cézanne which we have been enumerating, and which we spoke of as pressing conditions, were to figure in the web of projects which he was, they could have done so only by presenting themselves to him as *what* he had to live, leaving *how* to live it undetermined. An imposed theme at the start, they become, when replaced in the existence of which they are part, the monogram and the symbol of a life which freely interpreted itself.

But let us make no mistake about this freedom. Let us not imagine an abstract force which could superimpose its effects on life's "givens" or which cause breaches in life's development. Although it is certain that a man's life does not *explain* his work, it is equally certain that the two are connected. The truth is that *this work to be done called for this life.* From the very start, the only equilibrium in Cézanne's life came from the support of his future work. His life was the projection of his future work. The work to come is hinted at, but it would be wrong to take these hints for causes, although they do make a single adventure of his life and work. Here we are beyond causes and effects; both come together in the simultaneity of an eternal Cézanne who is at the same time the formula of what he wanted to be and what he wanted to do. There is a rapport between Cézanne's schizoid temperament and his work because the work reveals a metaphysical sense of the disease: a way of seeing the world reduced to the totality of frozen appearances, with all expressive values suspended. Thus the illness ceases to be an absurd fact and a fate and becomes a general possibility of human existence. It becomes so when this existence bravely faces one of its paradoxes, the phenomenon of expression. In this sense to be schizoid and to be Cézanne come to the same thing. It is therefore impossible to separate creative liberty from that behavior, as far as possible from deliberate, already evident in Cézanne's first gestures as a child and in the way he reacted to things. The meaning Cézanne gave to objects and faces in his paintings presented itself to him in the world as it appeared to him. Cézanne simply released this meaning: it was the objects and the faces themselves as he saw them which demanded to be painted, and Cézanne simply expressed what they *wanted* to say. How, then, can any freedom be involved? True, the conditions of existence can only affect consciousness by way of a detour through the *raisons d'être* and the justifications consciousness offers to itself. We can only see what we are by looking ahead of ourselves, through the lens of our aims, and so our life always has the form of a project or of a choice and therefore seems spontaneous. But to say that we are from the start our way of aiming at a particular future would be to say that our project has already stopped with our first ways of being, that the choice has already been made for us with our first breath. If we experience no external constraints, it is because we are our whole exterior. That eternal Cézanne whom we first saw emerge and who then brought upon the human Cézanne the events and influences which seemed *exterior* to him, and who planned all that happened to him—that attitude toward men and toward the world which was not chosen through deliberation—free as it is from external causes, is it free in respect to itself? Is the choice not pushed back beyond life, and can a choice exist where there is as yet no clearly articulated field of possibilities, only one probability and, as it were, only one temptation? If I am a certain project from birth, the given and the created are indistinguishable in me, and it is therefore impossible to name a single gesture which is merely hereditary or innate, a single gesture which is not spontaneous—but also impossible to name a single gesture which is absolutely new in regard to that way of being in the world which, from the very beginning, is myself. There is no difference between saying that our life is completely constructed and that it is completely given. If there is a true liberty, it can only come about in the course of our life by our going beyond our original situation and yet not ceasing to be the same: this is the problem. Two things are certain about freedom: that we are never determined and yet that we never change, since, looking back on what we were, we can always find hints of what we have become. It is up to us to understand both these things simultaneously, as well as the way freedom dawns in us without breaking our bonds with the world.

Such bonds are always there, even and above all when we refuse to admit they exist. Inspired by the paintings of Da Vinci, Valéry described a monster of pure freedom, without mistresses, creditors, anecdotes, or adventures. No dream intervenes between himself and the things themselves; nothing taken for granted supports his certainties; and he does not read his fate in any favorite image, such as Pascal's abyss. Instead of struggling against the monsters he has understood what makes them tick, has disarmed them by his attention, and has reduced them to the state of known things. "Nothing could be more free, that is, less human, than his judgments on love and death. He hints at them in a few fragments from his notebooks: 'In the full force of its passion,' he says more or less explicitly, 'love is something so ugly that the human race would die out (*la natura si perderebbe*) if lovers could see what they were doing.' This contempt is brought out in various sketches, since the leisurely examination of certain things is, after all, the height of scorn. Thus, he now and again draws anatomical unions, frightful cross-sections of love's very act." [2] He has complete mastery of his means, he does what he wants, going at will from knowledge to life with a superior elegance. Everything he did was done knowingly, and the artistic process, like the act of breathing or living, does not go beyond his knowledge. He has discovered the "central attitude," on the basis of which it is equally possible to know, to act, and to create because action and life, when turned into exercises, are not contrary to detached knowledge. He is an "intellectual power"; he is a "man of the mind."

Let us look more closely. For Leonardo there was no revelation; as Valéry said, no abyss yawned at his right hand. Undoubtedly true. But in "Saint Anne, the Virgin, and Child," the Virgin's cloak suggests a vulture where it touches the face of the Child. There is that fragment on the flight of birds where Da Vinci suddenly interrupts himself to pursue a childhood memory: "I seem to have been destined to be especially concerned with the vulture, for one of the first things I remember about my childhood is how a vulture came to me when I was still in the cradle, forced open my mouth with its tail, and struck me several times between the lips with it." [3] So even this transparent consciousness has its enigma, whether truly a child's memory or a fantasy of the grown man. It does not come out of nowhere, nor does it sustain itself alone. We are caught in a secret history, in a forest of symbols. One would surely protest if Freud were to decipher the riddle from what we know about the meaning of the flight of birds and about

2. "Introduction à la méthode de Léonard de Vinci," *Variété*, p. 185. [English translation by Thomas McGreevy, *Introduction to the Method of Leonardo da Vinci* (London, 1929).]

3. Sigmund Freud, *Un souvenir d'enfance de Léonard de Vinci*, p. 65. [English translation by A. A. Brill, *Leonardo da Vinci: A Study in Psychosexuality* (New York, 1947).]

fellatio fantasies and their relation to the period of nursing. But it is still a fact that to the ancient Egyptians the vulture was the symbol of maternity because they believed all vultures were female and that they were impregnated by the wind. It is also a fact that the Church Fathers used this legend to refute, on the grounds of natural history, those who were unwilling to believe in a virgin birth, and it is probable that Leonardo came across the legend in the course of his endless reading. He found in it the symbol of his own fate: he was the illegitimate son of a rich notary who married the noble Donna Albiera the very year Leonardo was born. Having no children by her, he took Leonardo into his home when the boy was five. Thus Leonardo spent the first four years of his life with his mother, the deserted peasant girl; he was a child without a father, and he got to know the world in the sole company of that unhappy mother who seemed to have miraculously created him. If we now recall that he was never known to have a mistress or even to have felt anything like passion; that he was accused—but ac-quitted—of homosexuality; that his diary, which tells us nothing about many other, larger expenses, notes with meticulous detail the costs of his mother's burial, as well as the cost of linen and clothing for two of his students—then we are on the verge of saying that Leonardo loved only one woman, his mother, and that this love left no room for any-thing but the platonic tenderness he felt for the young boys surround-ing him. In the four decisive years of his childhood he formed a basic attachment which he had to give up when he was recalled to his father's home and into which he had poured all his resources of love and all his power of abandon. His thirst for life could only be turned toward the investigation and knowledge of the world, and, since he himself had been *"detached,"* he had to become that intellectual power, that man who was all mind, that stranger among men. Indifferent, incapable of any strong indignation, love or hate, he left his paintings unfinished to devote his time to bizarre experiments; he became a person in whom his contemporaries sensed a mystery. It was as if Leonardo had never quite grown up, as if all the places in his heart had already been spoken for, as if the spirit of investigation was a way for him to escape from life, as if he had invested all his power of assent in the first years of his life and had remained true to his childhood right to the end. His games were those of a child. Vasari tells how "he made up a wax paste and, during his walks, he would model from it very delicate animals, hollow and filled with air; when he breathed into them, they would float; when the air had escaped, they would fall to the ground. When the wine-grower from Belvedere found a very unusual lizard, Leonardo made wings for it out of the skin of other lizards and filled these wings with mercury so that they waved and quivered whenever the lizard moved; he likewise made eyes, a beard, and horns for it in the same way, tamed it, put it in a box, and used this lizard to terrify his friends." [4] He left his work unfinished, just as his father had abandoned him. He paid no heed to authority and trusted only nature and his own judgment in matters of knowledge, as is often the case with people who have not been raised in the shadow of a father's intimidating and protective power. Thus even this pure power of examination, this solitude, this curiosity—which are the essence of mind—became Leonardo's only in reference to his history. At the height of his freedom he was, *in that very freedom,* the child he had been; he was detached in one way only because he was attached in another. Becoming a pure consciousness is just another way of taking a stand about the world and other people; Leonardo learned this attitude in assimilating the situation which his birth and childhood had made for him. There can be no consciousness that is not sustained by its primordial involvement in life and by the manner of this involvement.

Whatever is arbitrary in Freud's *explanations* cannot in this context discredit *psychoanalytical intuition.* True, the reader is stopped more than once by the lack of evidence. Why this and not something else? The question seems all the more pressing since Freud often offers several interpretations, each symptom being "over-determined" according to him. Finally, it is obvious that a doctrine which brings in sexuality everywhere cannot, by the rules of inductive logic, establish its effectiveness anywhere, since, excluding all differential cases beforehand, it deprives itself of any counter-evidence. This is how one triumphs over psychoanalysis, but only on paper. For if the suggestions of the analyst can never be proven, neither can they be eliminated: how would it be possible to credit chance with the complex correspondences which the psychoanalyst discovers between the child and the adult? How can we deny that psychoanalysis has taught us to notice echoes, allusions, repetitions from one moment of life to another—a concatenation we would not dream of doubting if Freud had stated the theory behind it correctly? Unlike the natural sciences, psychoanalysis was not meant to give us necessary relations of cause and effect but to point to motivational relationships which are in principle simply possible. We should not take Leonardo's fantasy of the vulture, or the infantile past which it masks, for a force which determined his future. Rather, it is like the words of the oracle, an ambiguous symbol which applies in advance to several possible chains of events. To be more precise: in every life, one's birth and one's past define categories or basic dimensions which do not impose any particular act but which can

4. *Ibid.,* p. 189.

be found in all. Whether Leonardo yielded to his childhood or whether he wished to flee from it, he could never have been other than he was. The very decisions which transform us are always made in reference to a factual situation; such a situation can of course be accepted or refused, but it cannot fail to give us our impetus nor to be for us, as a situation "to be accepted" or "to be refused," the incarnation for us of the value we give to it. If it is the aim of psychoanalysis to describe this exchange between future and past and to show how each life muses over riddles whose final meaning is nowhere written down, then we have no right to demand inductive rigor from it. The psychoanalyst's hermeneutic musing, which multiplies the communications between us and ourselves, which takes sexuality as the symbol of existence and existence as symbol of sexuality, and which looks in the past for the meaning of the future and in the future for the meaning of the past, is better suited than rigorous induction to the circular movement of our lives, where the future rests on the past, the past on the future, and where everything symbolizes everything else. Psychoanalysis does not make freedom impossible; it teaches us to think of this freedom concretely, as a creative repetition of ourselves, always, in retrospect, faithful to ourselves.

Thus it is true both that the life of an author can teach us nothing and that—if we know how to interpret it—we can find everything in it, since it opens onto his work. Just as we may observe the movements of an unknown animal without understanding the law which inhabits and controls them, so Cézanne's observers did not guess the transmutations which he imposed on events and experiences; they were blind to *his* significance, to that glow from out of nowhere which surrounded him from time to time. But he himself was never at the center of himself: nine days out of ten all he saw around him was the wretchedness of his empirical life and of his unsuccessful attempts, the leftovers of an unknown party. Yet it was in the world that he had to realize his freedom, with colors upon a canvas. It was on the approval of others that he had to wait for the proof of his worth. That is the reason he questioned the picture emerging beneath his hand, why he hung on the glances other people directed toward his canvas. That is the reason he never finished working. We never get away from our life. We never see our ideas or our freedom face to face.

2 / Metaphysics and the Novel

> "What surprises me is that you are touched in such a concrete way by a metaphysical situation."
> "But the situation is concrete," said Françoise, "the whole meaning of my life is at stake."
> "I'm not saying it isn't," Pierre said. "Just the same, this ability of yours to put body and soul into living an idea is exceptional."
>
> S. de Beauvoir, *L'Invitée*

I

THE WORK of a great novelist always rests on two or three philosophical ideas. For Stendhal, these are the notions of the Ego and Liberty; for Balzac, the mystery of history as the appearance of a meaning in chance events; for Proust, the way the past is involved in the present and the presence of times gone by. The function of the novelist is not to state these ideas thematically but to make them exist for us in the way that things exist. Stendhal's role is not to hold forth on subjectivity; it is enough that he make it present.[1]

It is nonetheless surprising that, when writers do take a deliberate interest in philosophy, they have such difficulty in recognizing their affinities. Stendhal praises ideologists to the skies; Balzac compromises his views on the expressive relations of body and soul, economics and civilization, by couching them in the language of spiritualism. Proust sometimes translates his intuition about time into a relativistic and skeptical philosophy and at other times into hopes of immortality which distort it just as much. Valéry repudiated the philosophers who wanted at least to annex the *Introduction à la méthode de Léonard de Vinci.* For a long time it looked as if philosophy and literature not only had different ways of saying things but had different objects as well.

---

1. As he does in *Le Rouge et le noir:* "Only I know what I might have done . . . , for others I am at most a 'perhaps.' " "If they had notified me of the execution this morning, at the moment when death seemed ugliest to me, the public eye would have spurred me on to glory. . . . A few perceptive people, if there are any among these provincials, could have guessed my weakness. . . . But nobody would have *seen* it."

Since the end of the 19th century, however, the ties between them have been getting closer and closer. The first sign of this reconciliation was the appearance of hybrid modes of expression having elements of the intimate diary, the philosophical treatise, and the dialogue. Péguy's work is a good example. Why should a writer from then on need to use simultaneous references to philosophy, politics, and literature in order to express himself? Because a new dimension of investigation was opened up. "Everyone has a metaphysics—explicit or implicit—or he does not exist." [2] Intellectual works had always been concerned with establishing a certain attitude toward the world, of which literature and philosophy, like politics, are just different expressions; but only now had this concern become explicit. One did not wait for the introduction of existential philosophy in France to define all life as latent metaphysics and all metaphysics as an "explicitation" of human life.

That in itself bears witness to the historical necessity and importance of this philosophy. It is the coming to consciousness of a movement older than itself whose meaning it reveals and whose rhythm it accelerates. Classical metaphysics could pass for a speciality with which literature had nothing to do because metaphysics operated on the basis of uncontested rationalism, convinced it could make the world and human life understood by an arrangement of concepts. It was less a matter of explicitating than of explaining life, or of reflecting upon it. What Plato said about "same" and "other" doubtless applies to the relations between oneself and other people; what Descartes said about God's being the identity of essence and existence pertains in a certain way to man and, in any event, pertains to that locus of subjectivity where it is impossible to distinguish the recognition of God from thought's recognition of itself. What Kant said about Consciousness concerns us even more directly. But after all, it is of "same" and "other" that Plato is speaking; it is God that Descartes is talking about in the end; it is Consciousness of which Kant speaks— not that other which exists opposite from me or that self which I am. Despite the most daring beginnings (for example: in Descartes), philosophers always ended by describing their own existence—either in a transcendental setting, or as a moment of a dialectic, or again in concepts, the way primitive peoples represent it and project it in myths. Metaphysics was superimposed in man upon a robust human nature which was governed by tested formulas and which was never questioned in the purely abstract dramas of reflection.

Everything changes when a phenomenological or existential phi-

2. Charles Péguy, *Notre Jeunesse*.

losophy assigns itself the task, not of explaining the world or of discovering its "conditions of possibility," but rather of formulating an experience of the world, a contact with the world which precedes all thought *about* the world. After this, whatever is metaphysical in man cannot be credited to something outside his empirical being—to God, to Consciousness. Man is metaphysical in his very being, in his loves, in his hates, in his individual and collective history. And metaphysics is no longer the occupation of a few hours per month, as Descartes said; it is present, as Pascal thought, in the heart's slightest movement.

From now on the tasks of literature and philosophy can no longer be separated. When one is concerned with giving voice to the experience of the world and showing how consciousness escapes into the world, one can no longer credit oneself with attaining a perfect transparence of expression. Philosophical expression assumes the same ambiguities as literary expression, if the world is such that it cannot be expressed except in "stories" and, as it were, pointed at. One will not only witness the appearance of hybrid modes of expression, but the novel and the theater will become thoroughly metaphysical, even if not a single word is used from the vocabulary of philosophy. Furthermore, a metaphysical literature will necessarily be amoral, in a certain sense, for there is no longer any human nature on which to rely. In every one of man's actions the invasion of metaphysics causes what was only an "old habit" to explode.

The development of a metaphysical literature, the end of a "moral" literature: this is what, for example, Simone de Beauvoir's *L'Invitée* signifies. Using this example, let us examine the phenomenon more closely, and, since the characters in the book provoked the literary critics to censure them for immorality, let us see whether there is not a "true morality" beyond the "morality" at which these characters jeer.

II

THERE IS a perpetual uneasiness in the state of being conscious. At the moment I perceive a thing, I feel that it was there before me, outside my field of vision. There is an infinite horizon of things to grasp surrounding the small number of things which I can grasp in fact. The whistle of a locomotive in the night, the empty theater which I enter, cause to appear, for a lightning instant, those things which everywhere are ready to be perceived—shows performed without an audience, shadows crowded with creatures. Even the things which surround me exceed my comprehension, provided I interrupt my usual intercourse with them and rediscover them, outside of the human or even the living world, in their role as natural things. In the silence of a country house, once the door has been shut against the odors of the shrubbery and the sounds of the birds, an old jacket lying on a chair will be a riddle if I take it just as it offers itself to me. There it is, blind and limited; it does not know what it is; it is content to occupy that bit of space—but it does so in a way I never could. It does not run off in all directions like a consciousness; it remains solidly what it is; it is in itself. Every object can affirm its existence only by depriving me of mine, and I am always secretly aware that there are other things in the world beside me and what I see. Ordinarily, however, I retain of this knowledge only what I need to reassure myself. I observe that, after all, the thing needs me in order to exist. Only when I discover the landscape hidden until then behind a hill does it fully become a landscape; one cannot imagine what a thing would be like if it were not about to, or able to, be seen by me. It is I who bring into being this world which seemed to exist without me, to surround and surpass me. I am therefore a consciousness, immediately present to the world, and nothing can claim to exist without somehow being caught in the web of my experience. I am not this particular person or face, this finite being: I am a pure witness, placeless and ageless, equal in power to the world's infinity.

It is thus that one surmounts or, rather, sublimates the experience of the Other. We easily escape from transcendence as long as we are dealing only with things: the transcendence of other people is more resistant. If another person exists, if he too is a consciousness, then I must consent to be for him only a finite object, determinate, *visible* at a certain place in the world. If he is consciousness, I must cease to be consciousness. But how am I then to forget that intimate attestation of my existence, that contact of self with self, which is more certain than any external evidence and which is the prior condition for everything else? And so we try to subdue the disquieting existence of others. "Their thoughts are the same to me as their words and their faces: objects which exist in my own particular world," says Françoise in *L'Invitée*. I remain the center of the world. I am that nimble being who moves about the world and animates it through and through. I cannot seriously mistake myself for that appearance I offer to others. I have no body. "Françoise smiled: she was not beautiful, yet she was very fond of her face; it always gave her a pleasant surprise when she caught a glimpse of it in a mirror. Most of the time she did not think she had one." Everything that happens is only a spectacle for this indestructible, impartial, and generous spectator. Everything exists just for her.

Not that she uses people and things for her private satisfaction; quite the contrary, because she has no private life: all other people and the whole world coexist in her. "Here I am, impersonal and free, right in the middle of the dance hall. I simultaneously contemplate all these lives, all these faces. And if I were to turn away from them, they would soon disintegrate like a forsaken landscape."

What strengthens Françoise' conviction is that, by an extraordinary piece of luck, even love has not made her realize her limits. Doubtless Pierre has come to be more to her than an object in her own particular world, a backdrop for her life as other men are. But for all that, he is not an Other. Françoise and Pierre have established such sincerity between them, have constructed such a machine of language, that they are together even when living apart from each other and can remain free in their union. "There was just one life and at its center one being, of which one could say neither that it was 'he' nor that it was 'I,' but only we.'" Every thought and every event of the day were communicated and shared, every sentiment immediately interpreted and made into a dialogue; the we-ness was sustained by all that happened to each one of them. For Françoise, Pierre is not an opaque being who masks everything else; he is simply a mode of behavior as clear to her as to himself, in harmony with a world which is not his private domain but belongs equally to Françoise.

To tell the truth, there are cracks in this construction right from the start. Simone de Beauvoir points out some of them: the book starts with a sacrifice on the part of Françoise. "Françoise looked at his fine green eyes beneath their curling lashes, the expectant mouth: If I had wanted to . . . Perhaps it still was not too late. But what could she want?" The consolation is convenient. I am losing nothing, Françoise tells herself, because I *am* my love for Pierre. Still, she is not at the point where she does not see Gerbert, does not consider an affair with him, nor does she tell Pierre all these first private thoughts. "Elsewhere" and "other" have not been eliminated; they have merely been repressed. Is Françoise wholly absorbed in the we-ness they have constructed? Is that common world, recreated and enlarged every day by their tireless conversations, really the world itself, or isn't it rather an artificial environment? Have they not exchanged the complacencies of the inner life for those of the life in common? Each questions himself before the other, but before whom are they questioned together? Françoise says ingenuously enough that the center of Paris is always where she is. This makes one think of children who also "have no inner life" and always believe themselves to be in the midst of the world because they project everything, including their dreams, into that world: they remain for all that no less in the midst of their subjectivity, since they do not distinguish these dreams from real things. Just as children do, Françoise always recoils before new things because they threaten to upset the environment she has constructed for herself. The real world, with all its harshness, does not permit so much precaution. If Françoise and Pierre arouse so much envy and even hatred around them, isn't it because the others feel shut out by this two-headed wonder, because they never feel accepted by them, but always betrayed by Françoise with Pierre, by Pierre with Françoise? Elisabeth and soon Xavière feel drained of their substance, receiving only strictly rationed kindnesses in return.

This eternal love of Pierre and Françoise is nonetheless temporal. Its not being threatened by Pierre's other love affairs is conditional on Pierre's telling Françoise about them, on their becoming objects of discussion, simple provinces in the world for two, and on Pierre's never really getting involved in any of them. It so happens that Pierre subscribes to these conditions of his own accord: " 'You know very well,' he said, 'that I never feel compromised by what goes on inside of me.' " For him, love means wanting to exist and to count for another. "To make her love me would be to impose myself upon her, to enter her world and to triumph there in accordance with her own values. . . . You know very well that I have an insane need of such triumphs." But do the women he "loves" ever really exist for him absolutely? His "adventures" are not his true adventure which he lives only with Françoise. His need for other love affairs is anxiety before the Other, a concern with having his mastery recognized and a quick way of verifying the universality of his life. Since Françoise does not feel free to love Gerbert, how could she leave Pierre free to love other women? No matter what she says, she does not love Pierre's *effective* liberty; she doesn't love him truly in love with another woman. She does not love him in his liberty unless it is a freedom to be indifferent, free of all involvements. Françoise, like Pierre, remains free to be loved but not to love. They are confiscated by each other, which is why Françoise draws back before an affair with Gerbert that would mean a genuine involvement and instead seeks Xavière's tenderness. The latter, so she thinks at least, will anchor her more securely in herself. "What delighted her most of all was to have annexed this sad little existence to her own life . . . ; nothing gave Françoise greater joy than this type of possession; Xavière's gestures, her face, her very life needed Françoise in order to exist." Just as the nations of Europe sensed French imperialism beneath the "universalist" policies of the National Convention, other people cannot help feeling frustrated if they are only dependencies in the world of Pierre and Françoise, and people sense beneath the generosity of these two a highly calculated enterprise. The other person is never admitted between them except warily, as a guest. Will he be satisfied with this role?

The metaphysical drama which Pierre and Françoise had succeeded in forgetting by dint of generosity is abruptly revealed by the presence of Xavière. Each in his own way has achieved the appearance of happiness and fulfillment by means of a general renunciation. " 'I for one,' said Xavière, 'was not born resigned.' " They thought they had overcome jealousy by the omnipotence of language; but when Xavière is requested to verbalize her life, she replies, " 'I don't have a public soul.' " One should make no mistake about the fact that if the silence she demands is perhaps that of equivocations and ambiguous feelings, it may also be that in which true commitment develops beyond all arguments and all motives. " 'Last night,' she said to Pierre, with an almost painful sneer, 'you seemed to be living things for once, and not just talking about them.' " Xavière challenges all the conventions by which Françoise and Pierre had thought to make their love invulnerable.

The dramatic situation of *L'Invitée* could be set forth in psychological terms: Xavière is *coquettish*, Pierre *desires* her, and Françoise is *jealous*. This would not be wrong. It would be merely superficial. What is coquetry if not the need to count for another person, combined with the fear of becoming involved? What is desire? One does not simply desire a body—one desires a being which one can occupy and rule over. Pierre's desire is mixed with his consciousness of Xavière as a valuable creature, and her value comes from her being completely what she feels, as her gestures and her face show at every moment. Finally, to say that Françoise is jealous is only another way of saying that Pierre is *turned toward* Xavière, that he is for once living a love affair, and that no verbal communication, no loyalty to the conventions established between himself and Françoise can re-integrate that love into Françoise's universe. The drama is therefore not psychological but metaphysical: Françoise thought she could be bound to Pierre and yet leave him free; not make a distinction between herself and him; will herself by willing him, as each wills the other in the realm of Kantian ends. The appearance of Xavière not only reveals to them a being from whom their values are excluded but also reveals that each of them is shut off from the other, and from himself. Among Kantian consciousnesses harmony can always be taken for granted. What the characters in this book discover is inherent individuality, the Hegelian self which seeks the death of the other.

The pages in which Françoise witnesses the ruin of her artificial world are perhaps the most beautiful in the book. She is no longer at the heart of things as if this were a natural privilege of hers: the world has a center from which she is excluded, and it is the place where Pierre and Xavière are to meet. With the others, things retreat beyond her grasp and become the strange debris of a world to which she no longer holds the key. The future ceases to be the natural extension of the present, time is fragmented, and Françoise is no more than an anonymous being, a creature without a history, a mass of chilled flesh. She now knows there are situations which cannot be communicated and which can only be understood by living them. There was a unique pulsation which projected before her a living present, a future, a world, which animated language for her—and that pulsation has stopped.

Does one even have to say that Pierre loves Xavière? A feeling is the name conventionally given to a series of instants, but life, when considered lucidly, is reduced to this swarming of instants to which chance alone gives a common meaning. In any case, the love of Françoise and Pierre only seemed to defy time insofar as it lost its reality. One can escape the crumbling of time only by an act of faith which now seems to Françoise a voluntary illusion. All love is a verbal construction, or at best a lifeless scholasticism. They had been pleased to think they had no inner lives, that they were really living a life in common. But, in the last analysis, if it is true that Pierre does not accept complicity with anyone against Françoise, is it not at least in complicity with himself and, at each moment, is it not from his solitude where he judges her that he rushes once again into the inter-world they had built? Henceforth, Françoise can no longer know herself from inner evidence alone. She can no longer doubt that, under the glance of that couple, she is truly an object, and through their eyes she sees herself from the outside for the first time. And what is she? A thirty-year-old woman, a mature woman, to whom many things are already irrevocably impossible—who, for example, will never be able to dance well. For the first time she has the feeling of being her body, when all along she had thought herself a consciousness. She has sacrificed everything to this myth. She has grown incapable of a single act of her own, of living close to her desires, and it is for this reason that she has ceased to be precious to Pierre, as Xavière knows so well how to be. That purity, that unselfishness, that morality they used to admire become hateful to her because they were all part of the same fiction. She and Pierre thought they had gone beyond individuality; she believed she had overcome jealousy and selfishness. How was she to know? Once she has recognized in all seriousness the existence of another person and accepted the objective picture of her life which she sees in the glances of other people, how could Françoise take as indubitable her own feeling about herself? How is one to recognize an inner reality? Has Pierre stopped loving her? And Françoise, is she jealous? Does she really scorn jealousy? Isn't her very doubt of this scorn itself a construction? An alienated consciousness can no longer believe in itself. At the moment when all projects thus collapse, when even the self's hold on itself is broken, death—which one's projects had traversed without even suspecting it up to now—becomes the only reality, since it is in death that the pulverization of time and life is consummated. Life has rejected Françoise.

The illness which comes over her is a sort of temporary solution. In the clinic to which she has been brought she neither asks herself any more questions, nor does she any longer feel abandoned because she has broken with her life. For the moment, the center of the world is in that room, and the most important event of the day is being X-rayed or having her temperature taken or the first meal she is going to get. All things have mysteriously regained their value: this container of orangeade on the table, that enameled wall are interesting in themselves. Every passing moment is replete and self-sufficient, and when her friends come up from Paris, they come out of nowhere each time they appear and are as intermittent as characters in a play. The petty discussions they bring to her bedside have no reality beside her solitude, which is no longer isolation. She has withdrawn from the human world where she was suffering into the natural world where she finds a frozen peace. As ordinary language so well expresses it, she *took* sick. Or would the crisis which is now subsiding perhaps have been less violent if it had not been for fatigue and the oncoming illness? Françoise herself will never know. All life is undeniably ambiguous, and there is never any way to know the true meaning of what we do. Indeed, perhaps our actions have no *single* true meaning.

Likewise, there is no way to tell whether the decisions Françoise reaches when, with renewed strength, she resumes her place between Pierre and Xavière are more truthful in themselves or whether they merely express the well-being and optimism of recovery. Xavière and Pierre have grown closer to each other during her absence and have ended by agreeing that they love one another. This time there must be no giving in to any ambiguous suffering. And after all, perhaps the only reason Françoise feels abandoned is that she remains aloof. Perhaps she can overtake this couple already formed without her; perhaps they can all live the same life if only Françoise will also accept responsibility for the enterprise of the trio. But she now knows that there is such a thing as solitude, that everyone decides for himself, that everyone is condemned to his own actions. She has lost the illusion of unobstructed communication, of happiness taken for granted, and of purity. But what if the only obstacle had been her own refusal, if happiness could be *made*, if freedom did not consist in cutting oneself off from all earthly involvements but in accepting and so going beyond them? What if Xavière had rescued them from the scholasticism which was killing their love? "What if she were finally to decide to plunge forward with all her might, instead of standing stock still, with limp and empty arms?" "It was so simple: this love which suddenly made her heart swell with sweetness had always been within arm's reach; she had only to stretch out her hand, that shy, greedy hand."

She will, then, reach out her hand. She will succeed in sticking with Pierre in his jealous passion for Xavière, right up to the moment when he spies on Xavière through a keyhole. And the trio will fail nevertheless. Just because it is a trio? True, the enterprise is a strange one. It is essential for love to be total, since the lover loves *a person,* not just *qualities,* and the beloved wants to feel justified in his very existence. The presence of a third person, even though and, in fact, just because he too is loved, introduces a mental reservation in each one's love for the other. The trio would really exist only if one could no longer distinguish two pairs of lovers and one pair of friends, if each one loved the other two *with equal feeling,* and if the good hoped for from them in return were not just their love for him but their love for one another as well; if, finally, they really lived as a threesome, instead of living two by two in alternating complicities with a general reunion every now and then. This is impossible; but a couple is hardly less impossible, since each partner remains in complicity with himself, and the love one receives is not the same as the love one gives. The immediate lives even of two people cannot be made one; it is the common tasks and projects that make the couple. The human couple is no more a *natural* reality than the trio. The failure of the trio (like the success of a couple) cannot be credited to any natural propensity. Are Xavière's defects then to be held responsible? She is jealous of Pierre, jealous of Françoise, jealous of their affection for their friends. Perversely, she upsets all this diplomacy "just to see what will happen." She is egoistic, which is to say that she never goes beyond herself and never puts herself in another's place: "Xavière did not care about making other people happy; she took a selfish delight in the pleasure of giving pleasure." She never lends or gives herself to any project. She will not work at becoming an actress or cross Paris to see a movie. She never sacrifices the immediate, never goes beyond the present moment. She always sticks to what she feels. Thus there is a certain kind of intimacy she will always evade; one may live beside her but never with her. She remains focused on herself, locked in moods one is never sure of truly understanding, about which perhaps there is no truth to be understood. But who knows? Can we tell what Xavière would be like in *another situation?* Here as everywhere, moral judgment does not go very far.

Françoise' love for Pierre succeeds in accepting Pierre's love for Xavière because it is deeper and older; and for this very reason Xavière can never accept the love between Pierre and Françoise. She senses a harmony between them which is over her head. Before meeting her they lived a whole *amour à deux* which is more essential than their predilection for her. Is it not precisely the torture of the trio that makes her incapable of loving either Pierre or Françoise in earnest?

It is not "Xavière's fault," nor Françoise', nor Pierre's; yet it is the fault of each of them. Each one is totally responsible because, if he acted differently, the others in turn would have treated him differently; and each can feel innocent because the others' freedom was invisible to him, and the face they offered to him was as fixed as fate. It is impossible to calculate each one's role in the drama, impossible to evaluate the responsibilities, to give a true version of the story, to put the events into their proper perspective. There is no Last Judgment. Not only do we not know the truth of the drama, but there is no truth—no other side of things where true and false, fair and unfair are separated out. We are inextricably and confusedly bound up with the world and with others.

Xavière sees Françoise as a forsaken, jealous woman, "armed with a bitter patience." There is not one word of this judgment, much as it rouses her indignation, which Françoise has not secretly said to herself. She has felt isolated, she has wished she might be loved as Xavière was, and she has put up with, not wished for, Pierre's love for Xavière. This does not mean that Xavière *is right*. If Françoise really had been forsaken, Xavière would not have felt so strongly how much she meant to Pierre. If Françoise had been jealous, she would not have suffered with him when he himself was jealous of Xavière: she loved Pierre in his liberty. One might answer, it is true, that Françoise' jealousy diminishes in direct proportion to the diminishing happiness of Pierre's love for Xavière. And so on, and so forth, *ad infinitum*. The truth is that our actions do not admit of any one motivation or explanation; they are "over-determined," as Freud so profoundly said. " 'You were jealous of me,' " Xavière says to Françoise, " 'because Labrousse was in love with me. You made him loathe me and took Gerbert away from me as well, to make your revenge even sweeter.' " Is this true, or is it false? Who is Françoise? Is she what she thinks of herself or what Xavière thinks of her? Françoise did not *intend* to hurt Xavière. She finally yielded to her fondness for Gerbert because she had come to understand that each of us has his own life and because she wanted to confirm her own existence after so many years of renunciation. But is the meaning of our actions to be found in our *intentions* or in the effect they have on others? And then again, are we ever completely unaware of what the consequences will be? Don't we really desire these consequences too? That secret love for Gerbert would be bound to look like revenge to Xavière—which Françoise could have guessed; and in loving Gerbert she implicitly accepted this consequence. Can one even say "implicitly"? "Strict as an order—as austere and pure as an icicle. Devoted, disdained, stuck in moral ruts. And she had said: No!" Françoise wanted to shatter the image of herself she had seen in Xavière's eyes. Is this not her way of saying that she wanted to get even with Xavière? We must not speak of the unconscious here. Xavière and the history of the trio are quite plainly at the root of the affair with Gerbert. It is simply that all of our actions have several meanings, especially as seen from the outside by others, and all these meanings are assumed in our actions because others are the permanent coordinates of our lives. Once we are aware of the existence of others, we commit ourselves to being, among other things, what they think of us, since we recognize in them the exorbitant power to *see us*. As long as Xavière exists, Françoise cannot help being what Xavière thinks she is. From this there follows the crime which, though it is no solution, since Xavière's death makes her dying image of Françoise eternal, ends the book.

Was there any solution? One might imagine a repentant or sick Xavière summoning Françoise to her side in order to confess her deceit. But Françoise would have been silly indeed to let this pacify her. There is no privilege inherent in the exaltation of repentance or of the last moments. One may very well feel that one is concluding one's life, dominating it, and solemnly handing out pardons or curses, but there is no proof that the convert or the dying man understands himself or others any better than before. We have no other resource at any moment than to act according to the judgments we have made as honestly and as intelligently as possible, as if these judgments were incontestable. But it would be dishonest and foolish ever to feel acquitted by the judgment of others. One moment of time cannot blot out another. Xavière's avowal could never obliterate her hatred, just as Pierre's return to Françoise does not annul the moments when he loved Xavière more than anything else.

III

THERE IS no absolute innocence and—for the same reason—no absolute guilt. All action is a response to a factual situation which we have not completely chosen and for which, in this sense, we are not absolutely responsible. Is it Pierre's fault or Françoise' that they are both thirty years old and Xavière twenty? Again, is it their fault if their simple presence condemns Elisabeth to feelings of frustration and alienation? Is it their fault they were born? How can we ever feel totally accountable for any of our actions, even those we have deliberately chosen, since at least the necessity of choosing has been imposed on us from the outside and since we have been cast into the world without first being consulted? All personal guilt is conditioned and overwhelmed by the general and original culpability with which fate burdens us by causing us to be born at a certain time, in a certain environment, and with a certain face; and if we can never feel justified no matter what we do, doesn't our conduct cease to matter? The world is such that our actions change their meaning as they issue and spread out from us. Sift through her memories as Françoise may, the moments she spent with Gerbert in that country inn contain nothing that is not radiant or pure. But the same love appears base to Xavière. Since this is how it always is, since it is our inevitable fate to be seen differently from the way we see ourselves, we have every right to feel that accusations from the outside do not quite pertain to us. The fundamental contingency of our lives makes us feel like *strangers* at the *trial* to which others have brought us. All conduct will always be absurd in an absurd world, and we can always decline responsibility for it, since in our heart of hearts, "We are not of the world" (Rimbaud).

It is true that we are always free to accept or refuse life. By accepting it we take the factual situations—our bodies, our faces, our way of being—upon ourselves; we accept our responsibilities; we sign a contract with the world and with men. But this freedom, the condition of all morality, is equally the basis of an absolute immoralism because it remains entire, in both myself and others, after every sin and because it makes new beings of us at every instant. How could an invulnerable liberty prefer any one line of conduct, any one relationship to another? Whether one emphasizes the conditioning of our existence or, on the contrary, our absolute liberty, our actions have no intrinsic and objective value—in the first case, because there are no degrees of absurdity, and no conduct can prevent us from bungling; and, in the second, because there are no degrees of freedom, and no conduct can lead us to perdition.

The fact is that the characters in *L'Invitée* lack any "moral sense." They do not find good and evil in things. They do not believe that human life, by itself, makes any definite demands, or that it follows a self-contained law as trees or bees do. They consider the world (including society and their own bodies) as an "unfinished piece of work"—to use Malebranche's profound phrase—which they question with curiosity and treat in various ways.

It is not so much their actions which bring down censure on these characters. Books, after all, are full of adultery, perversion, and crime, and the critics have come across them before this. The smallest town has more than one *ménage à trois*. Such a "family" is still a family. But how is one to accept the fact that Pierre, Françoise, and Xavière are totally ignorant of the holy natural law of the couple and that they try in all honesty—and without, moreover, any hint of sexual complicity—to form a trio? The sinner is always accepted, even in the strictest societies, because he is part of the system and, as a sinner, does not question its principles. What one finds unbearable in Pierre and Françoise is their artless disavowal of morality, that air of candor and youth, that absolute lack of gravity, dizziness, and remorse. In brief, they think as they act and act as they think.

Are these qualities only acquired through skepticism, and do we mean that absolute immoralism is the last word in an "existential" philosophy? Not at all. There is an existentialism which leans toward skepticism, but it is certainly not that of *L'Invitée*. On the pretext that every rational or linguistic operation condenses a certain thickness of existence and is obscure for itself, one concludes that nothing can be said with certainty. On the pretext that human acts lose all their meaning when detached from their context and broken down into their component parts (like the gestures of the man I can see but do not hear through the window of a telephone booth), one concludes that all conduct is senseless. It is easy to strip language and actions of all meaning and to make them seem absurd, if only one looks at them from far enough away: this was Voltaire's technique in *Micromégas*. But that other miracle, the fact that, in an absurd world, language and behavior do have meaning for those who speak and act, remains to be understood. In the hands of French writers existentialism is always threatening to fall back into the "isolating" analysis which breaks time up into unconnected instants and reduces life to a collection of states of consciousness.[3]

As for Simone de Beauvoir, she is not vulnerable to such criticism. Her book shows existence understood between two limits: on the one hand, there is the immediate closed tightly upon itself, beyond any word and any commitment (Xavière); and, on the other, there is an absolute confidence in language and rational decision, an existence which grows empty in the effort to transcend itself (Françoise at the beginning of the book).[4] Between these fragments of time and that

3. Sartre criticized Camus for giving way to this tendency in *L'Étranger*. [English translation by Stuart Gilbert, *The Stranger* (New York, 1954).]

4. I am keenly aware of how regrettable it is to write such a weighty commentary about a novel. But the novel has won its place in the public esteem and has nothing to lose or gain from my remarks.

eternity which erroneously believes it transcends time, there is an effective existence which unfolds in patterns of behavior, is organized like a melody, and, by means of its projects, cuts across time without leaving it. There is undoubtedly no *solution* to human problems; no way, for example, to eliminate the transcendence of time, the separation of consciousnesses which may always reappear to threaten our commitments; no way to test the authenticity of these commitments which may always, in a moment of fatigue, seem artificial conventions to us. But between these two extremes at which existence perishes, total existence is our decision by which we enter time in order to create our life within it. All human projects are contradictory because they simultaneously attract and repel their realization. One only pursues a thing in order to possess it, and yet, if what I am looking for today must someday be found (which is to say, passed beyond), why bother to look for it? Because today is today and tomorrow, tomorrow. I can no more look at my present from the point of view of the future than I can see the earth from Sirius.[5] I would not love a person without the hope of being recognized by him, and yet this recognition does not count unless it is always free, that is, never possessed. But, after all, love does exist. Communication exists between the moments of my personal time, as between my time and that of other people, and in spite of the rivalry between them. It exists, that is, if I will it, if I do not shrink from it out of bad faith, if I am of good faith, if I plunge into the time which both separates and unites us, as the Christian plunges into God. True morality does not consist in following exterior rules or in respecting objective values: there are no ways to *be* just or to *be* saved. One would do better to pay less attention to the unusual situation of the three characters in *L'Invitée* and more to the good faith, the loyalty to promises, the respect for others, the generosity and the seriousness of the two principals. For the value is there. It consists of actively being what we are by chance, of establishing that communication with others and with ourselves for which our temporal structure gives us the opportunity and of which our liberty is only the rough outline.

5. This idea has been developed in Simone de Beauvoir's essay *Pyrrhus et Cinéas*.

3 / A Scandalous Author

AT FIRST GLANCE Sartre's literary fate presents a mystery to those who know him: no man could be less provocative, and yet as an author he creates a scandal. I met him one day twenty years ago when the Ecole Normale unleashed its fury against one of my schoolmates and myself for having hissed the traditional songs, too vulgar to suit us. He slipped between us and our persecutors and contrived a way for us to get out of our heroic and ridiculous situation without concessions or damages. During the year he spent as a prisoner of war, this anti-Christ established cordial relationships with a great many priests and Jesuits, who consulted him as a sensible man about certain aspects of Marian theology. Literary colleagues who dislike his ideas try to make him angry by suggesting the theses which they believe are most contrary to his own. He reflects, nods his head, says he agrees, and gives his interlocutors a hundred good reasons to persevere in their chosen direction. This corrupter of youth will tell those who consult him about some personal problem that their situation is unique, that no one can decide for them, and that they must judge for themselves. This man with a genius for publicity will loan unpublished manuscripts to friends who lose them or to obscure personalities who carry them off to other countries. He will throw out young flatterers, because they have time to learn about life, but listen to boring old men, because they are old men. This "demoniacal" novelist—to use Claudel's expression—has never been known to lack tact in dealing with the worst petitioners as long as they are as simple as himself. To say "Hell is other people" does not mean "Heaven is me." If other people are the instruments of our torture, it is first and foremost because they are indispensable to our salvation. We are so intermingled with them that we must make what order we can out of this chaos. Sartre put Garcin in Hell not for being a coward but for having made his wife suffer. This disrespectful author scrupulously observes in his relations with others the Stendhalian rule condemning "lack of consideration."

This type of goodness is projected into the characters of his novels. In *L'Âge de raison*, Mathieu accepts the role of husband and father.[1] Marcelle would only have to say the word. He does not seduce Ivitch because he scorns the ceremony of seduction: words running contrary to actions, insistence, indirection, deceitful behavior, and, in the last analysis, because he does not claim any rights over her, because he respects her and wishes her to be free. In Sartre's novels one will not find those dagger-sharp words which so delight the critics of Bernstein, unless they are uttered in Hell. There is no twilight zone, no self-satisfaction, no sensuality except as satire and in the characters he later sacrifices. Sartre's favorite characters have a rare good will and propriety. How does it happen, then, that the newspaper critics have spoken with almost one voice of filth, immorality, and spinelessness? There must be something in the very virtues of his heroes which makes them invisible or even hateful to common opinion. Let us try to solve the riddle.

It is revealing to examine the complaints most often made about him—the charge, for example, that his books are full of ugliness. Emile Henriot, who does indeed seem a "man of taste," has cited as horrible the passage in *L'Âge de raison* where Ivitch drinks foolishly and makes herself sick. This is the scene that ends with two sacrilegious lines which stand a good chance of becoming famous: "A sharp little smell of vomit escaped from her pure mouth. Mathieu passionately inhaled that smell." The chapter in *Le Sursis* which describes the beginnings of love between two invalids, recounting all the humiliations caused them by their illness, has been proclaimed "intolerable" by Henriot or some other author.[2] The critics seem to think all is said and done when they have proved that Sartre has a certain fondness for the horrible.

But the real question is: What purpose does the horrible serve in the work of Sartre, and what does it signify? We are in the habit—and perhaps it is no more than that—of defining art by the beauty of its objects. All Hegel could see in this was the formula of a classical art which had disappeared before the dawn of Christianity; and the essence of romantic art which follows is not the harmony of the mind and appearances wherein lies the beauty of the Greek god, but rather their disharmony. "Romantic art no longer aspires to reproduce life in the state of infinite serenity . . . : on the contrary, it turns its back on

1. English translation by Eric Sutton, *The Age of Reason* (New York, 1947).— Trans.

2. English translation of *Le Sursis* by Eric Sutton, *The Reprieve* (New York, 1947).—Trans.

this pinnacle of beauty and brings interiority into juxtaposition with all that is accidental in exterior formations, giving unlimited place to features characterized by what is the antithesis of the beautiful." The ugly or horrible is the basic clash of inner and outer. The appearance of the spirit among things is a scandal among them, and, reciprocally, things in their bare existence are a scandal for the spirit. Romantic art "stamps an accidental character both inside and out, establishes a separation between these two aspects which means the very negation of art, and reveals the need for consciousness to discover higher forms than those of art in order to know the truth." [3] If inner and outer are reunited, their meeting will not be harmonious or beautiful but will have, rather, the violence of the sublime.

Well, one need neither elevate the tone nor hunt for the paradox to find a "minor sublimity" in the sentence from *L'Âge de raison* which so shocked Emile Henriot, a sublimity without eloquence or illusions which is, I believe, an invention of our time. It is nothing new to call man a combination of angel and animal, but most critics lack Pascal's boldness. They are reluctant to mix the angelic and the bestial in man. They need something above and beyond human disorder, and if they do not find this in religion, they seek it in a religion of the beautiful.

The complaint against ugliness here joins another, more general complaint. When Sartre wrote that every work of art expresses a stand taken about the problems of human life (including political life), and when he recently tried to rediscover the vital decision through which Baudelaire arrived at the themes of his suffering and his poetry, the same uneasiness or anger was apparent, this time among eminent authors. "You are leading us back into the dark ages," said Gide in effect. And those who cannot bear for Flaubert or Baudelaire to be questioned about the use they made of their lives keep on repeating, for their own consolation, that *Sartre is no artist.*

The religion of art risks becoming a technique for making things pretty if it refuses to mingle intimately with life. Gide, in what is itself an overly pretty phrase, has said that "there are no problems in art for which the work of art is not an adequate solution." Sartre least of all would deny that the work of art belongs to the world of imagination, that in this sense it transforms the prose of daily life, and that expression poses problems. Nonetheless, he believes that the writer's imaginative and effective lives work together or, rather, that they issue from one source: the way he has chosen to treat the world, other people, death and time. No author has been so little concerned with biography as Sartre; he has never stated his ideas except in his works

3. *Esthétique*, trans. Jankélévitch, II, 254. [English translation of Hegel's *Ästhetik* by F. P. B. Osmaston, *The Philosophy of Fine Art* (4 vols.; London, 1920).]

and has not as yet given us any intimate diary.[4] No one, therefore, would be less tempted to explain ideas or works by the circumstances of the author's life. The question here is quite different, one of going back to the undivided choice which is at one and the same time the choice of a life and of a certain kind of art. He questions the artist, as he does all men, about his basic decision—not to reduce the artistic process to the proportions of everyday language, but, quite the contrary, because he believes that the moment of self-expression or self-creation is to be found in each of us. Everything happens on the level of life because life is metaphysical.

The misunderstanding between Sartre and the "artists" stems from the artists' unwillingness to question the dichotomy of art and culture and their nostalgic wish to retain order and harmony as human attributes. After the defeat of 1940, Gide spent his time reading and rereading: he plunged into *Alexandre,* took up *Hermann et Dorothée* again, discussed assonances and the use of conjunctions, amused himself with finding a hemistich of Mallarmé in Victor Hugo. He lived in the world of culture and the "exquisite." One would have thought that all men, and Gide himself, were on earth just to make works of art and beauty possible, as plants exist to grow flowers. But here one must call Gide to witness against Gide. Whenever a meeting or an incident occurs, Gide is always sensitive and attentive to the occasion, and concrete humanity breaks into his *Journal.* Thus, Gide regrets not having seen the war from closer up, not having had more adventures. And so contact is re-established with raw life, and that admirable insight into others—which alternates with the religion of art as Gide's fundamental passion—once again appears. Man is then no longer simply the bearer of works of art; his bare, fortuitous existence is itself the absolute value, and Gide's response to the question of man's ultimate meaning is practically that of Sartre. "The more one thinks about it . . . , the more one is overwhelmed by this obvious truth: it has neither rhyme nor reason (Antoine Thibault). But why the devil should it? Man is an uninteresting miracle (Jean Rostand). But what in the world would it take for this miracle to acquire importance in your eyes, for you to deem it worthy of interest?" [5] Beyond the serenity of the work of art it is man's unjustified existence which is interesting.

Perhaps Sartre is scandalous just as Gide was: because he considers man's value to be his imperfection. "I do not like men," said Gide. "I like what consumes them." Sartre's freedom consumes organ-

4. Only lately has Sartre begun his autobiography with an account of his childhood, *Les Mots* (Paris, 1964).—Trans.

5. *Journal, 1939–1942.* [English translation by Justin O'Brien, *Gide: Journals,* Vol. IV (New York, 1951).]

ized humanity. Matter, sky, harvests, animals are beautiful. Man's attitudes, his very clothes, bear witness to the fact that he is of a different order. He is a flaw in the diamond of the world. Beneath the gaze of this being who is no being at all, who has no fixed instincts, no still point of equilibrium and repose, objects lose their self-sufficiency and self-evidence and, in a sudden reversal, appear arbitrary and superfluous, but he too is superfluous in the world of objects. Ugliness is the collision of man as nothingness or freedom with nature as plenitude and fate.

If humanism is the religion of man as a natural species, or the religion of man as a perfected creature, Sartre is as far from humanism today as he ever was. Nothing man does is absolutely pure or venerable, not even, especially not, the "perfect moments" he contrives for himself in life or in art. At the end of *La Nausée* a strain of music at last offered something incontestable, but it was no accident that Sartre selected "Some of These Days" for this final elevation.[6] He thus refused in advance the religion of art and its consolations. Man may get beyond his contingency in what he creates, but all expression, even what is known as Great Art, is an act born of man. The miracle takes place everywhere at ground-level, not in the privileged heaven of fine arts. The principles of order and disorder are one; the contingency of things and our liberty which dominates it are cut from the same cloth. If Sartre today calls himself a humanist, it does not mean that he has changed his mind: what he respects in man is still that basic imperfection which allows him—and only him—to create himself. The savagery of *La Nausée* is still there; it is only that Sartre has come to realize that men were close to his heart, even when he judged them most severely. "I can't help it," he said one day, in front of the swarming Gare du Luxembourg, "these fellows *interest me*." He became aware that all attempts to live apart were hypocritical because we are all mysteriously related, because others see us and so become an inalienable dimension of our lives—become, in fact, ourselves. The bonds of blood or species count for nothing: each of us is generic at our most individual, since our freedom waits for the recognition of other people and needs them to become what it is. The threat of war and the experience of the Occupation brought out the positive value hidden beneath the sarcasms of *La Nausée*. Fifteen years ago Sartre said that politics was unthinkable (as is, in every respect, the Other—that is, a consciousness seen from the outside). Since then he has discovered that it must indeed be thought, since it must be lived, and that there must be something valid in it, since through politics we have experi-

6. English translation by Lloyd Alexander, *Nausea* (Norfolk, Conn., 1949). —Trans.

enced absolute evil. The problem is to instill that radical freedom, which is the negation of humanity as a given species and which is an appeal for a self-created humanity, into human relations and to transmute it into history.

It is safe to predict that this new language will not win anyone over to Sartre's side: Christians and Marxists seem equally eager to forget whatever was wild and harsh at the start of the two traditions. Mathieu in *L'Âge de raison* may indeed be a man of good will, ready to sacrifice his own wishes; but this will not be reckoned to his credit. Personal forbearance is not what was asked of him. He is called to sacrifice in the name of a natural law. He is astounded at being a man and a father, but he is, on the other hand, ready to accept the consequences of this situation. He should revere it, be glorified by it. The decadence which threatens religious thought makes any slightly violent description of the human paradox seem shocking and diabolical. As if Christianity had anything to do with nature fetishism, as if it had not destroyed blood and family ties to create the bonds of the spirit. The Christians of fifty years ago found themselves face to face with a concise rationalism which regarded religion as pure absurdity. But the old-school rationalists did not question the customs of organized humanity, being content simply to base them on reason, and their freedom was one of good company. This is why the Catholics, after having polemicized against them for so long, now seem to miss them and reserve their severity for Sartre.

An analogous phenomenon occurs among the Marxists: in general, they seem more curious about the 18th century than about Hegel or Marx. They talk about dialectic much less than about science (which, carried over into politics, produces Comte and, through him, Maurras). They try to outdo each other in their distrust of the subjective, to the very point of explaining Descartes without once mentioning the *cogito*. Even though Marxism is completely based on the idea that there is no such thing as destiny, that sociological "laws" are valid only within the framework of a certain historical state of society, that it is up to men to regain control of the social apparatus and change a history that is undergone into one that is willed; even though Marxism consequently assumes a view of history which sees it as open, of man as maker of his fate, and should be sympathetic to all forms of radical criticism—one notes, on the contrary, a surprising timidity in most Marxists. Their criticism no longer surpasses and conquers: it warns, restrains, and lectures. Marxism's dominant virtue is no longer daring but prudence; it wonders learnedly whether the artist's liberty is compatible with morality and with the functioning of society. . . .

It is doubtful that Sartre's moral theory, when he publishes it, will disarm his critics. Were he even, in his way, to lay the foundation for an objectivity of values, were he to admit that these values are given by our situation at the same time as we invent them, he would still be criticized for making them subject to our unconditional recognition and consent—which was, however, what a philosopher like Lagneau did in less timid times. Well, Sartre will not give an inch on that point. "When people speak to me about freedom," he used to say, "it is as if they were speaking about myself." He identifies himself with that transparency or that agility which is not of the world and which, as he has written, makes freedom "mortal." That is an intuition from which one may go forward but cannot turn back—and which those who wish to remain asleep will always find disagreeable. The story is told of a French journalist who sent one of Sartre's recently published lectures to a Soviet critic, having excused himself beforehand for anything "backward" in it, and who was surprised to have the work highly praised in reply. "It has a spark we have been needing for a long time," is more or less what the critic said. He was right—but will he be heard? The same Cartesian virtue of generosity which makes Sartre's behavior human and reassuring will always make his books disturbing, since they reveal the prehuman root of such virtue. What makes the man winning makes the author scandalous.

And so he will go his way, between the total esteem of some and the wrath of others. There is no need to fear that the spark will go out. Sartre at first protested when the journalists labeled him an "existentialist." Then one day he said to himself that he had no right to refuse the label, which is what others see of him, and he valiantly took existentialism's side. Those who assume he is dogmatic do not know him very well, however: even when he is bending to the work fate has laid out for him, he does so with a smile. One might wish that this freedom would materialize in more solid literary images, but one cannot speak too highly of it; it is truly the salt of the earth. There are no indications that we are going to run out of sleepers and valets. It is good that from time to time there is a free man.

4 / The Film
and the New Psychology[1]

CLASSICAL PSYCHOLOGY considers our visual field to be a
sum or mosaic of sensations, each of which is strictly dependent on
the local retinal stimulus which corresponds to it. The new psychology
reveals, first of all, that such a parallelism between sensations and the
nervous phenomenon conditioning them is unacceptable, even for our
simplest and most immediate sensations. Our retina is far from homogeneous: certain parts, for example, are blind to blue or red, yet I do
not see any discolored areas when looking at a blue or red surface. This
is because, starting at the level of simply seeing colors, my perception
is not limited to registering what the retinal stimuli prescribe but re-
organizes these stimuli so as to re-establish the field's homogeneity.
Broadly speaking, we should think of it not as a mosaic but as a system
of configurations. Groups rather than juxtaposed elements are principal and primary in our perception. We group the stars into the same
constellations as the ancients, yet it is *a priori* possible to draw the
heavenly map many other ways. Given the series:

a b c d e f g h i j
· · · · · · · · · ·

we will always pair the dots according to the formula a-b, c-d,
e-f, etc., although the grouping b-c, d-e, f-g, etc. is equally probable in
principle. A sick person contemplating the wallpaper in his room will
suddenly see it transformed if the pattern and figure become the
ground while what is usually seen as ground becomes the figure. The
idea we have of the world would be overturned if we could succeed in
seeing the intervals between things (for example, the space between
the trees on the boulevard) as *objects* and, inversely, if we saw the

1. Lecture delivered March 13, 1945, at l'Institut des Hautes Etudes Cinémato-
graphiques.

[48]

things themselves—the trees—as the ground. This is what happens in puzzles: we cannot see the rabbit or the hunter because the elements of these figures are dislocated and are integrated into other forms: for example, what is to be the rabbit's ear is still just the empty interval between two trees in the forest. The rabbit and the hunter become apparent through a new partition of the field, a new organization of the whole. Camouflage is the art of masking a form by blending its principal defining lines into other, more commanding forms.

The same type of analysis can be applied to hearing: it will simply be a matter of temporal forms rather than spatial ones. A melody, for example, is a figure of sound and does not mingle with the background noises (such as the siren one hears in the distance during a concert) which may accompany it. The melody is not a sum of notes, since each note only counts by virtue of the function it serves in the whole, which is why the melody does not perceptibly change when transposed, that is, when all its notes are changed while their interrelationships and the structure of the whole remain the same. On the other hand, just one single change in these interrelationships will be enough to modify the entire make-up of the melody. Such a perception of the whole is more natural and more primary than the perception of isolated elements: it has been seen from conditioned-reflex experiments, where, through the frequent association of a piece of meat with a light or a sound, dogs are trained to respond to that light or sound by salivating, that the training acquired in response to a certain series of notes is simultaneously acquired for any melody with the same structure. Therefore analytical perception, through which we arrive at absolute value of the separate elements, is a belated and rare attitude—that of the scientist who observes or of the philosopher who reflects. The perception of forms, understood very broadly as structure, grouping, or configuration should be considered our spontaneous way of seeing.

There is still another point on which modern psychology over-throws the prejudices of classical physiology and psychology. It is a commonplace to say that we have five senses, and it would seem, at first glance, that each of them is like a world out of touch with the others. The light or colors which act upon the eye do not affect the ears or the sense of touch. Nevertheless it has been known for a long time that certain blind people manage to represent the colors they cannot see by means of the sounds which they hear: for example, a blind man said that red ought to be something like a trumpet peal. For a long time it was thought that such phenomena were exceptional, whereas they are, in fact, general. For people under mescaline, sounds are regularly accompanied by spots of color whose hue, form, and vividness vary with the tonal quality, intensity, and pitch of the sounds. Even normal subjects speak of hot, cold, shrill, or hard colors, of sounds that are clear, sharp, brilliant, rough, or mellow, of soft noises and of penetrating fragrances. Cézanne said that one could see the velvetiness, the hardness, the softness, and even the odor of objects. My perception is therefore not a sum of visual, tactile, and audible givens: I perceive in a total way with my whole being; I grasp a unique structure of the thing, a unique way of being, which speaks to all my senses at once.

Naturally, classical psychology was well aware that relationships exist between the different parts of my visual field just as between the data of my different senses—but it held this unity to be a construction and referred it to intelligence and memory. In a famous passage from the *Méditations* Descartes wrote: I say that I see men going by in the street, but what exactly do I really see? All I see are hats and coats which might equally well be covering dolls that only move by springs, and if I say that I see men, it is because I apprehend "through an inspection of the mind what I thought I beheld with my eyes." I am convinced that objects continue to exist when I no longer see them (behind my back, for example). But it is obvious that, for classical thought, these invisible objects subsist for me only because my judgment keeps them present. Even the objects right in front of me are not truly seen but merely thought. Thus I cannot *see* a cube, that is, a solid with six surfaces and twelve edges; all I ever see is a perspective figure of which the lateral surfaces are distorted and the back surface completely hidden. If I am able to speak of cubes, it is because my mind sets these appearances to rights and restores the hidden surface. I cannot see a cube as its geometrical definition presents it: I can only think it. The perception of movement shows even more clearly the extent to which intelligence intervenes in what claims to be vision. When my train starts, after it has been standing in the station, I often "see" the train next to mine begin to move. Sensory data are therefore neutral in themselves and can be differently interpreted according to the hypothesis on which my mind comes to rest. Broadly speaking, classical psychology made perception a real deciphering of sense data by the intelligence, a beginning of science, as it were. I am given certain signs from which I must dig out the meaning; I am presented with a text which I must read or interpret. Even when it takes the unity of the perceptual field into account, classical psychology remains loyal to the notion of sensation which was the starting point of the analysis. Its original conception of visual data as a mosaic of sensations forces it to base the unity of the perceptual field on an operation of the intelligence. What does *gestalt* theory tell us on this point? By resolutely rejecting the notion of sensation it teaches us to stop distinguishing between signs and their significance, between what is sensed and what is judged. How could we define the exact color of an object without mentioning the substance of which it is made, without saying, of this blue rug, for example, that it is a "woolly blue"? Cézanne asked how one is to distinguish the color of things from their shape. It is impossible to understand perception as the imputation of a certain significance to certain sensible signs, since the most immediate sensible texture of these signs cannot be described without referring to the object they signify.

Our ability to recognize an object defined by certain constant properties despite changes of lighting stems, not from some process by which our intellect takes the nature of the incident light into account and deduces the object's real color from it, but from the fact that the light which dominates the environment acts as *lighting* and immediately assigns the object its true color. If we look at two plates under unequal lighting, they will appear equally white and unequally lighted as long as the beam of light from the window figures in our visual field. On the other hand, if we observe the same plates through a hole in a screen, one will immediately appear gray and the other white; and even if we *know* that it is nothing but an effect of the lighting, no intellectual analysis of the way they appear will make us see the true color of the two plates. When we turn on the lights at dusk, the electric light seems yellow at first but a moment later tends to lose all definite color; correlatively, the objects, whose color was at first perceptibly modified, resume an appearance comparable to the one they have during the day. Objects and lighting form a system which tends toward a certain constancy and a certain level of stability—not through the operation of intelligence but through the very configuration of the field. I do not think the world in the act of perception: it organizes itself in front of me. When I perceive a cube, it is not because my reason sets the perspectival appearances straight and thinks the geometrical definition of a cube with respect to them. I do not even notice the distortions of perspective, much less correct them; I am at the cube itself in its manifestness through what I see. The objects behind my back are likewise not represented to me by some operation of memory or judgment; they are present, they *count* for me, just as the ground which I do not see continues nonetheless to be present beneath the figure which partially hides it. Even the perception of movement, which at first seems to depend directly on the point of reference chosen by the intellect is in turn only one element in the global organization of the field. For, although it is true that, when either my train or the one next to it starts, first one, then the other may appear to be moving, one should note that the illusion is not arbitrary and that I cannot willfully induce it by the completely intellectual choice of a point of reference. If

I am playing cards in my compartment, the other train will start moving; if, on the other hand, I am looking for someone in the adjacent train, then mine will begin to roll. In each instance the one which seems stationary is the one we have chosen as our abode and which, for the time being, is our environment. Movement and rest distribute themselves in our surroundings not according to the hypotheses which our intelligence is pleased to construct but according to the way we settle ourselves in the world and the position our bodies assume in it. Sometimes I see the steeple motionless against the sky with clouds floating above it, and sometimes the clouds appear still and the steeple falls through space. But here again the choice of the fixed point is not made by the intelligence: the looked-at object in which I anchor myself will always seem fixed, and I cannot take this meaning away from it except by looking elsewhere. Nor do I give it this meaning through thought. Perception is not a sort of beginning science, an elementary exercise of the intelligence; we must rediscover a commerce with the world and a presence to the world which is older than intelligence.

Finally, the new psychology also brings a new concept of the perception of others. Classical psychology unquestioningly accepted the distinction between inner observation, or introspection, and outer observation. "Psychic facts"—anger or fear, for example—could be directly known only from the inside and by the person experiencing them. It was thought to be self-evident that I can grasp only the corporal *signs* of anger or fear from the outside and that I have to resort to the anger or fear I know in myself through introspection in order to interpret these signs. Today's psychologists have made us notice that in reality introspection gives me almost nothing. If I try to study love or hate purely from inner observation, I will find very little to describe: a few pangs, a few heart-throbs—in short, trite agitations which do not reveal the essence of love or hate. Each time I find something worth saying, it is because I have not been satisfied to coincide with my feeling, because I have succeeded in studying it as a way of behaving, as a modification of my relations with others and with the world, because I have managed to think about it as I would think about the behavior of another person whom I happened to witness. In fact, young children understand gestures and facial expressions long before they can reproduce them on their own; the meaning must, so to speak, adhere to the behavior. We must reject that prejudice which makes "inner realities" out of love, hate, or anger, leaving them accessible to one single witness: the person who feels them. Anger, shame, hate, and love are not psychic facts hidden at the bottom of another's consciousness: they are types of behavior or styles of conduct which are visible from the outside. They exist *on* this face or *in* those gestures, not hidden behind them. Psychology did not begin to develop until the day it gave up the distinction between mind and body, when it abandoned the two correlative methods of interior observation and physiological psychology. We learned nothing about emotion as long as we limited ourselves to measuring the rate of respiration or heartbeat in an angry person, and we didn't learn anything more when we tried to express the qualitative and inexpressible nuances of lived anger. To create a psychology of anger is to try to ascertain the *meaning* of anger, to ask oneself how it functions in human life and what purpose it serves. So we find that emotion is, as Janet said, a disorganizing reaction which comes into play whenever we are stuck. On a deeper level, as Sartre has shown, we find that anger is a magical way of acting by which we afford ourselves a completely symbolic satisfaction in the imagination after renouncing effective action in the world, just as, in a conversation, a person who cannot convince his partner will start hurling insults at him which prove nothing or as a man who does not dare strike his opponent will shake his fist at him from a distance. Since emotion is not a psychic, internal fact but rather a variation in our relations with others and the world which is expressed in our bodily attitude, we cannot say that only the signs of love or anger are given to the outside observer and that we understand others indirectly by interpreting these signs: we have to say that others are directly manifest to us as behavior. Our behavioral science goes much farther than we think. When unbiased subjects are confronted with photographs of several faces, copies of several kinds of handwriting, and recordings of several voices and are asked to put together a face, a silhouette, a voice, and a handwriting, it has been shown that the elements are usually put together correctly or that, in any event, the correct matchings greatly outnumber the incorrect ones. Michelangelo's handwriting is attributed to Raphael in 36 cases, but in 221 instances it is correctly identified, which means that we recognize a certain common structure in each person's voice, face, gestures and bearing and that each person is nothing more nor less to us than this structure or way of being in the world. One can see how these remarks might be applied to the psychology of language: just as a man's body and "soul" are but two aspects of his way of being in the world, so the word and the thought it indicates should not be considered two externally related terms: the word bears its meaning in the same way that the body incarnates a manner of behavior.

The new psychology has, generally speaking, revealed man to us not as an understanding which constructs the world but as a being thrown into the world and attached to it by a natural bond. As a result it re-educates us in how to see this world which we touch at every point of our being, whereas classical psychology abandoned the lived world for the one which scientific intelligence succeeded in constructing.

*   *   *   *

If we now consider the film as a perceptual object, we can apply what we have just said about perception in general to the perception of a film. We will see that this point of view illuminates the nature and significance of the movies and that the new psychology leads us straight to the best observations of the aestheticians of the cinema.

Let us say right off that a film is not a sum total of images but a temporal *gestalt*. This is the moment to recall Pudovkin's famous experiment which clearly shows the melodic unity of films. One day Pudovkin took a close-up of Mosjoukin with a completely impassive expression and projected it after showing: first, a bowl of soup, then, a young woman lying dead in her coffin, and, last, a child playing with a teddy-bear. The first thing noticed was that Mosjoukin seemed to be looking at the bowl, the young woman, and the child, and next one noted that he was looking pensively at the dish, that he wore an expression of sorrow when looking at the woman, and that he had a glowing smile for the child. The audience was amazed at his variety of expression although the same shot had actually been used all three times and was, if anything, remarkably inexpressive. The meaning of a shot therefore depends on what precedes it in the movie, and this succession of scenes creates a new reality which is not merely the sum of its parts. In an excellent article in *Esprit,* R. Leenhardt added that one still has to bring in the time-factor for each shot: a short duration is suitable for an amused smile, one of intermediate length for an indifferent face, and an extended one for a sorrowful expression.[2] Leenhardt drew from this the following definition of cinematographic rhythm: "A certain order of shots and a certain duration for each of these shots or views, so that taken together they produce the desired impression with maximum effectiveness." There really is, then, a cinematographic system of measurements with very precise and very imperious requirements. "When you see a movie, try to guess the moment when a shot has given its all and must move on, end, be replaced either by changing the angle, the distance, or the field. You will get to know that constriction of the chest produced by an overlong shot which brakes the movement and that deliciously intimate acquiescence when a shot fades at the right moment." Since a film consists not only of montage (the selection of shots or views, their order and length) but also of cutting (the selection of scenes or

2. *Esprit,* 1936.

sequences, and their order and length), it seems to be an extremely complex form inside of which a very great number of actions and reactions are taking place at every moment. The laws of this form, moreover, are yet to be discovered, having until now only been sensed by the flair or tact of the director, who handles cinematographic language as a man manipulates syntax: without explicitly thinking about it and without always being in a position to formulate the rules which he spontaneously obeys.

What we have just said about visual films also applies to sound movies, which are not a sum total of words or noises but are likewise a *gestalt*. A rhythm exists for sounds just as for images. There is a montage of noises and sounds, as Leenhardt's example of the old sound movie *Broadway Melody* shows. "Two actors are on stage. We are in the balcony listening to them speak their parts. Then immediately there is a close-up, whispering, and we are aware of something they are saying to each other under their breath. . . ." The expressive force of this montage lies in its ability to make us sense the coexistence, the simultaneity of lives in the same world, the actors as they are for us and for themselves, just as, previously, we saw Pudovkin's visual montage linking the man and his gaze to the sights which surround him. Just as a film is not merely a play photographed in motion and the choice and grouping of the shots constitutes an original means of expression for the motion picture, so, equally, the soundtrack is not a simple phonographic reproduction of noises and words but requires a certain internal organization which the film's creator must invent. The real ancestor of the movie soundtrack is not the phonograph but the radio play.

Nor is that all. We have been considering sight and sound by turns, but in reality the way they are put together makes another new whole, which cannot be reduced to its component parts. A sound movie is not a silent film embellished with words and sounds whose only function is to complete the cinematographic illusion. The bond between sound and image is much closer, and the image is transformed by the proximity of sound. This is readily apparent in the case of dubbed films, where thin people are made to speak with the voices of fat people, the young have the voices of the old, and tall people the voices of tiny ones—all of which is absurd if what we have said is true—namely, that voice, profile, and character form an indivisible unit. And the union of sound and image occurs not only in each character but in the film as a whole. It is not by accident that characters are silent at one moment and speak at another. The alternation of words and silence is manipulated to create the most effective image. There are three sorts of dialogue, as Malraux said in *Verve* (1940). First may be noted expository dialogue, whose purpose is to make the circumstances of the dramatic action known. The novel and the film both avoid this sort of dialogue. Then there is *tonal* dialogue, which gives us each character's particular accent and which dominates, for example, in Proust where the characters are very hard to visualize but are admirably recognizable as soon as they start to talk. The extravagant or sparing use of words, their richness or emptiness, their precision or affectation reveal the essence of a character more surely than many descriptions. Tonal dialogue rarely occurs in movies, since the visible presence of the actor with his own particular manner of behaving rarely lends itself to it. Finally we have dramatic dialogue which presents the discussion and confrontation of the characters and which is the movies' principal form of dialogue. But it is far from continuous. One speaks ceaselessly in the theater but not in the film. "Directors of recent movies," said Malraux, *"break into* dialogue after long stretches of silence, just as a novelist breaks into dialogue after long narrative passages." Thus the distribution of silences and dialogue constitutes a metrics above and beyond the metrics of vision and sound, and the pattern of words and silence, more complex than the other two, superimposes its requirements upon them. To complete the analysis one would still have to study the role of music in this ensemble: let us only say that music should be incorporated into it, not juxtaposed to it. Music should not be used as a stopgap for sonic holes or as a completely exterior commentary on the sentiments or the scenes as so often happens in movies: the storm of wrath unleashes the storm of brass, or the music laboriously imitates a footstep or the sound of a coin falling to the ground. It should intervene to mark a change in a film's style: for example, the passage from an action scene to the "inside" of the character, to the recollection of earlier scenes, or to the description of a landscape. Generally speaking, it should accompany and help bring about a "rupture in the sensory balance," as Jaubert said.[3] Lastly, it must not be another means of expression juxtaposed to the visual expression. "By the use of strictly musical means (rhythm, form, instrumentation) and by a mysterious alchemy of correspondences which ought to be the very foundation of the film composer's profession, it should recreate a sonorous substance beneath the plastic substance of the image, should, finally, make the internal rhythm of the scene physically palpable without thereby striving to translate its sentimental, dramatic, or poetic content" (Jaubert). It is not the job of words in a movie to add ideas to the images, nor is it the job of music to add sentiments. The ensemble tells us something very precise which is neither a thought nor a reminder of sentiments we have felt in our own lives.

3. *Ibid.*

What, then, does the film *signify:* what does it mean? Each film tells a *story:* that is, it relates a certain number of events which involve certain characters and which could, it seems, also be told in prose, as, in effect, they are in the scenario on which the film is based. The talking film, frequently overwhelmed by dialogue, completes this illusion. Therefore motion pictures are often conceived as the visual and sonic representation, the closest possible reproduction of a drama which literature could evoke only in words and which the movie is lucky enough to be able to photograph. What supports this ambiguity is the fact that movies do have a basic realism: the actors should be natural, the set should be as realistic as possible; for "the power of reality released on the screen is such that the least stylization will cause it to go flat" (Leenhardt). That does not mean, however, that the movies are fated to let us see and hear what we would see and hear if we were present at the events being related; nor should films suggest some general view of life in the manner of an edifying tale. Aesthetics has already encountered this problem in connection with the novel or with poetry. A novel always has an idea that can be summed up in a few words, a scenario which a few lines can express. A poem always refers to things or ideas. And yet the function of the pure novel or pure poetry is not simply to tell us these facts. If it were, the poem could be exactly transposed into prose and the novel would lose nothing in summary. Ideas and facts are just the raw materials of art: the art of the novel lies in the choice of what one says and what one does not say, in the choice of perspectives (this chapter will be written from the point of view of this character, that chapter from another's point of view), in the varying tempo of the narrative; the essence of the art of poetry is not the didactic description of things or the exposition of ideas but the creation of a machine of language which almost without fail puts the reader in a certain poetic state. Movies, likewise, always have a story and often an idea (for example, in *l'Etrange sursis* the idea that death is terrible only for the man who has not consented to it), but the function of the film is not to make these facts or ideas known to us. Kant's remark that, in knowledge imagination serves the understanding, whereas in art the understanding serves the imagination, is a profound one. In other words, ideas or prosaic facts are only there to give the creator an opportunity to seek out their palpable symbols and to trace their visible and sonorous monogram. The meaning of a film is incorporated into its rhythm just as the meaning of a gesture may immediately be read in that gesture: the film does not mean anything but itself. The idea is presented in a nascent state and emerges from the temporal structure of the film as it does from the coexistence of the parts of a painting. The joy of art lies in its showing how something

takes on meaning—not by referring to already established and acquired ideas but by the temporal or spatial arrangement of elements. As
we saw above, a movie has meaning in the same way that a thing does:
neither of them speaks to an isolated understanding; rather, both
appeal to our power tacitly to decipher the world or men and to coexist
with them. It is true that in our ordinary lives we lose sight of this
aesthetic value of the tiniest perceived thing. It is also true that the
perceived form is never perfect in real life, that it always has blurs,
smudges, and superfluous matter, as it were. Cinematographic drama
is, so to speak, finer-grained than real-life dramas: it takes place in a
world that is more exact than the real world. But in the last analysis
perception permits us to understand the meaning of the cinema. A
movie is not thought; it is perceived.

This is why the movies can be so gripping in their presentation of
man: they do not give us his *thoughts,* as novels have done for so long,
but his conduct or behavior. They directly present to us that special way
of being in the world, of dealing with things and other people, which we
can see in the sign language of gesture and gaze and which clearly
defines each person we know. If a movie wants to show us someone
who is dizzy, it should not attempt to portray the interior landscape of
dizziness, as Daquin in *Premier de cordée* and Malraux in *Sierra de
Terruel* wished to do. We will get a much better sense of dizziness if we
see it from the outside, if we contemplate that unbalanced body
contorted on a rock or that unsteady step trying to adapt itself to who
knows what upheaval of space. For the movies as for modern
psychology dizziness, pleasure, grief, love, and hate are ways of
behaving.

*   *   *   *

This psychology shares with contemporary philosophies the common feature of presenting consciousness thrown into the world, subject
to the gaze of others and learning from them what it is: it does not,
in the manner of the classical philosophies, present mind *and* world,
each particular consciousness *and* the others. Phenomenological or
existential philosophy is largely an expression of surprise at this
inherence of the self in the world and in others, a description of this
paradox and permeation, and an attempt to make us *see* the bond
between subject and world, between subject and others, rather than to
explain it as the classical philosophies did by resorting to absolute
spirit. Well, the movies are peculiarly suited to make manifest the
union of mind and body, mind and world, and the expression of one
in the other. That is why it is not surprising that a critic should evoke

philosophy in connection with a film. Astruc in his review of *Défunt récalcitrant* uses Sartrian terms to recount the film, in which a dead man lives after his body and is obliged to inhabit another. The man remains the same *for himself* but is different *for others,* and he cannot rest until through love a girl recognizes him despite his new exterior and the harmony between the *for itself* and the *for others* is re-established. The editors of *Le Canard enchaîné* are annoyed at this and would like to send Astruc back to his philosophical investigations. But the truth is that both parties are right: one because art is not meant to be a showcase for ideas, and the other because contemporary philosophy consists not in stringing concepts together but in describing the mingling of consciousness with the world, its involvement in a body, and its coexistence with others; and because this is movie material *par excellence.*

Finally, if we ask ourselves why it is precisely in the film era that this philosophy has developed, we obviously should not say that the movies grew out of the philosophy. Motion pictures are first and foremost a technical invention in which philosophy counts for nothing. But neither do we have the right to say that this philosophy has grown out of the cinema which it transposes to the level of ideas, for one can make bad movies; after the technical instrument has been invented, it must be taken up by an artistic will and, as it were, re-invented before one can succeed in making real films. Therefore, if philosophy is in harmony with the cinema, if thought and technical effort are heading in the same direction, it is because the philosopher and the moviemaker share a certain way of being, a certain view of the world which belongs to a generation. It offers us yet another chance to confirm that modes of thought correspond to technical methods and that, to use Goethe's phrase, "What is inside is also outside."

PART II

Ideas

5 / Hegel's Existentialism

JEAN HYPPOLITE, who first became known through his annotated translation of the *Phénoménologie de l'esprit*, has since published his *Genèse et structure de la Phénoménologie de l'esprit*, which is bound to mark a decisive step in French studies of Hegel.[2] All the great philosophical ideas of the past century—the philosophies of Marx and Nietzsche, phenomenology, German existentialism, and psychoanalysis—had their beginnings in Hegel; it was he who started the attempt to explore the irrational and integrate it into an expanded reason which remains the task of our century. He is the inventor of that Reason, broader than the understanding, which can respect the variety and singularity of individual consciousnesses, civilizations, ways of thinking, and historical contingency but which nevertheless does not give up the attempt to master them in order to guide them to their own truth. But, as it turns out, Hegel's successors have placed more emphasis on what they reject of his heritage than on what they owe to him. If we do not despair of a *truth* above and beyond divergent points of view, if we remain dedicated to a new classicism, an organic civilization, while maintaining the sharpest sense of subjectivity, then no task in the cultural order is more urgent than re-establishing the connection between on the one hand, the thankless doctrines which try to forget their Hegelian origin and, on the other, that origin itself. That is where their common language can be found and a decisive confrontation can take place. Not that Hegel himself offers the truth we are seeking (there are several Hegels, and even the most objective historian will be led to ask which of them went furthest), but all our antitheses can be found in that single life and work. There would be no

1. Concerning J. Hyppolite's lecture of the same title, delivered on Feb. 16, 1947, to l'Institut d'Etudes germaniques.
2. English translation of Hegel's *Phänomenologie des Geistes* by J. B. Baillie, *Phenomenology of Mind* (New York, 1931).—Trans.

paradox involved in saying that interpreting Hegel means taking a
stand on all the philosophical, political, and religious problems of our
century. The great interest of Hyppolite's lecture is that, as far as
existentialism is concerned, it begins the translation which will
illuminate the discussions of our time. As is quite natural, the historian
tempered the philosopher every step of the way. Since our own aims are
non-historical, let us follow this lecture freely rather than textually, to
disagree occasionally and constantly to comment.

Kierkegaard, the first to use "existence" in the modern sense of the
word, deliberately set himself up in opposition to Hegel. The Hegel he
had in mind was the late Hegel, who treated history as the visible
development of a logical system, who sought in the relationships
between ideas the final explanation of events, and who subordinated
the individual experience of life to the life appropriate to ideas, as to
a destiny. This Hegel of 1827 offers us nothing but a "palace of ideas,"
to use Kierkegaard's phrase, where all historical antitheses are overcome, but only by thought. Kierkegaard is right in objecting that mere
thought is not enough to enable the individual to overcome the
contradictions facing him, that he is faced with dilemmas neither term
of which he can accept. This last Hegel has understood everything
except his own historical situation; he has taken everything into
account except his own existence, and the synthesis he offers is no true
synthesis precisely because it pretends ignorance of being the product
of a certain individual and a certain time. Kierkegaard's objection,
which is in profound agreement with that of Marx, consists in
reminding the philosopher of his own inherence in history: where are
you speaking from when you judge the world's development and
declare that it attains perfection in the Prussian state, and how can you
pretend to be outside all situations? Here the reminder of the thinker's
own existence and subjectivity merges with the recall to history.

But if the Hegel of 1827 may be criticized for his idealism, the same
cannot be said of the Hegel of 1807. The *Phénoménologie de l'esprit* is a
history not only of ideas but of all the areas which reveal the mind at
work: customs, economic structures, and legal institutions as well as
works of philosophy. It is concerned with recapturing a total sense of
history, describing the inner workings of the body social, not with
explaining the adventures of mankind by debates among philosophers.
Absolute knowledge, the final stage in the evolution of the spirit as
phenomenon wherein consciousness at last becomes equal to its
spontaneous life and regains its self-possession, is perhaps not a
philosophy but a way of life. It is a militant philosophy that we find in
the *Phénoménologie de l'esprit*, not as yet a victorious one. (And
besides, up until the *Principes de la philosophie du droit*, Hegel clearly

states that philosophers do not create history but always give voice to a situation already established in the world before their appearance on the scene.) [3] The real debate between Marx and Hegel has nothing to do with the relationship of ideas to history; rather, it involves the conception of historical movement, which ends for the Hegel of 1827 in a hierarchical society whose meaning is accessible to none except the philosopher but which the Hegel of 1807 perhaps saw culminating in a genuine reconciliation between men.

What is certain in any case is that the *Phénoménologie de l'esprit* does not try to fit all history into a framework of pre-established logic but attempts to bring each doctrine and each era back to life and to let itself be guided by their internal logic with such impartiality that all concern with system seems forgotten. The introduction states that the philosopher should not put himself in the place of human experiences; his task is simply to collect and decipher these experiences as history makes them available. It is in this sense that we can begin to speak of "Hegelian existentialism," since he does not propose to connect concepts but to reveal the immanent logic of human experience in all its sectors. The question is no longer limited, as it was in the *Critique de la raison pure théorique,* to discovering what conditions make scientific experience possible but is one of knowing in a general way how moral, aesthetic, and religious experiences are possible, of describing man's fundamental situation in the face of the world and other men, and of understanding religions, ethics, works of art, economic and legal systems as just so many ways for man to flee or to confront the difficulties of his condition.[4] Experience here no longer simply means our entirely contemplative contact with the sensible world as it did in Kant; the word reassumes the tragic resonance it has in ordinary language when a man speaks of what he has lived through. It is no longer a laboratory test but is a trial of life.

To be more exact, Hegel's thought is existentialist in that it views man not as being from the start a consciousness in full possession of its own clear thoughts but as a life which is its own responsibility and which tries to understand itself. All of the *Phénoménologie de l'esprit* describes man's efforts to reappropriate himself. At every period of history he starts from a subjective "certainty," makes his actions conform to the directions of that certainty, and witnesses the surprising consequences of his first intention, discovering its objective "truth." He then modifies his project, gets under way once more, again

3. English translation of Hegel's *Grundlinien der Philosophie des Rechts* by T. M. Knox, *Philosophy of Right* (Oxford, 1945).—Trans.
4. English translation of Kant's *Kritik der reinen Vernunft* by Norman Kemp-Smith, *Critique of Pure Reason* (London, 1933).—Trans.

becomes aware of the abstract qualities of his new project, until subjective certainty finally equals objective truth and in the light of consciousness he becomes fully what he already obscurely was. As long as this last stage of history remains unattained—and should it ever be reached, man, deprived of movement, would be like an animal—man, as opposed to the pebble which is what it is, is defined as a place of unrest (*Unruhe*), a constant effort to get back to himself, and consequently by his refusal to limit himself to one or another of his determinations. "Consciousness . . . therefore immediately becomes the act of surpassing the limit and, when it has incorporated this limit into itself, of surpassing itself. . . . Consciousness thus suffers at its own hand the violence by which it spoils all limited satisfactions. Feeling this violence, anxiety may well shrink before the truth, may aspire and tend to save the very thing which is threatened with loss, but there is no calming this anxiety: its attempt to sink into a thoughtless inertia is in vain. . . ." [5] Whatever relationships may be shown to exist between consciousness and the body or brain, all the discoveries of phrenology will not suffice to make consciousness a *bone*, for a bone is still a thing or a being, and if the only components of the world were things or beings, there would not be even a semblance of what we call man—that is, a being which is not, which denies things, an existence without an essence.

Today this idea is trite, but it regains its force if one applies it, as did Hegel, to the relationships between life and our consciousness of it. Of course, all we say about life has to do in reality with consciousness of life, since we who talk about it are conscious of it. However, consciousness re-appropriates as its own limit and source what preconscious life would have been. It would have been a force which disperses itself wherever it acts, a "dying and becoming" which would not even be aware of itself as such. For there to be consciousness of life, that dispersion would have to be ended; it would have to become total and aware of itself—which is in principle impossible for life. An absence of being would have to come into the world, a nothingness from which being would be visible, such that consciousness of life, taken radically, is consciousness of death. Even the doctrines which would imprison us in our racial or local peculiarities and hide our humanity from us can only do so—since they are doctrines and propaganda—by forsaking the immediate life and borrowing shamefully from consciousness of death. Nazi ideology is not to be reproached for reminding men of the tragic but for using the tragic and the vertigo

5. *Phénoménologie de l'esprit,* trans. J. Hyppolite, Introduction, p. 71.

of death to give a semblance of force to prehuman instincts; in short, for obscuring the awareness of death. To be aware of death and to think or reason are one and the same thing, since one thinks only by disregarding what is characteristic of life and thus by conceiving death.

Man cannot be made unaware of death except by being reduced to the state of an animal, and then he would be a poor animal if he retained any part of his consciousness, since consciousness implies the ability to step back from any given thing and to deny it. An animal can quietly find contentment in life and can seek salvation in reproduction; man's only access to the universal is the fact that he exists instead of merely living. This is the price he pays for his humanity, and it is the reason why the idea of the sound man is a myth, closely related to Nazi myths. "Man is the sick animal," said Hegel in an old text of his *Realphilosophie* published by Hoffmeister. Life can only be thought of as revealed to a consciousness of life which denies it.

All consciousness is therefore unhappy, since it knows it is a secondary form of life and misses the innocence from which it senses it came. Judaism's historical mission has been to spread this sense of separation throughout the entire world, and, as Hyppolite said to his students during the war, we are all Jews to the extent that we care about the universal, refuse to resign ourselves to merely being, and want to exist.

Consciousness of death is, however, neither a dead-end nor an outer limit. There are two ways of thinking about death: one pathetic and complacent, which butts against our end and seeks nothing in it but the means of exacerbating violence; the other dry and resolute, which integrates death into itself and turns it into a sharper awareness of life. The young Hegel speaks more willingly of death; the older Hegel prefers to speak of negativity. The Hegel of the *Phénoménologie* juxtaposes the pathetic and logical vocabularies and makes us understand what role consciousness of death plays in the advent of humanity. Death is the negation of all particular given beings, and consciousness of death is a synonym for consciousness of the universal, but it is only an empty or abstract universal as long as we remain at this point. We cannot in fact conceive nothingness except against a ground of being (or, as Sartre says, against the world). Therefore, any notion of death which claims to hold our attention is deceiving us, since it is in fact surreptitiously using our consciousness of being. To plumb our awareness of death, we must transmute it into life, "interiorize" it, as Hegel said. The abstract universal which starts out opposed to life must be made concrete. There is no being without nothingness, but nothingness can exist only in the hollow of being, and so consciousness of death carries with it the means for going beyond it.

The only experience which brings me close to an authentic awareness of death is the experience of contact with another, since under his gaze I am only an object just as he is merely a piece of the world under my own. Thus each consciousness seeks the death of the other which it feels dispossesses it of its constitutive nothingness. But I do not feel threatened by the presence of another unless I remain aware of my subjectivity at the very moment his gaze is reducing me to an object; I do not reduce him to slavery unless he continues to be present to me as consciousness and freedom precisely when he is an object in my eyes. We cannot be aware of the conflict unless we are aware of our reciprocal relationship and our common humanity. We do not deny each other except by mutual recognition of our consciousness. That negation of everything and of others which I am is completed only by reduplicating itself through another's negation of it. And just as my consciousness of myself as death and nothingness is deceitful and contains an affirmation of my being and my life, so my consciousness of another as an enemy comprises an affirmation of him as an equal. If I am negation, then by following the implication of this universal negation to its ultimate conclusion, I will witness the self-denial of that very negation and its transformation into coexistence. By myself I cannot be free, nor can I be a consciousness or a man; and that other whom I first saw as my rival is a rival only because he is myself. I discover myself in the other, just as I discover consciousness of life in consciousness of death, because I am from the start this mixture of life and death, solitude and communication, which is heading toward its resolution.

Domination, sadism, and violence destroy themselves just as consciousness of death goes beyond itself. If each participant in the duel of consciousnesses, of fraternal enemies, succeeded in fatally wounding the other, nothing would be left; there would not even be a place for that hatred of the other and that affirmation of self which is the principle behind the struggle. Thus, the man with the most exact awareness of the human situation is not the master (since the master pretends ignorance of the foundation of being and communication underlying the play of his despair and pride) but the slave. The slave has been truly afraid, has given up trying to conquer by the sword, and he is the only one with experience of death because he alone has known the love of life. The master wants to exist for no one but himself, but in fact he seeks recognition of his mastery from someone and so is weak in his strength. The slave consents to exist only for others, but nevertheless it is he who chooses to go on living on these terms, and he therefore has strength in his weakness. Since he is better acquainted with man's vital core than the master, it is he who will finally have the only possible mastery—at the expense of nature, not of other people. His life is more frankly rooted in the world than is the master's, which is precisely why he knows better than the master what death means: he has really experienced anxiety, the "fluidification of everything stable." Human existence, which had been risk and guilt, becomes history through him, and mankind's successive decisions can be concentrated in one single act by which consciousness is made whole, and God becomes man or, if you prefer, man becomes God.

This is where Hegel's thought abandons its initial pessimism. Learning the truth about death and struggle is the long maturation process by which history overcomes its contradictions and fulfills the promise of humanity—present in the consciousness of death and in the struggle with the other—in the living relationship among men. This is also where Hegel stops being an existentialist, Hyppolite adds. Whereas for Heidegger we exist for the sake of death and the awareness of death remains fundamental to philosophy as well as to behavior, Hegel transmutes death into a higher form of life. He therefore moves from the individual to history, whereas for Sartre there can be no remedy for the contradictions of the *for itself* and the *for others,* with the result that his dialectic is truncated. One might say that in this sense the *Phénoménologie de l'esprit* makes possible a Communist philosophy of the party or a philosophy of the Church rather than a philosophy of the individual such as existentialism. It is true, adds Hyppolite again, that there are other ways of understanding existentialism. This last statement seems the most accurate, since we should note that, even in Heidegger, consciousness of death is not authentic life; the only attitude which does not deceive us is the one which also has a place for the fact of our existence. The decision we must make is to accept death, but that cannot be separated from the decision to live and to get a new grip on our fortuitous existence. As for the existence of the other and the historicity which results, Heidegger does not deny it. It has apparently been forgotten that the last part of *Sein und Zeit* is devoted to the notion of history.[6] One might even say that what Heidegger lacks is not historicity but, on the contrary, an affirmation of the individual: he does not mention that struggle of consciousnesses and that opposition of freedoms without which coexistence sinks into anonymity and everyday banality. It is even more certain that French existentialists are not arrested at an awareness of death. "My death

6. English translation of Heidegger's *Sein und Zeit* by J. Macquarrie and E. Robinson, *Being and Time* (London, 1962).—Trans.

interrupts my life only when I die, and that only from the point of view of others. Death does not exist for me while I am alive; my project goes right through it without meeting any obstacles. The full impetus of my transcendence runs into no barriers; it alone determines when it shall run down, like the sea which strikes against a smooth shore and stops at a certain point, to go no further." [7] And so I live not for death but forever, and likewise, not for myself alone but with other people. A more complete definition of what is called existentialism than we get from talking of anxiety and the contradictions of the human condition might be found in the idea of a universality which men affirm or imply by the mere fact of their being and at the very moment of their opposition to each other, in the idea of a reason immanent in unreason, of a freedom which comes into being in the act of accepting limits and to which the least perception, the slightest movement of the body, the smallest action, bear incontestable witness.

7. Simone de Beauvoir, *Pyrrhus et Cinéas*, p. 61.

6 / The Battle over Existentialism

IT HAS BEEN two years since the publication of Jean-Paul Sartre's *L'Être et le néant*.[1] At first a profound silence settled over this 700-page book: were the critics holding back their ink? Does their respect for the united front extend even to philosophy? Were they waiting until a free discussion would again be possible? In any case, the silence has now been broken. On the Left, weeklies and reviews are bombarded with critical articles which they do or do not publish. On the Right the anathemas are piling up. High-school girls are warned against existentialism as if it were the sin of the century. The June 3d edition of *La Croix* speaks of a danger "graver than 18th-century rationalism and 19th-century positivism." It is remarkable how a thoroughgoing discussion is almost always put off until later, while criticism takes the form of a warning to the faithful. Sartre's book is labeled a poison of which we must beware instead of a philosophy which we might discuss; it is condemned for its horrible consequences instead of for its intrinsic falsity. It is a matter of first things first, and the first thing to do is to enforce a quarantine. For the established doctrines to refuse discussion is no indication of strength. If it is true that many young people are welcoming the new philosophy with open arms, it will take more than these peevish criticisms, which deliberately avoid the question raised by Sartre's work, to convince them to reject it.

The question is that of man's relationship to his natural or social surroundings. There are two classical views: one treats man as the result of the physical, physiological, and sociological influences which shape him from the outside and make him one thing among many; the

1. English translation by Hazel E. Barnes, *Being and Nothingness* (New York, 1956).—Trans.

other consists of recognizing an a-cosmic freedom in him, insofar as he is spirit and represents to himself the very causes which supposedly act upon him. On the one hand, man is a part of the world; on the other, he is the constituting consciousness of the world. Neither view is satisfactory. After Descartes one can object to the first on the grounds that, if man were indeed one thing among many, he could not know any of them because he would be locked in his own limits like this chair or that table, *present* at a certain location in space and therefore incapable of *representing* to himself all the others. We must grant man a very special way of being—intentional being—which consists of being oriented towards all things but of not residing in any. But if we tried to conclude from this that our fundamental nature makes us absolute spirit, our corporal and social ties with the world and our insertion in it would become incomprehensible, and we would give up thinking about the human condition. The merit of the new philosophy is precisely that it tries, in the notion of existence, to find a way of thinking about our condition. In the modern sense of the word, "existence" is the movement through which man is in the world and involves himself in a physical and social situation which then becomes his point of view on the world. All involvement is ambiguous because it both affirms and restricts a freedom: my undertaking to do a certain thing means both that it would be possible for me not to do it and that I exclude this possibility. My involvement in nature and history is likewise a limitation of my view on the world and yet the only way for me to approach the world, know it, and do something in it. The relationship between subject and object is no longer that *relationship of knowing* postulated by classical idealism, wherein the object always seems the construction of the subject, but a *relationship of being* in which, paradoxically, the subject *is* his body, his world, and his situation, by a sort of exchange.

We are not saying that *l'Être et le néant* makes this paradox of consciousness and action entirely clear. In our opinion the book remains too exclusively antithetic: the antithesis of my view of myself and another's view of me and the antithesis of the *for itself* and the *in itself* often seem to be alternatives instead of being described as the living bond and communication between one term and the other. It is obvious that the author's primary concern in dealing with the subject and freedom is to present them as uninvolved in any compromise with things and that he is putting off the study of the "realization" of nothingness in being—which is action and which makes morality possible—until some other time. *L'Être et le néant* is first of all a demonstration that the subject is freedom, absence, and negativity and that, in this sense, there is nothingness. But that also means that the subject is *only* nothingness, that he needs being to sustain himself, that he can only be thought of against a background of the world, and, finally, that he feeds on being like the shadows in Homer feed on the blood of the living. We can therefore expect all manner of clarification and completion after *l'Être et le néant*. But it cannot be denied that Sartre's descriptions pose the central problem of philosophy, as it appears after the acquisitions of the last centuries, pointedly and with new profundity. After Descartes, it was impossible to deny that existence as consciousness is radically different from existence as thing and that the relationship of the two is that of emptiness to plenitude. After the 19th century and all it taught us about the historicity of the spirit, it was impossible to deny that consciousness always exists in a situation. It is up to us to understand both things at once. Simply reaffirming one classical position or the other is not a solution for either Catholics or Marxists. This is impossible in itself and even impossible according to the internal logic of Christianity and Marxism.

*   *   *   *

The intuition of the *in itself* is the first thing rejected by Catholic critics; yet we are in the world, which is to say that our thoughts, our passions, and our worries revolve around the things that we perceive. All consciousness is consciousness of something; it is essential for us to move toward things, and consciousness seeks in them, so to speak, a stability which it lacks. Our actions and our given surroundings are the starting-point of our self-knowledge, each of us being for himself a stranger to which things hold up a mirror. It is therefore essential for the subject to perceive the object as older than himself. He senses that he has appeared in a world which was not made for him and which would have been more perfect without him. Of course, this is not strictly true, since reflection shows that being is inconceivable without any witnesses. But such indeed is our initial situation: we feel ourselves to be the indispensable correlative of a being which nevertheless resides in itself. Such is the contradiction which links us to the object. We cannot help but envy that plenitude of nature—crops growing and seasons succeeding one another in accordance with their perpetual law. In the face of this "order," man is the creature who never achieves completion. He is a rift, as it were, in the peaceful fabric of the world. "But are we not here coming back," wonders Gabriel Marcel, "to the epiphenomenalist conception of consciousness as a case of imperfect adaptation?" And he speaks elsewhere of the "crudely materialistic basis of the doctrine." [2] But is giving the word "being" its full meaning therefore materialistic? How can a religion which affirms the incarnation of God and the resurrection of the body find it surprising that consciousness—in all senses of the word—adheres to the world and that the being of the world always seems to it the very type of being?

Correlatively, the Catholic critics reject the intuition that the subject is nothingness. Since it radically distinguishes us from things and snatches us from their defining repose, Sartre thinks that liberty is exactly nothing—but a nothing which is everything. It is like a curse and at the same time the source of all human grandeur. It is indivisibly the principle of chaos and the principle of human order. If, in order to be subject, the subject must cut himself off from the order of things, man will have no "state of consciousness," no "feeling" which is not part of this consuming freedom and which is purely and simply what it is, the way things are. From this follows an analysis of ways of behaving which shows them all to be ambiguous. Bad faith and inauthenticity are essential to man because they are inscribed in the intentional structure of consciousness which is presence both to itself and to things. The very will to be good makes goodness false, since it directs us toward ourselves at the moment we should be directed toward the other. The very decision to respect the other smacks of selfishness, for it is still my generosity to which the other owes my recognition of him and about which I am self-satisfied. "To give is to obligate." Thus, nothing in man is pure; there is not one single act with which we can feel satisfied and in which a noble soul or a good conscience can find the consolation or the assurance which it loves. But these pessimistic propositions involve a reciprocal optimism: insofar as freedom destroys the unity of nature, there is not a single human act or passion which does not testify to man's humanity. There is not a single love which is simply a bodily mechanism and which—even and most of all when it attaches itself insanely to its object—does not prove our ability to put ourselves to the test, our power of absolute self-dedication, our metaphysical significance. The principles of good and evil are therefore but one principle. Man's wretchedness can be seen in his grandeur and his grandeur in his wretchedness. Sartre's philosophy, wrote another critic, "starts by putting out the light of the spirit." [3] Quite the contrary: it makes it shine everywhere because we are not

2. Gabriel Marcel, *Homo viator*, pp. 249, 248. [English translation by Emma Crawford, *Homo Viator* (Chicago, 1951).]

3. J. Mercier, "Le Ver dans le fruit," *Etudes* (Feb., 1945), p. 240.

body *and* spirit or consciousness *confronting* the world but spirit incarnate, being-in-the-world.

At bottom, what the Catholic critics want is evident. They challenge the intuition of an inert being together with that of a supple freedom because they would like things to be capable of proclaiming the glory of God and man to have a destiny like a thing. The first obstacle they run into is Pascal: "The eternal silence of these infinite spaces terrifies me." Let us take this to mean that there is something horrible, repulsive, and unchallengeable about things which simply are, which *express* nothing. By "Nothing stops the volubility of our spirit," let us understand: The spirit is that which can have no resting place—not in any proof, not in any pre-established destiny, not in any pharisaism. With Pascal, Catholics repudiate the Cartesian tradition, the distinction between the *res extensa*—the thing without spirit—and existence as consciousness—the spirit with no support in nature. Malebranche spoke of a primary glory of God which comes to Him from the perfection of things and distinguished this "architect's glory" from that which is afforded Him by the free sacrifice of men when they recognize Him, restore the world to Him, and cooperate, as it were, in Creation. This meant making a sharp distinction between the God of things and the God of men; it said that human order begins with freedom. This perspective reveals the basis of the debate: it is not Christianity and Marxism colliding here but Aristotle and Descartes, or St. Thomas and Pascal. The Catholic critics wish for things to reveal a God-directed orientation of the world and wish for man—like things—to be nothing but a nature heading toward its perfection. They would like to endow things with spirit and turn the human spirit into a thing. Gabriel Marcel appeals to "common sense" and "a certain secular wisdom" to localize that disturbing, all pervasive freedom in certain privileged acts. Our freedom would still consist only in putting us back under a law which already resides within us, in turning our potentiality into actuality. M. Marcel speaks favorably of a "natural virtue," of a "certain confidence, both spontaneous and metaphysical, in the order which encompasses our existence," of a "nuptial bond between man and life," and finally of a "piety which is not Christian but prechristian or, more precisely, perichristian." [4] Thus it is indeed the idea—itself prechristian—of a natural finality of man which underlies Marcel's criticism of *l'Être et le néant*. The same is true of Mme J. Mercier. An Aristotelian idea of a Good identical with being motivates her entire polemic against the Sartrean nothingness and leads her to blame it for undermining the virtues by

4. *Homo viator*, pp. 225–26.

introducing freedom. There is a Cartesian and Pascalian piety to which we owe the profoundest descriptions of man as an incomprehensible, contradictory monster whose old self-imposed habits are the only nature he possesses and who is grand because of his wretchedness, wretched because of his grandeur. The Catholic critics want nothing more to do with that philosophy, preferring the Aristotelian idea of man with his prescribed end, like plants with their prescribed form. One may well ask on which side is the "materialism."

Perhaps they are right in the end, when all is said and done. Perhaps the only way to sustain Christianity as theology is on the basis of Thomism, perhaps the Pascalian concept of being as a blind thing and of spirit as volubility leaves room only for mystical action with no dogmatic content and for a faith which, like Kierkegaard's, is not faith in any being. Perhaps in the end the religion of God-made-man arrives by an unavoidable dialectic at an anthropology and not a theology. Sartre says that consciousness tending, by the constant movement of intentionality, toward thingness without ever achieving it seems to testify to an ideal synthesis between itself and being, "not that the two ever become one, but, on the contrary, just because this integration is always indicated and always impossible." Pure nonsense, replies Gabriel Marcel: "How indeed could something which has never really been integrated really disintegrate?" But when M. Marcel offers his own solution some lines farther down, it consists of saying that "reflecting on itself, consciousness is led to consider itself degraded, without being able, however, to think in concrete terms about the world before the Fall." [5] If the original oneness is as unthinkable for M. Marcel as it is for Sartre, then it can be affirmed only by an act of faith devoid of notional content, and the only distinction between the two conclusions is that M. Marcel—instead of asserting the dialectic of the *for itself* and the *in itself*—declares it intolerable and wants to overcome it through action. Even this step is not forbidden in Sartre's perspective: indeed, it could well be the principle of morality. All of this is not a proof or even an affirmation of God but is an affirmation of man. To maintain Christianity's foothold on this slippery ground, one must reject the starting point, the very notion of spirit as negativity.

But can a Christian do this? For in the last analysis, even if man's freedom does consist in realizing his pre-established nature and his form, as the Thomists would have it, one has to admit that this realization is voluntary in man and dependent on him, and one must therefore introduce a second freedom, radical this time, which is his

5. *Ibid.*, p. 254.

absolute power to say yes or no. From this point, all that one has been able to do to subject human liberty to divine pre-ordination is again open to question. If I can say yes or no to my destiny, then the Good is not my good unless I agree to it, nothing has value in itself, and man's freedom is, as Descartes thought, in a sense equal to God's. On this point Thomism is far from being the only Christian tradition. It was even somewhat suspect at the time of the Jansenist *Augustinus,* and the Jesuits kept a firm hold on the absolute power of choice in spite of divine prescience. The question is to know what part freedom plays and whether we can allow it something without giving it everything. We said earlier that *l'Être et le néant* seems to require further development on this point and that one would expect the author to elaborate a theory of passivity. It is sure, however, that the book highlights this question and that it cannot be dismissed without first being understood. By ignoring the problem, Catholic criticism is deliberately placing itself beneath the level it fearlessly maintained three centuries ago, perhaps because there was less hesitation about confronting fundamental difficulties at a time when belief was a matter of course.

*   *   *   *

Whereas Catholic critics accuse Sartre of materialism, a Marxist like H. Lefebvre comes close to reproaching him with residual idealism.[6] According to Lefebvre, tarrying over the description of being and the establishment of the existence of others is already going too far. Only a consciousness long confined to solitude would find these truths new. Forgetting that Engels held that "the great question fundamental to all philosophy, and especially modern philosophy, concerns the relation of thinking and being," Lefebvre proposes that we "immediately admit" what Sartre has rediscovered.[7] Doesn't showing that Sartre's problems are meaningful for the Christian prove their meaninglessness for the Marxist, and if one justifies Sartre before Gabriel Marcel, doesn't one condemn him before Lefebvre?

There is, to be sure, a Marxism which from the very start places itself above Sartre's problems, the Marxism which absolutely denies interiority, which treats consciousness as a part of the world, a reflection of the object, a by-product of being, and, finally, to use a language which has never been Marxist, as an epiphenomenon. The

6. "Existentialisme et Marxisme," *Action* (June 8, 1945).

7. Engels, *Ludwig Feuerbach* (Editions Sociales, 1945), p. 13. [English translation, "Ludwig Feuerbach and the End of Classical German Philosophy," in *Basic Writings on Politics and Philosophy: Karl Marx and Friedrich Engels,* ed. Lewis S. Feuer (Garden City, N. Y., 1959).]

greatest Marxist writers have formulas which tend in this direction. When Engels writes that ideas should be considered as "the intellectual reflections of objects and of the movements of the real world," when he asks that one re-establish the true relationships between the real world and the ideas produced by the human brain, which after all is itself just a product of this real world," [8] when Lenin writes that "the picture of the world is a picture which shows how matter dies and how matter thinks" or that "the brain is the organ of thought," [9] then we agree that it is hard to build a bridge between these formulas and the Cartesian *cogito*. But one must add that most Marxists consider them inadequate. They find in them—and with good reason—the expression of a metaphysical philosophy which links all phenomena to one single substance, matter, not of a dialectical philosophy which necessarily admits of reciprocal relationships between the different orders of phenomena and the emergence of relationships or original structures on the basis of material phenomena.

If, in the name of Marxism, one wants to exclude the problems of subjectivity and, indeed, the very notion of it, it is not on these remnants of metaphysical materialism that one must base his case. Marxism contains a much deeper reason for abandoning the subject to concentrate on the object and history: the idea that we have no choice, that we are through and through the product of history, thrown without reservation into the world. For Marxism, whatever subjective justifications may be brought forth, exclusive reference to the interior is objectively an abstention and a way of avoiding the concrete tasks imposed on us from the outside. In a word, we are involved. It would be consistent with the purest Marxism to say that all philosophy is idealistic because philosophy always presupposes reflection, i.e., breaking with the immediate, and that therein lies the condemnation of philosophy. It is a special type of estrangement, a way of fleeing to the great beyond, a refusal to be, an anxiety in the face of revolution, a bourgeois guilty conscience. The philosopher who becomes aware of himself as nothingness and as freedom gives the ideological formula of his time, translating into concepts that phase of history where man's essence and existence are still separated, where man is not himself because he is bogged down in the contradictions of capitalism. The very idea of a *speculative* philosophy which would try to grasp an eternal essence of man and the world, testifies to the philosopher's existential refusal, underlying his ideas, to work at transforming the world, to his anxiety

8. Engels, *Socialisme utopique et socialisme scientifique* (Editions du Parti communiste, 1944), p. 13. [English translation by E. Aveling, *Socialism Utopian and Scientific* (New York, 1935).]

9. Lenin, *Oeuvres* (Edition russe), XIII, pp. 288, 125.

before the real humanity which *creates* itself through work and through praxis rather than seeking to define itself once and for all. The only way to obtain what philosophy seeks—a complete grasp of the world—is to connect ourselves with history instead of contemplating it. As Marx said in a famous text, the only way to fulfill philosophy is to destroy it.

Marxism's strongest argument against a philosophy of the subject is therefore an "existential" argument. It comes down to saying that any reflexive philosophy is inadequate to what it wants to grasp—that is, man's existence—because it itself is a certain way of existing apart from the world and history. "Philosophers," said Marx, "have only *interpreted* the world in various ways; the point, however, is to *change* it." [10] Gabriel Marcel likewise criticizes Sartre for imprisoning himself within the vicious cycle of being and nothingness. "There would hardly be any point," he adds, "in claiming that he is forced into it by the given facts or the structural conditions of our existence. Isn't the one authentic transcendence (no doubt it would be better to say 'the one authentic transcending') that act by which we free ourselves from these data and these conditions, replacing them with fresh facts and conditions?" [11] Both sides thus make the same appeal to action as the way of getting beyond dialectical oppositions (except that Marx does not claim that by earthly praxis we can rejoin a synthesis which has already been completed in heaven, and he situates synthesis in our future instead of outside time). At this point Kierkegaard and Marx, the two halves of Hegelian posterity, come together, but their very *rapprochement* is good evidence that Marxist praxis should become clearer about its own ends and means if it wishes to remain distinct from mystical action or pragmatism. It is all very well to invite us to be what we are, to become a conscious part of the movement of history in which we are involved in any case. But we still have to know what this movement of history is, who we can count on to help us complete it; we still have to know *what to do.* And from the minute these questions are raised, one invites the individual to understand and decide; in the last analysis one puts him back in control of his life and agrees that the meaning history will have for him depends on the meaning he sees in it. Every man, even a Marxist, is obliged to agree with Descartes that our knowledge of some outside reality depends on our having apprehended within ourselves that process by which we come to know. No *in itself* would be accessible to us if it were not at the very same time *for us,* and the meaning we find in it depends on our consent. No man can reject the *cogito* and

10. XIe "Thèse sur Feuerbach." [English translation, "Theses on Feuerbach," in *Basic Writings on Politics and Philosophy, op. cit.*]
11. *Homo viator,* p. 255.

deny consciousness, on pain of no longer knowing what he is saying and of renouncing all statements, even materialist ones. Marxist writers have said often and with good reason that Marxism does not deny the subjective conditions of history and is not a fatalism, that men create their history, and that ideologies, even if they express a clearly defined economic and social situation, have a bearing on history. But that is saying that they do not eliminate the subject as a factor in history. Let us remind those who shudder at the very word "subjectivity" of Marx's famous phrase: "The main thing wrong with all past materialism . . . is that it considers the thing, reality, the tangible world only as *object* or intuition, not as concrete human activity; as *practice,* not subjectively." [12]

M. Lefebvre lives subjectivity just like everyone else, though he would like to ignore this fact. Even he must sometimes stop thinking about politics for a few hours and return to it afterwards as to a duty. If his life has for him a political meaning, it is because he gives it this meaning through decisions of his own. In the same way, not all proletarians are Communists, which is to say that we can slip away from our class and from what we are. The dialectic between being and nothingness takes place not only in Sartre's mind but also in the mind of the down-hearted worker who is withdrawing from the struggle. Who would dare insist that no condemned man feel anguish at his death, even if he dies for his class and, through it, for the future of mankind? As soon as man is introduced as the subject of history—and Marxism so portrays him—one is no longer bringing in merely collective man or class but is also including individual man who retains his power to serve or to betray his class and who in this sense joins it of his own accord. Marx gives us an objective definition of class in terms of the effective position of individuals in the production cycle, but he tells us elsewhere that class cannot become a decisive historical and revolutionary factor unless individuals become aware of it, adding that this awareness itself has social motives, and so on. As a historical factor, class is therefore neither a simple objective fact, nor is it, on the other hand, a simple value arbitrarily chosen by solitary consciousnesses. It is more in the nature of a fact-value or an incarnate value, for which the theory remains to be worked out. Today, when other oppositions (the national opposition of France and Germany, both of them worn out and stripped of social consciousness by Hitlerism and the Vichy regime; the opposition between the new world of America and the old Western world, between rich countries and those which have been bled to death) mask class relationships to a greater extent

12. "Première Thèse sur Feuerbach" [*op. cit.*].

than ever, the French worker must make an individual effort to re-establish contact with the Italian worker despite the Fascist aggression of 1940; the individual Italian worker must make an effort to reforge the link with the French worker in spite of French projects to annex the Aosta Valley; restoring the ties between the American worker and his poor French relative, between the French worker and his rich American cousin, depends on the individual efforts of both, and the subject's role in establishing class as a historical factor is clearer than ever. We must analyze involvement, the moment when the subjective and objective conditions of history become bound together, how class exists before becoming aware of itself—in short, the status of the social and the phenomenon of co-existence. *L'Être et le néant* does not yet offer this social theory, but it does pose the problem of the reciprocal relations between consciousness and the social world as vigorously as possible by refusing to admit of freedom outside of a situation and by making the subject in no sense a reflection, as epiphenomenalism would have it, but a "reflecting reflection" in accordance with Marxism.

But there is more to be said. Marxism not only tolerates freedom and the individual but, as "materialism," even gives man a dizzying responsibility, as it were. Insofar as he reduced history to the history of the spirit, Hegel found the final synthesis heralded and guaranteed in his own consciousness, in his certainty at having understood history completely, and in the very realization of his philosophy. How could he help being optimistic, when history was consciousness's return to itself and the internal logic of the idea as he lived it in himself testified to the necessity of this return and to man's possibility of attaining totality and freedom from anxiety? That is the textbook Hegel, but there are other ways to interpret him: he could be, and we think he must be, made much more Marxist; one could base his logic on his phenomenology and not his phenomenology on his logic. But whether it bears the name of Hegel or Marx, a philosophy which renounces absolute Spirit as history's motive force, which makes history walk on its own feet and which admits no other reason in things than that revealed by their meeting and interaction, could not affirm *a priori* man's possibility for wholeness, postulate a final synthesis resolving all contradictions or affirm its inevitable realization. Such a philosophy continues to see the revolutionary event as contingent and finds the date of the revolution written on no wall nor in any metaphysical heaven. The breakdown of capitalism may lead the world to chaos instead of to the revolution if men do not understand the situation and do not want to intervene, just as childbirth may result in the death of both mother and baby if no one is there to assist nature. Although synthesis exists *de jure* in Hegel, it can never be more than *de facto* in Marxism. If there is a

Hegelian quietism, there is necessarily a Marxist unrest. Although Hegel's solid and enduring foundation in theology makes it possible for him blindly to leave everything to the natural course of events, Marxist praxis—which can rely on nothing but coexistence among men—does not have the same resource. It cannot assign history a particular end in advance; it cannot even affirm the dogma of "total man" before he actually comes into being. If all our contradictions are someday to be resolved, then that day will be the first we know of it. Engels' learned talk about the way necessity reabsorbs historical accidents is much admired, but how does he know that history is and will continue to be rational if he is no longer a theist or an idealist? Marxism is unique in that it invites us to make the logic of history triumph over its contingency without offering any metaphysical guarantees.

One might ask why existentialism is so eager to conciliate Marxism. M. Lefebvre's gracious supposition is that it is the better to devour it. The truth—which, as we shall see, is much more straightforward—is that many readers of Marx are in absolute agreement with analyses like *XVIII Brumaire*, for example, but feel unsatisfied with certain of Marx's own theoretical formulas and above all with those of his commentators. According to these readers, the Marxist discovery of social existence as the most "interior" dimension of our life, of class dynamics as an integral process where economic and cultural determinations endlessly intersect and inter-signify, not only admits but demands a new conception of consciousness on the theoretical plane, which would establish a basis for both its autonomy and its dependence by describing it as a nothingness which comes into the world and which could not keep its liberty without engaging itself at every moment. According to them, this is the conception of consciousness which Marxism has at least *practiced* in its most powerful concrete analyses, if not formulated in theory. A living Marxism should "save" and integrate existentialist research instead of stifling it.

7 / The Metaphysical in Man

Justifying a conception of the world within the limits of an article is out of the question. On the other hand, what everyone can briefly state is the meaning the word "metaphysical" has gradually assumed for him, what he opposes to it, and his intention in using it. This type of account, which only defines the concept in terms of its "use" value, so to speak, is not enough to justify the definition but is at least a legitimate contribution to the sociology of ideas if the latent metaphysics revealed in the use of the word is sufficiently widespread.

Metaphysics, which Kantianism reduced to the system of principles employed by reason in constituting knowledge or the moral universe (only to have its guiding function in turn radically contested by positivism) has not ceased to lead a sort of unlawful life, in literature and poetry, where critics come upon it today.[1] It even reappears in the sciences, not so as to restrict their field or erect barriers against them, but as the deliberate inventory of a type of being unknown to scientism and which the sciences have gradually learned to recognize. It is this metaphysics in action which we propose to define more clearly, starting by introducing it at the horizon of the sciences of man.

*   *   *   *

It would be hard to deny that gestalt psychology overturns what could be called the implicit ontology of science and forces us to revise our conception of the conditions and limits of scientific knowledge— for example, the ideal of an objective animal psychology. Koehler's

1. Cf., for example, Etiemble and Y. Gauclère, *Rimbaud*, p. 234: "Metaphysics is not necessarily the artificial association of noumena; Rimbaud felt this more keenly than anyone and restored a metaphysics of the concrete: he *saw* things in themselves, flowers in themselves."

work shows indisputably that, in addition to our own perceptual universe, we have to reconstitute the animal's universe in all its originality, with its "irrational" connections, its short-circuits, and its lacunae, and that any success we may have will come from taking our human experience of the animal as our starting point, describing the curve of its conduct as it appears *to us,* with its qualitative distinctions of "freshness" and "fatigue," "good solution" and "poor solution," "continuity" and "discontinuity," "optical contact" and "mechancial connection," so that ultimately one's research concludes not with quantitative stimulus-response laws which would be applicable to all species, but with an over-all view of how the chimpanzee, for example, elaborates on given stimuli, of the chimpanzee's behavioral universe as revealed by methodical interpretation of his conduct. The work is living proof that a descriptive science is possible and throws in relief the paradox that, to become truly scientific, psychology must not reject wholesale our human experience of the animal on the grounds that such experience is anthropomorphic, nor should it, in order to become truly scientific, restrict its questions about the animal to those physics asks about an atom or an acid. Measurable relationships, we find, have no monopoly on truth, and our notion of what is objective must be completely redefined. Koehler brought to light a certain structure of the animal universe being studied, an *"a priori of the species"* which is the condition of stimulus-response relationships, and he assigned psychology the task of describing this ensemble. This conception naturally spread to psychopathology and general psychology, which became an inventory of typical behavioral systems. If *Intelligence des singes supérieurs* proves anything, it is that one cannot attach the same meaning to intelligence when referring to animals as when referring to people.[2] The book invited psychologists to understand forms of behavior in terms of their law of internal organization instead of trying to find in them the result of a combination of simple and universal processes.

Strange to say, neither Koehler's book nor, in general, the research of this school has been acclaimed or criticized on the basis of its most novel contributions.[3] *Intelligence des singes supérieurs* impresses the

2. English translation of Wolfgang Koehler's *Intelligenzenprüfungen an Menschenaffen* by Ella Winter, *The Mentality of Apes* (New York, 1959).—Trans.

3. It is surprising, for example, that J. Piaget (*Psychologie de l'intelligence,* 1947) finds hardly anything more than a renewal of innateism in this psychology. [Translated by Malcolm Piercy and D. E. Berlyne, *The Psychology of Intelligence* (New York, 1950).] In fact, it has so little minimized the role of experience in development that Koffka (*Die Grundlagen der psyschischen Entwicklung*) dwells at length on the opposition of the categories of *Lernen* and *Reifen* and, in his *Psychologie* (*Die Philosophie in ihren Einzelgebieten*) describes the whole genesis

reader as a naturalistic anthropology. It is less sensitive to the contrast between the ways men and animals *gestalt* things than to the fact that animal behavior presupposes a *Gestaltung* just as human conduct does, and this purely formal analogy prevails over the most obvious descriptive differences. Instead of leading to a revision of the scientific ideal and methodology which had so long masked the reality of the *gestalt*, gestalt psychology only developed insofar as it breathed new life into the moribund methodology. The Berlin School proposed to describe the privileged forms of human conduct, on the one hand, and, on the other, to determine the conditions which elicited this conduct. The return to description and the appeal to phenomena as a legitimate source of psychological knowledge precludes in principle treating the *gestalt* as a lesser or derivative reality and allowing the linear processes and the isolatable sequences to retain the privilege granted them by scientism. But the Berlin School shrank before these consequences; they preferred to affirm—by a pure act of faith—that the totality of phenomena belonged to the universe of physics and merely to refer to a more advanced form of physics and physiology to make us understand how, in the last analysis, the most complex forms have their foundations in the most simple. Their favorite subject of study was those forms whose appearance, especially in the laboratory, is more or less regular, given a certain number of external conditions: the anonymous sensory functions. They were willing to pay any price for precision in their formulas, even if this meant abandoning to some extent the more complex forms which affect the entire personality, are less simply dependent upon given external conditions, and are for that very reason more difficult to discover but also more valuable for the knowledge of human behavior. The psychology of perception has taken over psychophysiology's old role as the center of psychological research. In reality the study of the psychophysiological functions, of vision (in the abstract

---

of *gestalts* and a whole series of transitory forms, from the child's syncretic liaisons to the *Und-Verbindungen* of the adult. It is not the role of experience, which is no greater in the one than in the other, which really distinguishes the Gestaltists from Piaget but the way in which they understand the relationship between exterior and interior, between given conditions and their biological and psychic elaboration. For the Gestaltists, the accumulation of experience merely makes possible a restructuring which will re-establish the equilibrium between the living being and his milieu at another level. Indeed, this is how Piaget himself describes development in his best passages; but he is apt to return to a quasi-empiricist notion of experience, perhaps because he fails to hold strictly to the Gestaltist principle that the whole is in no case the simple sum of its parts: in *La Construction du réel chez l'enfant* it sometimes seems that passing on to a higher type of perception and conduct can be explained simply as a more complete and more exact registering of experience, whereas this itself presupposes a reorganization of the perceptual field and the advent of clearly articulated forms. [Translated by Margaret Cook, *The Construction of Reality in the Child* (New York, 1954).]

sense of seeing colors, distances, or contours), should never have been pursued at the expense of the study of the more complex forms of behavior which bring us into contact not merely with stimuli but with other men, with vital and social situations. Psychoanalysis—saved from its own dogmas—is the normal extension of a consistent gestalt psychology. By treating what is merely the periphery of psychology as its core (as if the psychology of elementary functions was later bound to yield the psychology of the whole simply by the accumulation of research in special areas); by allowing the sensory functions and their laws to retain an undeserved privilege because they are more or less suited to quantitative treatment; by thus concentrating the efforts of the new psychology on the "functional" and the "objective" when it had sought to rediscover all that is "descriptive" and "phenomenal"—by doing these things scientism retarded the development of a psychological science.

If, on the other hand, we want to give an unprejudiced definition of gestalt psychology's philosophical meaning, we would have to say that, by revealing "structure" or "form" as irreducible elements of being, it has again put into question the classical alternative between "existence as thing" and "existence as consciousness," has established a communication between and a mixture of, objective and subjective, and has conceived of psychological knowledge in a new way, no longer as an attempt to break down these typical ensembles but rather an effort to embrace them and to understand them by reliving them.

It goes without saying that the example of one school, and a school about which there is still disagreement, can prove nothing by itself. However, the work of the school would become significant if one could show that in general each of the sciences of man is oriented in its own way toward the revision of the subject-object relation. Now this is just what we note in linguistics. If one wants to apply rigorous methods to the study of language, one has first to repudiate the prescientific or animistic conceptions which represent each language as an organism or a rational entity whose evolution merely gradually reveals its invariable essence. It was therefore proposed that language be treated as a thing, and one tried to discover the laws whose interplay would explain the facts of language. But language, like behavior, eluded scientistic treatment. The notion of law was challenged even as pertains to phonetics, which would seem to offer an especially suitable field of endeavor. The attempt to detach the law from the facts, to make the facts disappear ideally into the law, had to be abandoned. "The phrase 'c plus a becomes ch in French between the fifth and eighth centuries' is just as much an expression of a historical event which took place once and for all as the phrase 'the Bourbons ruled in France from

1589 to 1791.' " [4] Along with the ideal of a system of laws "truer" than facts, the very conception of language as pure object was again called into question. Already Saussure thought that the repudiation of the old comparative grammar had been too hasty. "There are," he said, "certain images which we cannot do without. To insist that we use no terms but those corresponding to the realities of language is to claim that these realities no longer hold any mystery for us." [5] Just as gestalt psychology demands the use of descriptive concepts which are borrowed from our human experience and which can in no way be *replaced* by functional concepts based on measurements of correlative variations, so Saussure's linguistics legitimates, in the study of language—beyond the perspective of casual explanation which links each fact with a previous fact and thus spreads language before the linguist like a natural object—the perspective of the speaking subject who lives in his language (and who may in some cases change it). From the first point of view, language is a mosaic of facts with no "interior"; from the second, in contrast, it is a totality. A scholar as rigorous as Meillet formulates this progress of linguistic reflection by saying that "linguistic facts are qualitative" and, elsewhere, that "every language forms a system," which means that it admits of a principle of internal organization. Saying that linguistic facts are qualitative says further that they need the mediation of consciousnesses in their connection and development. However, one cannot conclude from this that consciousness is the locus or matrix of language or that language is an abstraction and speaking subjects the only reality; for each speaking subject, even if he modifies the language, feels compelled to use those modes of expression which will make him comprehensible to others. Just as psychology, torn between the "objective method" and "introspection," finally reached equilibrium in the idea of a form of behavior accessible both from the outside and from within, so linguistics finds itself confronted by the task of going beyond the alternative of language as thing and language as the product of speaking subjects. Language must *surround* each speaking subject, like an instrument with its own inertia, its own demands, constraints, and internal logic, and must nevertheless remain open to the initiatives of the subject (as well as to the brute contributions of invasions, fashions, and historical events), always capable of the displacement of meanings, the ambiguities, and the functional substitutions which give this logic its lurching gait. Perhaps the notion of *gestalt,* or structure, would here perform the same service it did for psychology, since both cases involve ensembles

4. W. von Wartburg, *Problèmes et méthodes de la linguistique* (1947), p. 19.

5. F. Saussure, *Cours de linguistique générale* (1916), p. 19, n. 1. [English translation by Wade Baskin, *Course in General Linguistics* (New York, 1959).]

which are not the pure manifestations of a directive consciousness, which are not explicitly aware of their own principles, and which nevertheless can and should be studied by proceeding from the whole to the parts. At the heart of every language one should find laws of equilibrium, maybe even a theme, a fundamental project, or, as G. Guillaume says, a "sublinguistic schema" which escapes notice when we work with the categories of common sense or of the old grammar but which reveals its effective life when the linguist sets up the new categories required to coordinate the facts. For example, Greek or Latin have a characteristic view of time.[6] This view fixed in the conjugational forms solicits every member of the linguistic community from the day he is born, yet is the work of none of them. It nevertheless is not inevitable, remaining exposed to the influences, to the obsolescence through which the language is finally transformed into another tongue. That general spirit which we all constitute by living our life in common, that intention already deposited in the given system of the language, preconscious because the speaking subject espouses it before he becomes aware of it and elevates it to the level of knowledge, and yet which only subsists on the condition of being taken up or assumed by speaking subjects and lives on their desire for communication—this, in the field of linguistics, is indeed the equivalent of the psychologists' "form," equally alien to the objective existence of a natural process as to the mental existence of an idea. Being neither thing nor idea, language, like individual consciousness, can be approached only by a method of "comprehension" which finds amid the multiplicity of facts a few intentions or decisive aims, the "profound and in a way secret facts upon which rest the construction of the language." [7]

One might arrive at the same conclusion by examining the development of sociology from the moment Durkheim gave it what he believed to be a scientific method. In fact, a consideration of his famous work on the *Formes élémentaires de la vie religieuse* tempts us to say that, although he energetically called attention to the study of the social, he may have stripped it of its most interesting features by advising that it

6. G. Guillaume, *L'architectonique du temps dans les langues classiques* (Copenhagen, 1945).

7. *Ibid.*, p. 16. This deciphering of the fundamental intention must of course be strictly controlled: "The method we use—one long deliberated and very close to the method of modern physics—might be defined as combining, in whatever proportion is best, close concrete observation with deep abstract reflection, in which the former of course always has the last word since it alone is qualified to make final decisions about the true nature of things; reflection's role in the alliance it contracts with observation is in no way to reach conclusions in its place but to guide, sharpen, deepen observation—in a nutshell, to endow it with a 'power' which it would lack if it had to depend on no strength but its own." *Ibid.*, p. 17.

be treated "like a thing." [8] It will be remembered that he nominally defines the religious by the sacred, goes on to show that in totemic society the experience of the sacred coincides with its moments of greatest cohesion, and concludes that religious life—at least in its elementary forms and doubtless in its higher forms as well—is nothing but society's way of attaining self-awareness. It would be out of place to question the definition of the religious in terms of the sacred, since Durkheim presents it as preliminary and nominal; one can only observe that it does not yet allow us to penetrate the inner workings of religion, and one may express reservations about a method which is more concerned with assembling concepts taken extensionally than with the exploration of their content. The identification of the sacred with the social justifies such reservations, for this is either all too obvious and begs the whole question, or else it is taken to be an *explanation* of the religious by the social, in which case it hides the problem from us. That religious experience always occurs in an actual or virtual collectivity; that it implies an idea of interpersonal relations; that, as reflection or counterpart, it directly or indirectly expresses the actual human relationships in a given civilization; that any conception of spirit both carries with it a certain conception of the relationship between consciousnesses and, inversely, owes something to our experience of communication—all this is certain, just as it is certain that literature, art, science, and language are social facts in the sense of facts of communication. But even when that has been recognized, one has still done nothing toward explaining the religious phenomenon (or the literary, aesthetic, or linguistic phenomena). The passage from the religious to the social does not lead us from darkness into light; we explain nothing and only find the same obscurity or the same problem hiding under another name, leaving us with the task of grasping each civilization's particular mode of interpersonal relationship and communication. Recourse to social ties cannot be considered an explanation of religion or of the sacred unless one makes an immutable substance of the social, an all-round cause, a vague force defined only by its power of coercion; that is, if one makes oneself blind to the ever-original operation of a society in the process of establishing the system of collective meanings through which its members communicate. Nothing is gained by basing the religious or the sacred on the social, since one comes upon the same paradoxes, the same ambivalence, and the same blend of union and repulsion, desire and fear which already existed in the sacred and made it a problem. Durkheim treats the social as a reality external to the individual and entrusts it

8. English translation by Joseph Ward Swain, *The Elementary Forms of the Religious Life* (New York and London, 1915).—Trans.

with explaining everything that is presented to the individual as what he has to become. But the social cannot perform this service unless it itself bears no resemblance to a thing, unless it envelops the individual, simultaneously beckoning and threatening him, unless each consciousness both finds and loses itself in its relationship with other consciousnesses, unless, finally, the social is not *collective consciousness* but intersubjectivity, a living relationship and tension among individuals. Sociology should not seek an explanation of the religious in the social (or, indeed, of the social in the religious) but must consider them as two aspects of the real and fantastic human bond as it has been worked out by the civilization under consideration and try to objectify the solution which that civilization invents, in its religion as in its economy or in its politics to the problem of man's relation with nature and with other men. If treating social facts like things means hunting for their constitutive elements or forging an external link from one to the other as cause and effect, then this famous precept is not practicable: sociology cannot recognize any permanent elements in the different wholes into which they are integrated, no facts external to one another, but, in the case of each society, should recognize a totality where phenomena give mutual expression to each other and reveal the same basic theme. "The spirit of a civilization makes up a totality of functions; it is an integration different from the sum of the parts." [9] For us to grasp this movement by which men assume and elaborate the given conditions of their collective life and crown them with original values and institutions, we must once again revise our idea of scientific or objective knowledge: at its highest point, sociological knowledge, like knowledge of a person, requires that, while taking all the objective indices as our guide, we recover the human attitude which makes up the spirit of a society.

Because the historian is concerned with the individual and remains in contact with an inexhaustible reality, his very position makes him better armed than the sociologist against the dream of a sovereign knowledge capable of immediate access to all times and of an absolute objectivity. To gain awareness of his task, the historian had nonetheless first to reject his claim to a Universal History completely unfolded before the historian as it would be before the eye of God. He must also recognize—and this is more difficult—that, far from guaranteeing us coincidence with the past, a certain rigorism or scientism in historical matters risks imprisoning us in our most subjective views. It will be remembered that Seignobos refused all putting into perspective and confined the historian to studying, for each event, the singular

9. M. Mauss, *Manuel d'ethnographie* (1947), p. 170.

constellation which had made its appearance possible.[10] According to him, one could not select a few conditions as "the principal" ones from among all the conditions nor start from there to make an induction. All the conditions had their part in producing the effect, and they were all equally its cause. There are no details in history, nothing that is accessory, therefore nothing that is essential. According to this method each event is the result of a conjunction and an accident. We are forbidden to discover any inner meaning in it, and the senseless tumult of history offers nothing to the understanding. If one applies this method to a revolution, for example, it will make it appear straight off as illusory or absurd. The men who make a revolution think they are resolving a problem which is posed in things; it seems to them that their will augments a requirement or responds to a solicitation of their time. Whether they are right is, of course, not sure—but we still cannot assume that they are wrong. The chances of error are the same whether, like Seignobos, we adopt the point of view of Sirius and refuse to grant any meaning to events, no matter what they may be, or whether we assume God's point of view, as did Bossuet, and find everything full of meaning. The resolution to ignore the meaning which men have themselves given to their action and to keep all historical efficacy reserved for the concatenation of facts—in short, to idolize objectivity—contains, according to a profound remark of Trotsky, the boldest sort of judgment when it has to do with a revolution, since it imposes *a priori* on the man of action, who believes in a logic of history and a truth of his action, the categories of the "objective" historian who has no such belief. The union of the peasants and the workers during the events of 1917 in Russia may be an accident, but another hypothesis is also possible: the workers' movement and the demands of the peasants converged toward a socialist revolution because the democratic phase with its liberal reforms was not viable in a country with no bourgeoisie and because the peasants could find no satisfaction for their demands except by going beyond such a phase. The structure of the Czarist State would then explain the "fortuitous" conjunction alluded to by the "objective" historian. Thus true objectivity demands that we examine the "subjective" components of the event—the way it was interpreted by its contemporaries and protagonists—in order to assign them their rightful role. But the historian must confront these views with the facts in order to correctly appraise their influence; he must on occasion measure the degree to which the facts and the interpretations deviate from each other; and, lastly, he must reach a decision about a Marxist interpretation of the

10. Charles Seignobos (1854–1942), French historian.—Trans.

events of 1917 which will always be personal to some extent because it has no basis other than the probable.[11] It is then that the task of history appears in all its difficulty: we must reawaken the past, reinstate it in the present, recreate the atmosphere of the age as its contemporaries lived it, without imposing any of our own categories upon it, and, once that has been done, go on to determine whether its contemporaries were mystified and who, of their number or ours, best understood the truth of that time. Once again, it is a problem of communication. As L. Febvre showed so well with respect to 16th-century unbelief, Rabelais' mental universe cannot be described in our language or thought of in terms of our categories.[12] There are many passages which prevent us from calling him a believer in our sense of the word, but it would be just as inexact to say that he was an unbeliever in the sense which the word took on two, three, or four centuries later. Religion was part of the mental equipment or gear of the 16th century. Even if it is not at the center of Rabelais' life and thought, it does delimit his horizon, at least as implicit thesis and established reality. To understand Rabelais would be to recreate the cultural environment which was his and is no longer ours, to rejoin his thoughts through our own historical situation. If we can make any progress toward an adequate knowledge of the past, it will not be—contrary to what Seignbos believed—by raising ourselves to the point of view of an absolute observer who thinks he dominates all times and who, *because of that very assumption,* knows nothing about them; rather, it will be by experiencing ever more clearly that this very conviction can be dated, that the very idea of a universe of truth deceives us, and by perceiving what the past meant to itself. We will arrive at the universal not by abandoning our particularity but by turning it into a way of reaching others, by virtue of that mysterious affinity which makes situations mutually understandable.

*   *   *   *

As presently oriented, the sciences of man are metaphysical or transnatural in that they cause us to rediscover, along with structure and the understanding of structure, a dimension of being and a type of knowledge which man forgets in his natural attitude. It is natural to

11. Even in a Marxist perspective effective history follows its internal logic to the very end only if men become aware of it, understand it in the Marxist sense, and complete the movement which is roughly indicated in things. The historian who writes the history of 1917 cannot, even if he is a Marxist, pretend that the revolution was predestined; he must show it was possible—even probable—but not prefabricated. The course of universal history is not predetermined even for him: socialism will come, but who knows when or by what paths?

12. L. Febvre, "La religion de Rabelais," *Le probleme l'incroyance au XVI*ᵉ *siècle* (Paris, 1943).

believe ourselves in the presence of a world and a time over which our thought soars, capable of considering each part at will without modifying the part's objective nature. This belief is taken up and systematized in the beginnings of science, which always takes for granted an absolute observer in whom all points of view are summed up and, correlatively, a true projection of all perspectives. But the sciences of man—not to mention the others—have made it evident that all knowledge of man by man, far from being pure contemplation, is the taking up by each, *as best he can,* of the acts of others, reactivating from ambiguous signs an experience which is not his own, appropriating a structure (e.g., the *a priori* of the species, the sublinguistic schema or spirit of a civilization) of which he forms no distinct concept but which he puts together as an experienced pianist deciphers an unknown piece of music: without himself grasping the motives of each gesture or each operation, without being able to bring to the surface of consciousness all the sediment of knowledge which he is using at that moment. Here we no longer have the positing of an object, but rather we have communication with a way of being. The universality of knowledge is no longer guaranteed in each of us by that stronghold of absolute consciousness in which the Kantian "I think"—although linked to a certain spatio-temporal perspective—was assured *a priori* of being identical to every other possible "I think." The germ of universality or the "natural light" without which there could be no knowledge is to be found ahead of us, in the thing where our perception places us, in the dialogue into which our experience of other people throws us by means of a movement not all of whose sources are known to us. Metaphysics begins from the moment when, ceasing to live in the evidence of the object—whether it is the sensory object or the object of science—we apperceive the radical subjectivity of all our experience as inseparable from its truth value. It means two things to say that our experience is our own: both that it is not the measure of all imaginable being in itself and that it is nonetheless co-extensive with all being of which we can form a notion. This double sense of the *cogito* is the basic fact of metaphysics: I am sure that there is being—on the condition that I do not seek another sort of being than being-for-me. When I am aware of sensing, I am not, on the one hand, conscious of my state and, on the other, of a certain sensuous quality such as red or blue—but red or blue are nothing other than my different ways of running my eyes over what is offered to me and of responding to its solicitation. Likewise, when I say that I see someone, it means that I am moved by sympathy for this behavior of which I am a witness and which holds my own intentions by furnishing them with a visible realization. It is our very difference, the uniqueness of our experience, which attests to our strange ability to enter into others and re-enact their deeds. Thus is founded a truth which, as Pascal said, we can neither reject nor completely accept. Metaphysics is the deliberate intention to describe this paradox of consciousness and truth, exchange and communication, in which science lives and which it encounters in the guise of vanquished difficulties or failures to be made good but which it does not thematize. From the moment I recognize that my experience, precisely insofar as it is my own, makes me accessible to what is not myself, that I am sensitive to the world and to others, all the beings which objective thought placed at a distance draw singularly nearer to me.[13] Or, conversely, I recognize my affinity with them; I am nothing but an ability to echo them, to understand them, to respond to them. My life seems absolutely individual and absolutely universal to me. This recognition of an individual life which animates all past and contemporary lives and receives its entire life from them, of a light which flashes from them to us contrary to all hope—this is metaphysical consciousness, whose first stage is surprise at discovering the confrontation of opposites and whose second stage is recognition of their identity in the simplicity of *doing*. Metaphysical consciousness has no other objects than those of experience: this world, other people, human history, truth, culture. But instead of taking them as all settled, as consequences with no premises, as if they were self-evident, it rediscovers their fundamental strangeness to me and the miracle of their appearing. The history of mankind is then no longer the inevitable advent of modern man in fixed stages starting with the cave men, that imperious growth of morality and science of which "all too human" textbooks chatter; it is not empirical, successive history but the awareness of the secret bond which causes Plato to be still alive in our midst.

Understood in this way, metaphysics is the opposite of system. If system is an arrangement of concepts which makes all the aspects of experience immediately compatible and compossible, then it suppresses metaphysical consciousness and, moreover, does away with morality at the same time. For example, if we wish to base the fact of rationality or communication on an absolute value or thought, either

13. It would obviously be in order to give a precise description of the passage of perceptual faith into explicit truth as we encounter it on the level of language, concept, and the cultural world. We intend to do so in a work devoted to "The Origin of Truth." [This is the volume on which Merleau-Ponty was working when he died. He variously referred to this work as "Being and Sense," "The Genealogy of Truth," or "The Origin of Truth." The manuscript for the first part of this volume has recently been published as *Le Visible et l'invisible* (Paris, 1964). An English translation of this work, by A. L. Lingis, will be published in 1967 as another of the Northwestern University Studies in Phenomenology and Existential Philosophy.]

this absolute does not raise any difficulties and, when everything has been carefully considered, rationality and communication remain based on themselves, or else the absolute descends into them, so to speak—in which case it overturns all human methods of verification and justification. Whether there is or is not an absolute thought and an absolute evaluation in each practical problem, my own opinions, which remain capable of error no matter how rigorously I examine them, are still my only equipment for judging. It remains just as hard to reach agreement with myself and with others, and for all my belief that it is in principle always attainable, I have no other reason to affirm this principle than my experience of certain concordances, so that in the end whatever solidity there is in my belief in the absolute is nothing but my experience of agreement with myself and others. Recourse to an absolute foundation—when it is not useless—destroys the very thing it is supposed to support. As a matter of fact, if I believe that I can rejoin the absolute principle of all thought and all evaluation on the basis of evidence, then I have the right to withdraw my judgments from the control of others on the condition that I have my consciousness for myself; my judgments take on a sacred character; in particular—in the realm of the practical—I have at my disposal a plan of escape in which my actions become transfigured: the suffering I create turns into happiness, ruse becomes reason, and I piously cause my adversaries to perish. Thus, when I place the ground of truth or morality outside ongoing experience, either I continue to hold to the probabilities it offers me (merely devalued by the ideal of absolute knowledge), or I disguise these probabilities as absolute certainties—and then I am letting go of the verifiable for the sake of truth, which is to say I drop the prey to catch its shadow. I waver between uncertainty and presumptuousness without ever finding the precise point of human resolution. If, on the other hand, I have understood that truth and value can be for us nothing but the result of the verifications or evaluations which we make in contact with the world, before other people and in given situations of knowledge and action, that even these notions lose all meaning outside of human perspectives, then the world recovers its texture, the particular acts of verification and evaluation through which I grasp a dispersed experience resume their decisive importance, and knowledge and action, true and false, good and evil have something unquestionable about them precisely because I do not claim to find in them absolute evidence. Metaphysical and moral conscious-ness dies upon contact with the absolute because, beyond the dull world of habitual or dormant consciousness, this consciousness is itself the living connection between myself and me and myself and others. Metaphysics is not a construction of concepts by which we try to make our paradoxes less noticeable but is the experience we have of these paradoxes in all situations of personal and collective history and the actions which, by assuming them, transform them into reason. One cannot conceive of a response which would eliminate such an inquiry; one thinks only of resolute actions which carry it further. Metaphysics is not a knowledge come to complete the edifice of knowledges but is lucid familiarity with whatever threatens these fields of knowledge and the acute awareness of their worth. The contingency of all that exists and all that has value is not a little truth for which we have somehow or other to make room in some nook or cranny of the system: it is the condition of a metaphysical view of the world.

Such a metaphysics cannot be reconciled with the manifest content of religion and with the positing of an absolute thinker of the world. These affirmations immediately pose the problem of a theodicy which has not taken one step forward since Leibniz and which in the last analysis perhaps consisted—even for Leibniz himself—of evoking the existence of this world as an insurpassable fact which from the first solicits creative actualization and therefore of rejecting the point of view of a worldless God. God then appears, not as the creator of this world—which would immediately entail the difficulty of a sovereign and benevolent power forced to incorporate evil in His works—but rather as an idea in the Kantian and restrictive sense of the word. God becomes a term of reference for a human reflection which, when it considers the world such as it is, condenses in this idea what it would like the world to be. A God who would not be simply for us but for Himself, could, on the contrary, be sought by metaphysics only behind consciousness, beyond our ideas, as the anonymous force which sustains each of our thoughts and experiences.[14] At this point religion ceases to be a conceptual construct or an ideology and once more becomes part of the experience of interhuman life. The originality of Christianity as the religion of the death of God is its rejection of the God of the philosophers and its heralding of a God who takes on the human condition. The role of religion in culture is not that of a dogma or even of a belief, a cry. But what else could it be and still be effective? The Christian teaching that the Fall is fortunate, that a world without

14. Any determination one would like to give of this foundation at once becomes contradictory—not with that fertile contradiction of human consciousness but with the inert contradiction of inconsistent concepts. I have the right to consider the contradictions of my life as a thinking and incarnate subject, finite and capable of truth, as ultimate and true because I have experienced them and because they are interconnected in the unquestionable perception of a thing or in the experience of a truth. I can no longer introduce a "transcendence in immanence" behind me as Husserl did (even transcendence qualified as hypothetical), for I am not God, and I cannot verify the co-existence of these two attributes in any indubitable experience.

fault would be less good, and, finally, that the creation, which made being fall from its original perfection and sufficiency, is nevertheless more valuable or was all to the good makes Christianity the most resolute negation of the conceived infinite.

Lastly, no matter if metaphysics conceived as system has clashed with scientism, as Bergson saw, there is much more than a concordat between a metaphysics which rejects system as a matter of principle and a science which is forever becoming more exact in measuring how much its formulas diverge from the facts they are supposed to express: there is a spontaneous convergence.[15] Philosophical self-consciousness does not make science's effort at objectification futile; rather, philosophy pursues this effort at the human level, since all thought is inevitably objectification: only philosophy knows that on this level objectification cannot become carried away and makes us conquer the more fundamental relationship of co-existence. There can be no rivalry between scientific knowledge and the metaphysical knowing which continually confronts the former with its task. A science without philosophy would literally not know what it was talking about. A philosophy without methodical exploration of phenomena would end up with nothing but formal truths, which is to say, errors. To do metaphysics is not to enter a world of isolated knowledge nor to repeat sterile formulas such as we are using here: it is thoroughly to test the paradoxes it indicates; continually to re-verify the discordant functioning of human intersubjectivity; to try to think through to the very end the same phenomena which science lays siege to, only restoring to them their original transcendence and strangeness. When it seems that

---

15. Bergson's *Introduction à la métaphysique* shows in a profound way that science should be considered not only with respect to its completed formulas but also with an eye to the margin of indetermination which separates these formulas from the data to be explained and that, taken in this way, it presupposes an intimacy with the still-to-be-determined data. Metaphysics would then be the deliberate exploration of this world prior to the object of science to which science refers. In all these respects it seems to us that Bergson has perfectly defined the metaphysical approach to the world. It remains to be seen whether he was true to this method and did not revert to the system in passing from the "curve of facts" to a vital or spiritual impulse of which they would be the manifestation or the trace and which could be perceived only from the absolute observer's viewpoint, thus transforming the effort and tension he first described into an eternal repose. If, for Bergson, intuition really makes us transcend the world, it is because Bergson is not fully aware of his own presuppositions and of that simple fact that all we live is lived against the background of the world. And if, on the other hand, his philosophy is finally to be understood as a philosophy of immanence, he may be reproached with having described the human world only in its most general structures (e.g., duration, openness to the future); his work lacks a picture of human history which would give a content to these intuitions, which paradoxically remain very general. [English translation of Bergson's book by T. E. Hulme, *An Introduction to Metaphysics* (New York and London, 1912).]

methodology has incontestably established that all induction is baseless in the absolute sense of the word and that all reflection always carries with it whole vistas of experience which tacitly cooperate to produce the purest of our evidence, it will undoubtedly be in order to revise the classical distinction between induction and reflection and to ask ourselves if two kinds of knowing are really involved or if there is not rather one single way of knowing, with different degrees of naïveté or explicitness.

A certain number of negations were necessary clearly to define the limits of this conception of metaphysics, but, taken in itself, such a conception is the essence of positiveness, and it is impossible to see what it could deprive us of. The glory of the evidence such as that of successful dialogue and communication, the common fate which men share and their oneness, which is not merely a biological resemblance but is a similarity in their most intimate nature—all that science and religion can effectively live is here brought together and rescued from the ambiguities of a double life.

8 / Concerning Marxism

THIERRY MAULNIER began writing about politics in the period of fascism's ascendancy. He has thought about it and written about it a great deal, sometimes fervently and sometimes with reserve. There is no doubt that he helped make fascism respected, precisely because he took it seriously and submitted it to sober examination, accepting this and rejecting that. As he himself wrote, the sincerity of a few men is a necessary auxiliary of historical mystifications.[1] Once that has been said, one must immediately add that our author comported himself in such a way as to escape polemics and tendentiousness and find a place on the level of political philosophy where opinions may be true or false but none deserve to be condemned. Let us remember that in May, 1940, when chance circumstances left him sole editor of a weekly paper, Thierry Maulnier brought out several resolutely "war-mongering" issues which two years later earned him the same paper's denunciation as a British agent. Between 1940 and 1944 he limited himself to the role of military critic in the newspapers on which he collaborated in the unoccupied zone and never permitted the interest he had shown in the Fascist phenomenon to be utilized by the propaganda of foreign fascisms. He thereby not only gave proof of his independence and sincerity—private virtues which are not decisive in politics—but he showed that he had a sense of historical responsibility, and he understood that a writer in an even partially occupied country, especially if he had been interested in fascism, could no longer put his name to a political chronicle. This is what gives him the complete right to publish his reflections today and gives us complete liberty to discuss them without any mental reservations.

His interest in fascism was conditional. For Thierry Maulnier the

1. *Violence et conscience*, p. 128.

problem of our time was to unite two forces which had up to this time been separate: the proletarian forces heading toward a classless society by means of economic and social revolution, and the forces which tended to preserve the nation, the form of Western European civilization. Looking at fascism in its first stages—and perhaps giving too much credit to the declarations of its theoreticians—he believed that the significance of the phenomenon lay in bringing about this union. This, he thought, was the historical *truth* of fascism, no matter how the different existing fascisms—which might or might not remain true to their mission—conducted themselves. On this point, Thierry Maulnier multiplied his reservations: "The recourse to Action, Race, Blood, the predestined Leader, the superior mission of one people—all the suspicious instruments of modern nationalism are nothing but the substitutes of faltering intelligence, man's appeal to shadows in order to regain control of a world in which knowledge is powerless to guide him." [2] His only hope was that "the confused instincts and contradictory tendencies associated with fragments of old doctrines, with resentments that are sometimes vulgar and interests that are sometimes sordid," would introduce into history a *true* fascism, one without racial persecutions, oppression, or war, wholly dedicated to solving the proletarian problem within the limits of the nation.[3]

It was therefore necessary to help fascism become aware of its true historical destination and in some way to transform it into itself. Fascism thus far had appealed to "moral relics, vague claims, to myths as vague as those of heroism, duty, and sacrifice, to the easiest and sometimes the most suspicious sources of exaltation." [4] The gold buried in that mud had to be mined. The question was whether restricted social reforms, racism, and the exaltation of the national community were not merely instruments designed to conjure away the social and proletarian problem according to the tested formulas of traditional nationalism or whether, on the contrary, one was to witness the emergence of a new type of society in Germany and Italy. We can understand how Munich, the occupation of Prague six months later, the war on Poland, and all the rest definitively enlightened Thierry Maulnier about fascism's relation to its historical "essence" and how he unhesitatingly refused the existing fascism the sympathy he had shown for a certain "possible" fascism.

The important thing is to draw from this historical experience all the lessons which it entails. We mean: Was Thierry Maulnier's fascism really a *possible* fascism? Was it by chance or through an unforesee-

2. *Au-dela du nationalisme*, p. 19.
3. *Ibid.*, p. 29.
4. *Ibid.*, p. 25.

able choice of certain individuals that naziism and fascism resorted in the end to war and conquest? Was it reasonable to expect it to solve the problems of our time? Are we free to give a regime the meaning we are pleased to find in it, or isn't there a way to grasp the concrete logic of the system, which leads it necessarily—or at least probably—to its ultimate decisions? Wasn't it possible, from 1938 on, to tell which of fascism's different aspects (innovating or traditional) would finally prevail? Abandoning the naïve method of intellectualism and looking for the latent content of fascism beneath its manifest content was all that would have been necessary. Thierry Maulnier drew up a finished design for fascism by putting together a few ideas he liked: the idea of a social revolution and the idea of a national civilization. He strove to show that these ideas are compatible. But political criticism is not concerned solely with ideas, for it must take account of the modes of behavior for which these ideas are more masks than expressions. Even if the nation and the revolution are not incompatible on the level of ideas, on the level of action and in the dynamics of history if a socialism is "national," it ceases to be a socialism; the bourgeois of all countries have understood very well that the addition of this prefix eliminates all that is disturbing about socialism. We must know how to decipher this language which the powers can read at a single glance. For now, let us only say that if you put the national problem and the proletarian problem on the same level, you are in reality corrupting the socialist consciousness: by making it fall from humanism to empiricism, or, if you like, from "open" to "closed" politics; because it will be qualitatively modified from that moment on; and because, by a vital logic against which good will is helpless, it ceases in fact to choose the revolution because it ceases to choose it absolutely. Marxism is well aware of this law of all or nothing, and its criticism of opportunism or social democracy contains a psychoanalysis of political life which will have to be developed one day. Six years of grief and mourning will be as nothing for political experience if we go on thinking that fascism *might have* made socialism a reality, if we do not understand that fascism chose the "solutions" (which were, moreover, illusory) of war and conquest from the very start when it shrank before the proletarian problem, if we have not learned to connect exterior and interior politics as two aspects of an undivided choice, if we have not learned to consider a regime or a political movement as a living organism in which everything is related to everything else.

It will be seen that *Violence et conscience* does not go that far. Thierry Maulnier's solutions are today still what they were seven years ago. He undertook to criticize fascism "from the inside." The young people who read the magazine *Combat* were obviously Fascist sympathizers, and this magazine taught them to severely criticize fascism's inadequacies in matters of social politics. As Thierry Maulnier so excellently puts it today, each fascism has an "avant-garde" which, unknown to itself, fulfills the double function of reassuring the Leftist elements which rally to the regime in the hope of a social revolution and of disquieting the Rightist elements which would pull the system in a reactionary direction were it not for this threat.[5] One cannot avoid the thought that Thierry Maulnier is reflecting on his own past conduct in writing these lines. His claim to go beyond both nationalism and Marxism is precisely what put him in the avant-garde of Fascist ideology. Even today, when he has long since (and as flatly as possible) withdrawn any sort of support for certain Fascist milieus, his position is scarcely different. He teaches that the proletarian problem is the problem of problems and that capitalism must be destroyed. But he usually addresses himself to the readers of *Figaro* and the *Carrefour*— and we will not step on anyone's toes if we say that they are not wholeheartedly dedicated to social revolution. Which paper devoted two front-page columns to *Violence et conscience* this summer? *Epoque*. What did it get out of the book? Precisely those quite timid conclusions which we shall have to discuss. In such a setting, Thierry Maulnier's ideas can only serve once more as a moral guaranty for reactionary politics, and in the end it is with good reason that Thierry Maulnier has remained sociologically a Rightist critic.

Such great lucidity, honesty, and vigor in his thought, such timidity in his choice of a public and in his conclusions: the only way to explain their co-existence within the author is in terms of some political complex. Thierry Maulnier's problem is the problem of the French intellectual Right, and men of thirty-five are all the more aware of that problem because at some moment it was theirs in one way or another. Around 1930 *Action Française* enjoyed such credit among the students as is unimaginable to the young people of today, and the reasons for this must be sought. It is fascinating in any case to see Thierry Maulnier gradually rejecting all that was hasty in his first views without, for all that, completely getting rid of them and to see how such a rigorous thought process sometimes is held back and falls short of Marxism and sometimes touches on Marxism's basic problems.

*   *   *   *

There was a healthy reaction against Kantian illusions of democracy in the Maurrasianism of 1900. Democratic optimism allows that,

5. *Violence et conscience*, pp. 112 ff.

in a State where the rights of man are guaranteed, no liberty any longer encroaches on any other, and the co-existence of men as autonomous and reasonable subjects is assured. This is to suppose that violence appears only episodically in human history, that economic relationships in particular tend of themselves to effect harmony and justice, and, finally, that the structure of the human and natural world is rational. We know today that formal equality of rights and political liberty mask rather than eliminate relationships based on force. And the political problem is then to institute social structures and real relationships among men such that liberty, equality, and right become effective. The weakness of democratic thinking is that it is less political than moral, since it poses no problem of social structure and considers the conditions for the exercise of justice to be given with humanity. In opposition to that particular moralism we all rallied to realism, if by that one means a politics concerned with realizing the conditions of existence for its chosen values. Maurrasian immoralism is something else again: it renounces equality and liberty instead of concluding that, since they have not been given, they must be created. Having acknowledged that the view of man which we get through consciousness is abstract and that a society is not a collection of pure, free, and equal consciousnesses but is first of all a system of institutions to which consciousnesses owe whatever effective reason and liberty they might have, Maurras definitively rejects the judgment of consciousnesses and makes politics a technique for order with no place for value judgments. Maurrasianism is in large part a criticism of the interior to the profit of the exterior. Justice and truth, whose source men think they possess insofar as they are consciousnesses, are in reality based upon law-courts, books, and traditions and are therefore fragile like these and, like them, are threatened by individual judgment. The individual's evaluations and his ability to think correctly depend upon his external supports, and it is essential that these be maintained. The political man is he who has recognized the price of existing things and defends them against private fantasy. The problem is to save historically constituted man from nature which, within us and outside of us, always threatens him because it is pure transition. We should therefore place no faith in the course of events and should revere the admirable happenstance which permitted the appearance of humanity; there can be no question of abandoning an inheritance to heirs who will squander it or of consulting them about how it should be used. There are those who know because they have understood history, and there are those who foolishly make their consciousness their only guide. This results in a pessimistic, cynical, and authoritarian *pathos* of which traces are to be found in all of Thierry Maulnier's works, as, for example, when he says that hatred and the passions catch fire more readily than good will or that "a large part of true politics doubtless consists in making what are conventionally called men's vices serve the general good and in keeping what one calls their virtues from harming them—insofar as this is possible." [6] Or when he evokes "the effective power of stupidity." [7] Or when he defines liberty as "the benefit demanded by those who aspire to power as long as they still are weak." [8] Or each time he speaks of democracy, and even today when he stresses the hazards of history.[9] Barrès and Maurras thought that the world and our life were a senseless confusion in which a few fragile and precious *forms* appear. Their ideas are rooted in the despair of 1900. Thierry Maulnier owes this sense of a possible chaos, this respect for man and scorn for men, to his earliest political awakening.

Yet as far back as his book of 1938 appears another idea which leads somewhere else. He rejects the idea of necessary progress but rejects as well the Maurrasian idea of an immutable human nature which reduces political problems to those of an immutable sociology of order. "It is ridiculous to deny that man is capable of progress; it is no less ridiculous to believe that such progress will set him free. . . . Every time man introduces a new element into the system of known relationships which constitute an old civilization, he transforms this whole system of relationships to an inestimable extent and can plant in it the seed of an immense disorganization; thus certain steps forward can be paid for by much greater setbacks. . . . Let us at least realize that we create nothing which must not later be faced. It is only on this condition that we will be able to tackle the problems posed by the modern world without the stupid disdain, the imbecile terror, and the inane optimism which are the masks of impotent thought." [10] Thus Thierry Maulnier introduced the idea of a social dynamics and a movement of history. Politics could therefore no longer restrict itself to the tested formulas of an art of governing and a happy use of chance. It required an analysis of the present situation and acknowledged a certain meaning in history which it had to take into account on pain of being ineffectual. One was led to make a distinction among empirical events between those which make history take a step it will not retrace, because they respond to the problems of the time, and those which are merely adventitious, since they are based on a conjunction of circumstances which they will not outlive.[11] There is no guarantee that power

6. *Au-delà du nationalisme*, p. 84.
7. *Ibid.*, p. 23.
8. *Ibid.*, p. 106.
9. *Violence et conscience*, p. 10.
10. *Au-delà du nationalisme*, pp. 5–16.
11. *Ibid.*, pp. 20–21.

will return to the men and the forces best able to dominate the difficulties of the moment. The course of history is contingent, and it is not always the best or the truest which carries the day. "History is full of lost chances, of squandered wealth, of blind paths embarked upon." [12] Success can crown the least rigorous ideologies—at least for a while. There are true doctrines which, as Péguy said, do not get written into history, and, inversely, there are conspicuous events which do not carry history one step further. But history is at least rational in that a movement which fails to perceive its historical destination and to pose the problems of its origin has every likelihood of getting off the track, of miscarrying, of being deleted from the course of things or of leaving only an "ephemeral rent" in the web of history.[13] The movement which is successful at one moment is not always the truest or the most valuable, but such it must be if it is to last. If, for example, fascism only overcomes class antagonism by the ephemeral exaltation of national feeling and by resorting anew to the good will of the oppressed, if it continues to ignore problems instead of resolving them, it will disappear for failing to rejoin, by an act of conscious will, the deep-lying motives which gave it birth and for not assuming responsibility for its own truth.

Thus one witnessed the emergence of the idea of a politics which is not created *ex nihilo* in the minds of individuals but is prepared and worked out in history—and not in the Maurrasian sense of a history which repeats itself but in the sense of a history which goes beyond itself and presents men with new situations to dominate. History contains vectors; it has a meaning—not that all things fall into place in terms of one end, but because it rejects the men and the institutions which do not respond to existing problems; not that everything which occurs deserves to happen, but because everything that disappears deserves to disappear. If, then, one grants that there are certain *effective problems* present at the core of history, the analysis of our present situation should not be concerned solely with men's wishes and ideas but should be total. Analysis should tackle the very arrangement of things and the economic situation which, like everything else, henceforth takes on a historical significance. The inevitable consequence of the idea of a logic of history is a certain historical materialism. Thierry Maulnier encountered Marxism from these two angles. What did he think of it?

First, he criticized it for having underestimated man's role in effecting history. For him, if history poses problems, it does not of itself offer any solution to them. The breakdown of capitalism does not carry

12. *Ibid.*, p. 21.
13. *Ibid.*, p. 31.

within itself the seeds of the regime which is to replace it. It is up to man freely to conceive the institutions which will extract a new order from chaos and preserve history on the brink of nothingness. On our view Thierry Maulnier was here just disagreeing with a superficial Marxism. Indeed, how can one deny the role of human initiative if a class is effective only insofar as it has become aware of itself? Since Marxism has always said that the revolution is not inevitable, for it as for Thierry Maulnier history is only "half-determined." [14] For Marxism as for Thierry Maulnier, the historical determination of effects by causes passes through human consciousness, with the result that men make their own history, although their doing so is neither disinterested nor lacking in motives. In conceding that political will is supported by a factual situation and projects given antagonisms toward their future solution, Thierry Maulnier has for his part granted Marxism all that it asks: since human decision is motivated by the course of events, it will therefore seem—at least in retrospect—to be called forth by these events, so that no rupture or hiatus between effects and causes will ever be discoverable in completed history. In this respect *Violence et conscience* formulates the consequences of a historical method in politics with perfect clarity. "From the moment it has been clearly understood that history is never given to men like an empty space where they may construct what they like but is given to them like a certain state of things produced by anterior causes which they cannot cause not to be and which they must keep in mind, whether they like it or not, in ordering their conduct—from this moment the freedom it leaves them is just the freedom to have a better or worse understanding of the world in which they find themselves and to behave to greater or less advantage in that world. From this point of view, if the fact of consciousness contains an infinite number of possible representations and modes of behavior, there is scarcely more than one possible representation and mode of behavior contained in the highest degree of consciousness. It is in the highest degree of consciousness that man simultaneously perfects and destroys the freedom which history has left him, just because he is conscious." [15]

As a matter of fact, from 1938 on the only thing that set Thierry Maulnier apart from Marxism was his manner of describing the basic situation of our time. As we said before, he saw in it two *equally essential* facts: first, the appearance in modern societies of a class antagonism which destroys national unity, with the proletariat justifiably feeling alien in a country where one is allowed to sell one's labor without retaining possession of the products of this labor; and, second, the

14. *Ibid.*, p. 209.
15. *Violence et conscience*, p. 139.

resistance of the nation and of the middle classes in particular to this process of decomposition. He viewed as abstract any analysis of the present which omitted either of these two facts or tried to subordinate one to the other. His complaint against Marxism was precisely that it provided only a fleshless schema of history because it reduced history to economic history and deformed even this latter by treating the resistance of the middle classes to proletariatization and their attachment to the values of national civilizations as a surface phenomenon. Thierry Maulnier thought it true that modes of being and thinking depend at every moment on the modes of production, but no less true that the manner of working and producing in a given country at a given moment depends on the mores, the accepted values, and the psychology of the country in question. The class struggle itself takes place only within a national community, on the basis of the cultural acquisitions which comprise the nation's unity even at the moment it is dividing against itself. "We cannot deduce from economic exchanges (except arbitrarily and verbally) the more complex social exchanges; on the contrary, we must consider the existence of a complex social milieu . . . as the vital condition of all economic exchange, even the most primitive. However considerable a role economic exchange may play in social life from the very beginning (and it is as considerable as the vital organic needs and the ways of satisfying them are in the life of an individual human being), it no more constitutes the structure of society than the need to eat, sleep, or clothe oneself constitutes the structure of individual life." [16]

On this point as well, Thierry Maulnier's criticism was less telling against Marxism itself than against the current accounts of it or against certain formulas which are authentically Marxist but which schematize the doctrine. Marxism is often presented as a *reduction* of cultural phenomena to economic phenomena, or as a reduction of history to *conflicts of interest.* Marxists often speak of the bourgeoisie as of an "economic personage" who always acts with a view to his own interests and for whom ideas and beliefs are only means. It is nonetheless true that these interpretations and formulas remain unequal to Marxism and perhaps miss its central intuition. The greatness of Marxism lies not in its having treated economics as the principal or unique cause of history but in its treating cultural history and economic history as two abstract aspects of a single process. Labor, which is the substructure of history in the Hegelian sense, is not the simple production of riches, but, in a more general way, it is the activity by which man projects a human environment around himself and goes

16. *Au-dela du nationalisme,* p. 64.

beyond the natural data of his life. The Marxist interpretation of history does not reduce it to the conscious play of interests; it simply admits that all ideologies—even, for example, a morality of heroism which prescribes that men should risk their lives—are bound up with certain economic situations through which they come into existence: only when the morality of the masters is embodied in the economic relation of master and slave and in a society based upon slave labor does it cease to be an individual concept and become an institution and receive historical existence. Marxist materialism consists in admitting that the phenomena of civilization and concepts of rights have a *historical anchorage* in economic phenomena, by means of which they escape the transitoriness of interior phenomena and are deposited outside as Objective Spirit. Economic life is not a separate order to which the other orders may be reduced: it is Marxism's way of representing the inertia of human life; it is here that conceptions are registered and achieve stability. More surely than books or teachings, modes of work hand the previous generations' ways of being on to the new generations. It is true that, in a given society at a given moment, the way of working expresses the mental and moral structure just as a living body's slightest reflex expresses the total subject's fundamental way of being in the world. But economic life is at the same time the historical carrier of mental structures, just as our body maintains the basic features of our behavior beneath our varying moods; and this is the reason one will more surely get to know the essence of a society by analyzing interpersonal relations as they have been fixed and generalized in economic life than through an analysis of the movements of fragile, fleeting ideas—just as one gets a better idea of a man from his conduct than from his thoughts. Thus Thierry Maulnier's criticism of Marxism as abstract materialism was to a large extent unjust. Thierry Maulnier took no more trouble than De Man—whom he names and from whom he perhaps drew his inspiration—to disentangle Marxism from the mechanistic and utilitarian ambiguities to which certain of its formulas may lend themselves. Criticizing these formulas leaves Marxism's principal thought—that there is an incarnation of ideas and values—intact; it does not authorize us to transcend or "go beyond" economic analysis or to drop the guideline of the class struggle.

In the end this is just what Thierry Maulnier did. On the pretext that, in each single event, the class struggle is never seen except through the medium of the particularities of a country and a time, and that in this sense it is never pure or uniquely responsible, he proceeded as if certain historical realities escaped its influence. He treated the national community, for example, as an equally essential fact. In short, because historical facts entail moral and psychological conditions in addition to their economic conditions, he refused to put things in perspective. But the plurality of conditions does not rule out treating one of them as the principal condition. This is what scientists do every day: even though everything in nature depends to some extent on everything else and there are no strictly isolatable phenomena, we do have laws—i.e., statistically true schemas which approximately apply to the course of nature—for the intervention of the most distant phenomena in what we observe here and now is only negligible, thanks to a kind of damping effect. Likewise, although economic and other conditions are inextricably combined in events taken one by one, we retain the right to give the former a privileged place in our analysis of phenomena, if it has been established that they give a more faithful indication of the course of things when one is considering a sufficiently broad segment of history. It would be impossible in any case to restrict economic analysis to certain sectors of history: it is all-pervasive. The reaction of the middle classes to the threat of proletariatization is not a phenomenon distinct from the class struggle and does not point to any failure of Marxist analysis; it has its place in the class dialectic, being a new phase and a new illustration of it. The nation, which Thierry Maulnier treats as an irreducible fact, is itself charged with the class struggle, whether it is the bourgeoisie invoking the national interest and the external danger to bring strikers back into line or the proletariat assuming responsibility for the national heritage abandoned by the bourgeoisie, as in 1793, 1871, or even in 1944. A strange postulate is involved in Thierry Maulnier's setting the proletarian movement against the demands of national safety, the proletarian fact against the national fact. For it may come about that the proletarian movement is the condition of the nation's safety instead of a threat to it. There are really two nations: the nation as crude reality, with its existing bourgeois framework—this nation undoubtedly threatened by the class struggle; and the nation as a fundamental mode of life and behavior, hard to imagine as having anything to fear from a worldwide proletarian revolution. One cannot cite the national fact as a residue which Marxist analysis is unable to assimilate, since we have seen how this "fact" splits in two precisely under the influence of the historical factors discovered by Marxist analysis. Any politics which claims to be based on the proletarian fact *and* the national fact, as if the first did not encompass the second, is, beneath the flattering guise of a "concrete" politics, really just a "diversionary" effort, as Thierry Maulnier now says fascism was.[17]

17. *Violence et conscience*, p. 93.

Only let us admit that we are better prepared to recognize these truths today than in 1938. Then we were facing fascism on the rise—that is to say, a forest of bayonets but also a "social" and "revolutionary" staging, which intellectuals at least found impressive. We learned what propaganda was after four years of reading articles in *Oeuvre* about "socialist" Europe and the work standard and then confronting them with the reality of Germany at war. Beneath our very eyes fascism *became,* first, an army in combat and, finally, a pile of scrap-iron and ruins where worn-out populations, with no political idea or will, somehow subsisted. It requires effort for us to remember how fascism looked seven years ago, to distinguish it from the war into which it sank, and to restore the prestige it enjoyed as a new society, "beyond Marxism." In another connection, Vichy and the sacrifice of so many French workers made it evident to us that anti-Communism could lead to treason and that the will to revolution could assume responsibility for the nation. Lastly, now that France has clearly ceased to be a power of the first magnitude and national existence seems to depend so strictly upon world imperialisms, our diminished power no longer permits us solemnly to set the drama of worldwide economic organization against the French national fact, as if they were facts of equal weight: our humiliation will perhaps free us of the *provincialism* that was so striking in prewar French politics, and especially in the politics of *Action Française*. These years of looking to the world for our salvation have perhaps taught us to pose problems in worldwide terms, and the knowledge we have gained of infrastructures makes it impossible for us any longer to remain unaware of the matter of history, just as a sick person can no longer remain unaware of his body.

What is certain is that Thierry Maulnier does justice to Marxism in his new book as he has never done before and proposes a view of history which retains all the essential Marxist elements. The idea of historical "mystification" seems to have illuminated the whole Marxist conception of history for him. "When capitalistic society has reached a certain stage of decay," he writes, "capitalism can no longer find any safeguard except in a resolutely anti-conservative attitude. The capitalistic caste can no longer find anyone capable of struggling against the proletarian revolt unless it looks outside its own ranks; the economic structure which entails the plundering of labor and the domination of money can no longer count on anything but the myths of disinterestedness and heroism to protract its slow decline. It is no longer a question of a head-on shattering of the anti-capitalistic revolutionary *élan* but is a question of giving that *élan* an oblique orientation which will diminish the force of the shock and preserve part of the existing institutions." [18] Since Thierry Maulnier elsewhere excludes the interpretation of fascism as an "authoritarian disguise for large-scale capitalism," he therefore means that for nearly everyone this holding maneuver is preconscious.[19] He is not sure after all that any member of the bourgeoisie—with the exception of a few "masters"—ever conceived the Fascist diversion as a deliberate project. The mysterious thing about history is precisely that, without any preconceived plan, individuals behave in all particulars as if they had an infinite power of foresight: for example, the "bourgeois" choice of views and values in all domains (politics, morality, religion, the art of war) falls with infallible certainty upon those which will in fact make it possible to maintain capitalism. Plot, premeditation, or coincidence? We asked ourselves this at the Pétain trial. It probably was none of these. But, as if by a sort of reflex, Pétain—formed and defined as he was by fifty years in a military, and ten years in a pre-Fascist, environment—adopted in every circumstance and, for example, when faced with the problem of the armistice, the attitude which ran the least risk of liberating the revolutionary forces. The logic of history does not operate in terms of clear ideas and individual projects; its instruments are the complex politics and anonymous projects which give a group of individuals a certain common style, "fascist," for example, or "proletarian." Insofar as we have not understood that our actions take on a certain statistical and objective meaning (which may be quite different from that which we give them) when they pass from us into things, we are surprised by them, do not recognize them, and are misled by the "mysterious power of autodetermination" with which, as Thierry Maulnier says, history seems endowed.[20] This is what accounts for that look of barely awakened sleepers seen in certain "traitors" when events suddenly show them the unfamiliar configuration of their own lives. It is neither ideas alone nor interests recognized as such which go to make up history, but interests disguised as ideas and ideas which have sunk to the state of worries and vague anxieties in the confused give-and-take of existence. "If the determining factors of the Second World War can in no case be reduced to the play of economic causes, and if the role played by the economic causes of the war cannot easily be disentangled from the confused web in which they operate, there is nonetheless in this historical complex—which includes the routes, angles of attack, and interferences of all the forces governing society—a system of disequilibrium the influence of which seems to guide the ebb and flow of the great struggle, almost in the way that the

18. *Ibid.*, p. 104.
19. *Ibid.*, p. 93.
20. *Ibid.*, p. 46.

movements of the ocean are guided by a planetary gravitation. That the war of 1939 was to a considerable degree the war of peoples for possession of the great sources of raw materials and for domination by means of these sources of raw materials is beyond doubt." [21] Here one sees the idea of a sort of global or lateral economic determinism, which allows the other sort of conditions free play in each particular case, content to deflect them in its own direction. The discussion of Marxism has long been conducted as if it were a question of assigning *the cause* of history and as if each event had to have a relationship of linear causality with another event, about which it then had to be determined whether it was "economic" or "ideological," and Marxism was thought vanquished when one pointed to examples of "ideological" causality. But it goes without saying that the ideology in turn cannot be separated from its economic context. If a materialistic history is rejected for being abstract, then an idealistic or spiritualistic history should be rejected on the same grounds. One will then conclude that each event entails all orders of determinants, and there are some who still believe that this slant gets them beyond Marxism, since no perspective is absolutely excluded. They do not see that it is precisely this idea, that nothing can be isolated in the total context of history, which lies at the heart of Marxism, with, in addition, the idea that because of their greater generality economic phenomena make a greater contribution to historical discourse—not that they explain everything that happens but that no progress can be made in the cultural order, no historical step can be taken unless the economy, which is like its schema and material symbol, is organized in a certain way. "We must be careful . . . ," says Thierry Maulnier, "not to let ourselves be carried too far by this apparent victory over 'materialism.' We have driven the 'production of material conditions' from the 'foundation' where Marx placed it, only to reintroduce it at the 'core' of social reality. It is not a question now of once again ousting productive labor from this core of human social reality where we came upon it, completely immersed in but also completely immersing that reality, associated with all its forms and manifestations by an infinite mutual penetration and full reciprocity. It is not a question of relegating the 'production of material conditions' to the outbuildings of history, the kitchens or waiting rooms of human society, as do the idealistic historians, ashamed and disgusted. Production of the material conditions of life is not the foundation of human history, but neither is it the passive, disgraced servant; it is securely installed in this history, exerting a continual, powerful influence upon it, determining it and

21. *Ibid.*, p. 120.

determined by it—*on an equal footing,* as it were. We can neither hypostatize it as some kind of transcendent priority nor relegate it to a shameful or contemptible area. The producer of material conditions, the man who wrenches the life of his fellows from the world, this man is not the creator of human society considered in its historical being—for he is himself created by it, along with his work—but neither is he its slave: he is the instrument of the powerful transformations it works upon itself through the medium of nature, which it combats and often controls. History does not spring from him; it does not pass over him; it passes through him. . . . It would be useless to deny the preponderant part which *homo faber's* efforts to assure man's continued survival in nature play in the activities of human society; and it goes without saying that this effort—itself radiating from every part of the social totality of which it is a function—does much to determine the other forms of human activity: the production and transformation of laws, customs, beliefs, styles of civilization, and, in sum, the comportment and content of consciousness. Thus we can conclude that although the superstructures of the social totality are not determined by an economic substratum which could be said to have produced them, one can say that this totality determines itself, mainly through the intermediary of the activities by means of which it assures its survival and transforms surrounding nature." [22] How much Thierry Maulnier has changed can be measured by recalling his summary protests against American and Soviet mechanism in *La Crise est dans l'homme.* If the economy is to the society what the heart is to the organism, the problem is not how to regiment economic progress; we must instead be on the lookout for what Balzac called "the mystery of civilization," of which such progress is perhaps the visible outline.

Thierry Maulnier would seem to have reversed his original positions. In a history in which a strange logic holds everything together, the man with a real political sense will not try to play on human passions in order to reach arbitrarily chosen goals. Thrown with other men into a drama which will not necessarily end well but which at all events is moving toward some end, he understands that conservatism is a utopia, finds nothing insignificant in either men or things, questions and listens to them; for he cannot make them into anything but what they are. The time of juvenile cynicism is long gone: "To govern man by his passions is to augment them dangerously. Flattery and constraint are the two faces of contempt: they do, of course, turn man into a good instrument—but making an instrument of man, that indeed is contempt." [23] Yet one changes philosophies faster than morals and

22. *Ibid.,* pp. 151, 153.
23. *Ibid.,* p. 116.

morals faster than politics. If we leave the philosophy of history and turn to practical conclusions, we will find Thierry Maulnier lagging behind his own ideas.

*　　*　　*　　*

If it is true that the class struggle is an essential fact, that class antagonism shatters the constituted forms of culture, and, lastly, that step by step the economic decay of capitalism corrupts all the ideas, all the values it had sanctioned, then it seems natural to conclude that the only way to return to an "organic" economy and civilization is by expropriating the property-holders and, as Lenin said, "stealing what had been stolen." Thierry Maulnier, on the other hand, imposes such a series of meticulous conditions on this recovery by man of his own life that for all practical purposes they are tantamount to refusing the revolution. Indeed he admits that the problem is to do away with wage-earning and to re-establish the link between the producer and his product. That fraction of labor which serves in the capitalistic system to multiply capital should be paid for, if not in money and with the right to use that money to buy consumable goods (for the possibility of new investments and a new technical development would then disappear along with the accumulation of wealth), then at least in a "currency of production" which would make the worker co-owner of the enterprises to be created. On this point Thierry Maulnier adds: "As for the owners of the present instruments of production, they may find themselves reasonably satisfied in that case to be left in possession of their property, only without the right to use this property for gratuitous self-appropriation of the surplus value of their employees' labor, so as to assure themselves a monopoly in the creation and ownership of new wealth." [24] And so the very author who described occupation of the State by the bourgeoisie in almost the same terms as the Marxists is expecting the revolution in a State which has not been liberated by the expropriation of the property-holders. How can one help seeing that one of two things will happen: either Thierry Maulnier's "reforms" really will abolish capitalism—in which case it would be naïve to believe that the owners of the instruments of production will be "reasonably satisfied" with the toy one has left them—or else their power will be maintained by some indirect means, in which case they will tolerate the reform but it will no longer be anything but a new mystification. Concretely speaking, *who* will bring about the reform? A parliamentary majority? But, as we shall see, it is not certain that

24. *Ibid.*, p. 173.

Thierry Maulnier will accept just any form of democracy; and besides, we know full well the means which the powerful have at their disposal—precisely under the aegis of freedom of the press—to stir up currents of opinion and manifestations which paralyze a parliamentary majority. The proletarian problem has been posed, says Thierry Maulnier; there is competition to solve it. "Who the winner of the universal contest will be and whether he holds sword, scepter, or hammer in his right hand does not make much difference to us, but only what his guiding thought will be." [25] And elsewhere: "Let us imagine the political means of a radical transformation of society (i.e., of the political State) in the hands of one man or a group of men endowed with enough boldness, decisiveness, and historical consciousness to abolish the proletariat *qua* class, that is, to impose upon society an economic structure which abolishes wage-earning. . . ." [26] So that is what we end up with: socialism brought about by the decrees of *one man* or *a group* of enlightened men! Did we think that Thierry Maulnier was won over to the idea—which is perhaps the most incontestable of Marxist ideas—that an effective politics is not one conceived by a few individuals gathered around their table but one which carries the movement of history farther and which is borne by historical forces? Who will support the decisions of our reformers if not those they are going to set free, and how are they to support them if not by strikes and seizing factories? Must one then explain to them that they are not to take possession of or even direct the factories which they occupy? And what if they continue to occupy them? Who is going to evacuate the factories if not the police, and who will benefit from this if not the present owners? Was it worth the trouble of reflecting about Marxism and peremptorily rejecting all manner of reformism just to end up with this new "plan"? If socialism is not an intellectual's notion but, as Thierry Maulnier said back in 1938, "that which demands to be born," the form of social existence which is taking shape in the alienation of the proletariat and its revolt against this alienation, then a non-proletarian socialism is a square circle.

As *Epoque's* commentator was well aware, Thierry Maulnier could afford to get ride of his prejudices on the philosophical level, since they remain effective when one gets down to concrete problems, which, after all, are the only ones that count in politics. His thought at this point becomes weak and banal. It is no longer himself speaking. Control of management by labor? "That involves an absurd contamination of the programs of economic reform by the theoretical principles of democracy,"—that is, "by methods which have proved their paralyzing

25. *Ibid.*, p. 58.
26. *Ibid.*, p. 165.

slowness and inefficiency in the political order." [27] That is easy to say. Is he serious in comparing political democracy, in which everyone is called upon to give his opinion on abstract problems and, above all, where a whole series of influences (which Thierry Maulnier himself has pointed out) come between the voter and legislative decisions, with the daily management of business by workers? Has he forgotten that among the workers are a certain number of engineers and directors who are as "competent" as the owner of the business or the chairman of the board in general business matters? One only needs to have observed a workshop in operation, a combat section under fire, or a fishing boat at sea to understand that technical authority is never challenged when it is not used to mask inadmissible interests. Men may not be good, but they are not all that stupid; and when one thinks of the great many sacrifices which they have not only endured but finally accepted when it was not at all evident that they had to, one may well wonder whether they would not accept even greater sacrifices to ensure the success of an economy in which they would feel personally involved and which would be *their* affair. The question is not whether the revolution would disrupt production at the start but what solutions there are to the proletarian problem besides this one. A politics "for the people" which is not developed "by the people" in the end is not developed at all: this is the ABC's of a *historical* politics. We are reminded of the results of De Man's experiment in Belgium. The plan, which was adopted by the Belgian Workers Party in particular, had been set forth before "concentrations" of the people which were to be crowned by a giant "concentration" in Brussels, along with the threat of a general strike. There were two possible methods: the reformist or parliamentary method and the revolutionary method. Either workers at all levels would regain possession of the economic apparatus and impose a welfare constitution on the government—which would be going from the revolution to political power; or else the workers would remain at work and the plan would be put into effect by maturely deliberated legislative decisions—which, said De Man, would be going from political power to the revolution. De Man chose the second method, in conformity with the ideology of a planned economy. We all know what happened: the plan was never put into operation. If one's goal is to liberate the proletariat, it is *historically* ridiculous to try to attain that goal by nonproletarian means, and choosing such means clearly indicates that one is renouncing one's pretended goal. End and means can only be distinguished in intellectual conceptions, not on the terrain

27. *Ibid.*, p. 193.

of history, and any politics which does not admit this principle remains inferior to Marxism on the pretext of "going beyond" it.

Let no attempt be made here to disguise a reactionary politics with the excuse that the revolution must be directed. The problem of directing the revolution exists, but it arises after the economy has been freed of its parasites, not before. A man like Lenin did, of course, run into it along his way. He did not think there was any speculatively perfect solution: a politics cannot be built either on mass opinion alone or solely on the decrees of the party or its leaders. The secret of Leninism was in the communication he managed to establish between the masses and the leaders, between the working class and its "conscience." This presupposes leaders who do not shut themselves up in their offices and who know how to explain to the masses what is being proposed to them; it presupposes a dialogue and an exchange between the masses, which are a constant barometer of the state of the *effective* revolution, and the center, where revolutionary *conceptions* and perspectives are worked out. It no doubt means opening the door to eloquence and introducing a possibility of deceit into the system. But we must admit that if there is any solution, it is this.

One senses a second conservative theme in *Violence et conscience:* the idea that culture is a fragile thing and that a proletarian revolution would destroy it along with its capitalistic props. The proletariat, which "has no homeland" because it is excluded from its nominal homeland, is a result of the decay of capitalism. How is it supposed to have the strength within itself to erect a new culture? "One of the most ingenious, but also one of the most debatable points of the Marxist interpretation of life undoubtedly is this fusion, in a single dialectical movement, of the principles of decline and dissociation with the principles of renewal, of the disintegrating with the constructive forces of life." [28] Marxism is not unaware of the problem. It makes a distinction between a proletariat drained of all cultural substance (and, moreover, of all revolutionary energy)—Marx's *Lumpenproletariat*—and a proletariat which remains capable of historical and cultural creation. Marx's analysis should be extended and renewed on this point: the decay of capitalism, which is much more advanced today than a century ago, and the "rotting" of the revolution, especially in its Fascist form, have corrupted, morally ruined, and politically annulled broad social strata which would have been capable of revolutionary action. All one need do to become convinced of this is think of the proletarian elements who were involved in traffic with the

28. *Ibid.*, p. 68.

Germans during the Occupation or who remain in black market circles as something other than consumers. Such annulment may make it unlikely that a revolutionary consciousness will be formed in the immediate future. However, it must be understood that the restoration of culture is equally compromised, for, according to Thierry Maulnier himself, since economic phenomena are at the heart of a society, economic decomposition will not leave the cultural heritage intact. It is a fact that, in our present situation, there is not one term in the moral vocabulary which has not become ambiguous, not one traditional value which has not been contaminated. If one is to be able to speak favorably of work, family, or country some day, it will be on the condition that these values have first been purified by the revolution of the ambiguities they served to foster. Which means that there can be no question of saving them from proletarian violence, since this violence is the only thing that can make them honorable once more. The only way to preserve what merits being kept of the past is by laying the foundation of a new future. A classless society will reunite the negative conditions of a renewed culture. Thierry Maulnier will ask whether the positive conditions will also be reunited; and it is here that a choice must be made. If one views humanity as Maurras did, i.e., as a completely fortuitous result of a few exceptional men and a few improbable circumstances, then the revolution necessarily seems the greatest possible risk. But Thierry Maulnier has rejected this basically pessimistic view. Against such a view should be set, not the basic optimism of the 18th century, but a methodical optimism, as it were. For, after all, however rare great and beautiful things may be, it is a remarkable fact that they are fairly generally understood and admired. Man might be defined by this ability of his to conceive or in any case to respect what he is not and has not. All several men need do is live together and be associated with the same task for some rudimentary rules and a beginning of law to emerge from their life in common. Looking at things in this way, one gets the feeling that man has immense resources. One need only go back to that very wide-spread idea that reason is rare, and one could show that in one sense it is everywhere in men, that they are in a way caught up in it, and that this opening to the possible is exactly what makes their instincts much less stable than those of animals, as Pascal—who was no optimist—was well aware. There is something to be said in favor of the "natural light." Men somehow secrete culture without even wanting to. The human world, however different it may be from the natural or animal world, is somehow *natural for man*. One could find many traces of 19th-century evolutionism in Maurras' pessimistic philosophy; if there is a radical difference between human and animal existence, one might doubtless be a little less suspicious of man. The stakes are high, of course, and the risk is great. We should perhaps avoid running it, if we could. But if the alternatives are socialism or chaos, then imprudence is on the side of those who help aggravate the chaos on the pretext that the revolution is risky. Boiled down to its essence, Marxism is not an optimistic philosophy but simply the idea that another history is possible, that there is no such thing as fate, that man's existence is open-ended. It is the resolute try for that future which no one in the world or out of the world can know will come or, if it comes, what it will be.

* * * *

Has Thierry Maulnier therefore absolutely no grounds for being hesitant about Marxism? On the contrary, we think his hesitation has a profound significance once it has been unburdened of its "reactionary" themes, and it is for the very purpose of extracting what we will call "the Marxist problem" in all its purity that we have formulated the above criticisms.

We know that Marx and Lenin imagined that the State as a coercive power would "wither away" in a late phase of socialist society, because it seemed to them that constraints become superfluous in a society where there is no more oppression or exploitation and where the class struggle has really been abolished. This meant assuming that the contradictions between the individual and society only occur in a capitalistic society and that once this society has been destroyed man will become integrated into all forms of collective existence effortlessly and without any problems. On this point Thierry Maulnier writes: "There is one kind of alienation which can be abolished because it is the result of a certain reformable state of the society. But there is another, irreducible kind: the only way that man could regain complete possession of himself is by ceasing to live in contact with his fellows." [29] The passage would be weak if one took it as an argument against the revolution, for even if there is an alienation of the *for others* to which no revolution will put an end and even if the individual does experience the law as yet another constraint once the revolutionary *élan* has subsided, these are not reasons to turn him aside from the revolutionary act in which, at least for a while, he assumes existence with others and which has a chance of reducing the constraints of co-existence to the inevitable minimum. Although this passage cannot serve to justify a reactionary politics, it does, however, show us what separates Thierry Maulnier from most Marxists: he considers certain

29. *Ibid.*, p. 87.

contradictions of the human condition definitive; he believes that it is basically irrational. Thierry Maulnier never says this in so many words, but it seems to us that the truth of his book, over and beyond its prejudices, lies in his having clearly perceived in history what J. Hyppolite calls "dialectical facts," without his being able to adhere to the idea of a unique dialectic of history. We are not concerned here with an external criticism of Marxism, which could be curtailed by a more complete examination of the doctrine; our real concern is with an internal difficulty which deserves the attention of the Marxists themselves.

Marxism, as we know, recognizes that nothing in history is absolutely contingent, that historical facts do not arise from a sum of mutually foreign circumstances but form an intelligible system and present a rational development. But the characteristic thing about Marxism—unlike theological philosophies or even Hegelian idealism—is its admission that humanity's return to order, the final sythesis, is not necessitated but depends upon a revolutionary act whose certainty is not guaranteed by any divine decree or by any metaphysical structure of the world. A Marxist believes both that the Russian Revolution of 1917 was not fated—that, for example, it might have failed for want of leaders capable of thinking the situation out and orienting the masses—and that the very presence of a remarkable revolutionary directorate as well as the weakness of the middle-class political personnel in the Russia of 1917 were no chance and were bound up with Russia's total situation at that moment: on the one hand, the radicalism of a newborn proletariat formed by levying a labor force from rural areas and, on the other, the semi-colonial regime in Russia, which foreign capitalism had forced to undergo rapid industrialization. It is therefore characteristic of Marxism to admit that history is both logical and contingent, that nothing is absolutely fortuitous but also that nothing is absolutely necessary—which is what we meant just now when we said that there are dialectical facts. But this completely empirical and experimental character of Marxism immediately poses a problem. If we admit that an event, whatever its probability, can always miscarry at any moment, just as chance may renew its offensive, it may turn out in the end that logic and history go separate ways and that what seems to be the logical consequence of history never materializes in empirical history. Doesn't the revolution cease to be the fundamental dimension of history when it loses the character of a necessary future; and, with regard to effective history— which, after all, is the only thing that matters—isn't the person who judges everything from the angle of the class struggle putting things into an arbitrary perspective? There are two ideas contained in the notion of a "logic of history": first, the idea that events of any order—and economic events in particular—have a human significance, that in all its aspects history is integral and makes up a single drama; and, second, the idea that the phases of this drama do not orderlessly follow one another but move toward a completion and conclusion. The contingency of history means that even if the diverse orders of events form a single intelligible text, they are nonetheless not rigorously bound together, that there is a certain amount of free play in the system. For example, economic development may be ahead of ideological development, ideological maturity may supervene when objective conditions are not yet or are no longer favorable for the revolution; or, on the other hand, the dialectic of history may get bogged down or veer off toward chance ventures without solving the problems which it brought to light. If we resolutely give up the theological idea of a rational basis of the world, the logic of history becomes nothing more than one possibility among others. Even though we are better able to understand a greater number of events through Marxist analysis than through any other analysis, we still do not know whether effective history is going to consist of a series of *diversions*—of which fascism was the first and of which Americanism or the Western bloc could be other examples—for as long as we live and perhaps even for centuries. The Marxist historian will of course always be able to show in retrospect that these systems were just so many forms of "resistance" to the class struggle, but one wonders if the most efficient politics for a given country might not consist in trying to make some sort of place for itself in this world of accidents such as it is, rather than ordering all its behavior in relation to the class struggle, which is a *general* principle of history. It no longer makes any sense to treat the class struggle as an *essential* fact if we are not sure that effective history will remain true to its "essence" and that its texture will not be the product of accidents for a long time or forever. History would then no longer be a coherent discourse whose conclusion we could await with assurance and in which each phrase had its necessary place. Instead, like the words of a drunken man, it would sketch an idea which would soon grow faint—only to keep on reappearing and disappearing without necessarily attaining its full expression. Marxism could then only be stated in terms of negative propositions: the world economy cannot be organized, and its internal contradictions cannot be overcome (barring the continuous sequence of chances upon which man, as a reasonable being, cannot count), as long as socialistic ownership of the instruments of production is not everywhere established. But we know neither that a universal socialist production would achieve equilibrium nor that the course of events, with all the accidents which help to shape it, is heading toward that outcome. Marxism would remain a politics which is as justified as any other. It would even be the only universal and human politics. But it would not be able to take advantage of a pre-established harmony with the course of events: the universal proletariat bearing down on all sides on the capitalistic apparatus and destroying it in order to substitute a socialistic civilization—that would be not a fact but a vow, not an existing force from which we could draw support but a force we would have to create, since the nations' working classes are in fact seduced by the "diversions" of history.

It might be easier to admit this as a problem for Marxism if we put it in terms of everyday politics. The foundations of the proletarian revolution were laid in Russia in 1917 and nowhere else as yet. That is a fact for which hindsight can undoubtedly furnish reasons: it was no accident, one might say, that the most economically backward country in Europe was the first to have its revolution. It was just because Russia, unlike the Western countries, had not effected its own industrialization that it offered a semi-colonial country, as it were, to the capital of "advanced" countries; and the brutal establishment there of modern production methods was bound to provoke a crisis which would lead directly to the proletarian revolution, without passing through a long democratic and bourgeois phase as in the countries of the West. One can even speak of a law of "unequal development," according to which the phases of social and economic evolution may be upset by the interaction of "advanced" and "backward" countries. But this law was only discovered after the event, and since it was likewise only after the event that the Russian phenomenon was reintegrated into the logic of history, other incidences and other after-effects, which cannot be foreseen with the help of given explanatory schemas, cannot be excluded from the future. Not only is this possible, it is inevitable. For even after the unexpected event has been classified under a new law and linked to the Marxist dialectic, its consequences and its interaction with the configuration of the world continue to confuse Marxist schemata. Once the foundations of socialism had been established in Russia, the politics of the new State was profoundly affected by the double necessity of accomplishing an industrialization supposedly given in Marxist schemata of the proletarian revolution and of protecting the new State against a possible coalition of capitalist powers. If the government of the U.S.S.R. brought "bourgeois" motives into its industrial-equipment enterprise, if it established salary differences comparable to or greater than those existing under a capitalist regime, the reason for this is doubtless to be found in the fact that the U.S.S.R. could not apply the socialist ideology in a country which had not yet acquired the infrastructure of socialism and that its problem was precisely the problem of first erecting this infrastructure. On the other hand, it is difficult not to agree that if the Russian Revolution had not looked "well-behaved" to the capitalist powers, if the U.S.S.R. had pursued a policy of supporting proletarian movements outside its borders, then either the coalition against Germany could not have been formed or else the Germans would have succeeded in splitting it apart. Even today, if the U.S.S.R. was not signing an agreement with Chiang Kai-Shek and was openly supporting the Chinese Communists, World War III would be close at hand. But all this comes down to the recognition that the politics of the U.S.S.R. can no longer be a universalist politics, with which Marxists of all countries can immediately concur. For a French Communist, the paths of revolution are at present very different from those foreseen by the doctrine; Marx's nice, simple guideline, "Workers of the world, unite," is no longer available to help him judge everything in politics and know what to do in every case. Whereas for traditional Marxism there could be no contradiction or even any difference between the revolution and everyday politics, between doctrine and tactics, between revolutionary energy and efficacy, between morality and politics, we have returned to the politics of cunning. Because the U.S.S.R. stood alone, we are not even sure that it is the "cunning of reason," and this unforeseeable fact shattered the rationality of history. The result is that if we want to apply Marxist analysis to the events which fill our time, our Marxism loses its way in cross-phenomena and unexpected reactions, runs after events without catching up to them, or in any case without ever getting ahead of them; and a clear-thinking Marxist comes to wonder, as he sees how the schema of the class struggle becomes diversified and takes on different shades of meaning, if the course of history from one diversion to another will really end up as the history of the class struggle or if he is not simply dreaming with his eyes open.

This central difficulty of Marxism is today more obvious than ever.[30] Generally speaking, Marxism is weak when faced with concrete events taken moment by moment. This should not make us forget how strong it appears when applied to a somewhat prolonged sequence of events. We are perhaps misled by the importance we inevitably assign to the present in which we live. If the class struggle should reappear tomorrow—as is possible or even probable after a war—and should

30. This is what Lenin had in mind in *La Maladie infantile du communisme* when he sought the criterion of validity for a Marxist compromise with the bourgeoisie. It would be appropriate to extend the practical conclusions which he adopts onto the theoretical plane. A theory of contingency in history could be drawn from his Marxist "perception" of situations.

show up in all the countries of the world, the broad Marxist lines of history would once again appear. When Lenin, in exile in Switzerland, was reflecting on Marxism, what indication was there that a few months later it would become a reality, even in one part of the world?

The only thing certain is that, having seen history multiply its diversions, we can no longer assert that it will not keep on inventing others until the world sinks into chaos, and consequently we can no longer count on an immanent force in things guiding them toward an equilibrium which is more probable than chaos. We are sure that the world will not become organized, will not stop rending itself, will not extricate itself from precarious compromises or rediscover beliefs and values unless the men who are least involved with the special interests of imperialisms regain possession of the economic apparatus. We know neither whether this necessary condition will be realized nor whether it is a sufficient condition, and consequently we do not know what is the correct value to assign to these pauses, these instants of peace which may be procured through capitalist compromises. It is up to us to observe the world during these years when it begins to breathe again, once the bottom has fallen out of fascism, once consciences have been demobilized. If the class struggle once again becomes the motivating force of history and, definitely, if the alternative of socialism or chaos becomes clearer, it is up to us to choose a proletarian socialism—not as a guaranty of happiness, since we do not know whether man can ever be integrated into co-existence or whether each country's happiness is compossible with that of the others, but as that unknown *other future* which we must reach, or die. Thierry Maulnier would find his *real* conclusion—which he has not written and which he may some day write—in this Marxism without illusions, completely experimental and voluntary, to which he unwittingly committed himself when he recognized both the logic and the contingency of history.

August 1945

9 / Marxism and Philosophy

> "To be a radical is to seize things by the root. For man, the root is man himself."—Marx, *Contribution à la critique de la Philosophie du droit de Hegel,* p. 97.

ONE WOULD GET a strange idea of Marxism and its relation to philosophy if one were to judge it on the basis of the writings of certain contemporary Marxists. They evidently consider philosophy as wholly a matter of words, with no content or meaning, and, like Auguste Comte in his first period, they want to replace it with science and reduce man to the state of a scientific object. P. Naville writes that political economy should borrow the method of the natural sciences, establishing the laws of "social nature" just as the natural sciences establish those of physical nature. In a recently published discussion with Sartre, he showed his annoyance with humanism and valiantly sided with naturalism. R. Garaudy, in *Lettres Françaises,* brings off the feat of writing several columns in praise of Descartes without even mentioning the *cogito.* Once more in honor of Descartes, G. Cogniot, in the large auditorium of the Sorbonne, put in their place the "café philosophers" who think they can define man, in contrast to things, as non-being, forgetting that it is Descartes who is principally responsible for these aberrations, as one may become convinced by opening the *Méditations.*[1] It is strictly everyone's right to adopt the philosophy of his taste: for example, the scientism and mechanism which have for so long taken the place of thinking in radical-socialist milieus. But it should be known and stated that this type of ideology has nothing in common with Marxism.

A Marxist conception of human society and of economic society

1. "I am not this assemblage of members which is called a human body. I am not a rarefied and penetrating air spread throughout all these members; I am not a wind, a breath, a vapor, or anything at all that I can imagine and picture to myself. . . ." (*Méd.* II). [English translation by Lawrence J. Lafleur (New York, 1951).]

in particular cannot subordinate it to permanent laws like those of classical physics, because it sees society heading toward a new arrangement in which the laws of classical economics will no longer apply. Marx's entire effort in *Das Kapital* is directed precisely to showing that these famous laws, often presented as the permanent features of a "social nature," are really the attributes (and the masks) of a certain "social structure," capitalism, which is evolving towards its own destruction. The notion of structure or totality, for which P. Naville has nothing but mistrust, is one of the basic categories of Marxism. A Marxist political economy can speak of laws only within qualitatively distinct structures, which must be described in terms of history. *A priori,* scientism seems a conservative idea since it causes us to mistake the merely momentary for the eternal. Throughout the history of Marxism, in fact, the fetishism of science has always made its appearance where the revolutionary conscience was faltering: the celebrated Bernstein exhorted Marxists to return to scientific objectivity. As Lukacs notes, scientism is a particular case of alienation or objectification (*Verdinglichung*) which deprives man of his human reality and makes him confuse himself with things.[2]

Explaining the (simultaneous or successive) totality of human society in terms of the combined action of permanent "natural" laws is all the more unjustified since this reduction is no longer possible even with respect to physical nature. Far from being able itself to eliminate structure, modern physics only conceives its laws within the framework of a certain historical state of the universe, which nothing tells us is definitive, and under the influence of empirical coefficients which are given for what they are and cannot be deduced. This means, then— Naville would say—that there is a dialectic even at the level of nature and that, in this sense, nature and society are homogeneous. Indeed, it is true that Engels took over from Hegel the bold idea of a dialectic in nature. But, apart from its being the most fragile part of the Hegelian heritage, how is the dialectic in nature to survive idealism? If nature is nature, that is, exterior to us and to itself, it will yield neither the relationships nor the quality needed to sustain a dialectic. If it is dialectical, then we are dealing with that nature perceived by man and inseparable from human action, of which Marx speaks in his *Thèses sur Feuerbach* and *l'Idéologie Allemande*. "This activity, this perceptible and continuous action and work, this production are . . . the basis of the entire perceptible world as it now exists."[3]

2. G. Lukacs, *Geschichte und Klassenbewusstsein* (Berlin, 1923), "Die Verdinglichung und das Bewusstsein des Proletariats."

3. Feuerbach is wrong not to "conceive the perceptible world as the total perceptible and living activity of the individuals who make it up" (*l'Idéologie*

Of course there are passages in Marx with positivistic overtones, which treat certain ideologies as absurd and apparently count on the bright day of science to dissipate them. For example *l'Idéologie Allemande* states: "These Germans, in short, are always concerned with resolving the nonsense of earlier writers into some other foolishness, which means presupposing that all this nonsense does in the end have a special 'sense' which must be discovered, whereas it is simply a matter of explaining these theoretical phrases from the actual existing conditions" (p. 189). One would say that Marx refuses to "understand" religion, to grant it any significance, and consequently rejects the very principle of a phenomenology of religion. Here we are on the brink of a "fleshless Marxism" which reduces history to its economic skeleton. Religion literally means nothing; it is all words, all wrong, nothing but an appearance or a play. That, however, is not Marx but Voltaire, and Marx, moreover, has said just the opposite: "Religion is the general theory of this world, its encyclopedic compendium, its logic in popular dress, its spiritualistic point of honor, its enthusiasm, its moral sanction, its solemn complement, its universal ground for consolation and justification. It is the realization in fantasy of the human essence, because this essence has no true reality. . . . Religion is . . . the soul of a world which lacks a heart, just as it is the spirit of an era which has no spirit." [4]

Thus it is a question not of denying religion all human significance but of treating it as the symbolic expression of the social and human drama. Communist thinking should yield more than religion, not less: that is, religion returned to its origins and to its truth—the concrete relationships of men with each other and with nature. It is not a question of replacing the religion of churches with the religion of the laboratories and of substituting a recording cylinder for the Eucharist. It is a matter of understanding religion as man's chimerical effort to rejoin other men in another world and of replacing this fantasy of communication with effective communication in this world. At the time when he still made interpersonal life the basis of history and when the world spirit had not yet withdrawn to the far side of things, the young Hegel said that reading the newspapers was the "realist's morning prayer." The human core of religion and, in the Heideggerian

---

Allemande, p. 164). He gets his inspiration from the natural sciences. "But where would the natural sciences be without industry and commerce? In fact, even these 'pure' natural sciences only get their goals and their materials from industry and commerce, from the perceptible activity of men" (*ibid.*, p. 163). The science of nature is part of the cultural world and must not be hypostatized, since it is ignorant of its own human premises. [English translation, *The German Ideology*, Parts I and III, ed. R. Pascal (London, 1938).]

4. *Contribution à la critique de la Philosophie du droit de Hegel*, p. 84.

sense, the "metaphysical" content of Marxism consist of men in the process of taking nature (to which they were at first subordinate) upon themselves, of rupturing the given structures of society, and of acceding through praxis to "the reign of liberty," [5] or, as Hegel said, to "absolute history." [6] Religion is more than a hollow appearance; it is a phenomenon based on interpersonal relationships. It is only in passing into these relationships that it will disappear as separate religion. There is a pseudo-Marxism according to which everything is false but the final phase of history and which corresponds, on the level of ideas, to that rudimentary communism—the "envy and desire for levelling"—for which Marx had no kind words.[7] Authentic Marxism wants to assume—in going beyond it—all that has been gained and in this sense admits that everything is true in its particular place and level in the total system of history, that everything has a meaning. We are given this sense of history as totality not by some physico-mathematical type of law but by the central phenomenon of alienation. In the movement of history, man, who has alienated himself for the benefit of his fetishes and has been drained of his very substance, regains possession of himself and of the world. Animals have neither economic life nor goods nor the fetishism of goods nor revolt against this fetishism. These phenomena are possible only because man is not a thing or even an animal, because he has the privilege of relating himself to something other than himself, because he not only is but "exists."

What lends credibility to the legend of a Marxist positivism is that Marx is fighting on two fronts. On the one hand, he is opposed to all forms of mechanistic thought; on the other, he is waging war with idealism. For Marx, even the spontaneous logic of ideas as well as Hegel's "World Spirit"—that cunning spirit which leads men without their knowing it and makes them accomplish its own designs—are further "chimerical realizations of the human essence." But this struggle against idealism has nothing in common with the positivist objectification of man. Marx, unlike Durkheim, would not even agree to speak of a collective consciousness whose instruments are individuals. "Above all we must avoid once again setting society up as an abstraction over against the individual." The individual is *social being*.[8] Man is "a being which exists for itself," thus, a *generic being*.[9] Society

5. *Das Kapital*, ed. Kautsky, III, 2, 355. [English translation by S. Moore and E. Aveling, *Capital* (New York, 1906).]

6. *Esthétique*, trans. Jankelevitch, II, 261.

7. Marx, *Economie politique et philosophie*, trans. Molitor, p. 20. [English translation by T. B. Bottomore, "Economic and Philosophical Manuscripts," in E. Fromm, *Marx's Concept of Man* (New York, 1961).]

8. *Ibid.*, p. 27.

9. *Ibid.*, p. 78.

for man is not an accident he suffers but a dimension of his being. He is not in society as an object is in a box; rather, he assumes it by what is innermost in him. This is why one can say that "man produces man himself and other men." [10] "As society itself produces man as man, so it is produced by him." [11]

If it is neither a "social nature" given outside ourselves, nor the "World Spirit," nor the movement appropriate to ideas, nor collective consciousness, *then what is, for Marx, the vehicle of history and the motivating force of the dialectic?* It is man involved in a certain way of appropriating nature in which the mode of his relationship with others takes shape; it is concrete human intersubjectivity, the successive and simultaneous community of existences in the process of self-realization in a type of ownership which they both submit to and transform, each created by and creating the other. The question has sometimes been raised, and with reason, as to how a materialism could be dialectical; how matter, taken in the strict sense of the word, could contain the principle of productivity and novelty which is called dialectic.[12] It is because in Marxism "matter"—and, indeed, "consciousness"—is never considered separately. It is inserted in the system of human coexistence where it forms the basis of a common situation of contemporary and successive individuals, assuring the generality of their projects and making possible a line of development and a sense of history. But if this situational logic is set in motion, developed, and completed, it is by means of human productivity, without which the play of given natural conditions would summon forth neither an economics nor, *a fortiori*, a history of economics. Domestic animals, asserts Marx, are a part of human life, but they are only products of it, not participants in it. Man, on the other hand, is always producing new modes of work and life. Thus man cannot be explained by taking either animals or, *a fortiori*, matter as a point of departure. There is no origin of man, "since, for socialist man, the whole of what is called world history is nothing but the creation of man by human labor, and the emergence of nature for man, he has therefore the evident and irrefutable proof of his self-creation, of his own origins." [13] If socialist man can have a presentiment of a "reign of liberty" which is yet to come and, in this perspective, live the present as a phase of capitalist alienation, it is because he has within his possession the assurance that man is productivity, a relation to something other than himself, and not an inert thing. Shall we then define man as consciousness? This would

10. *Ibid.*, p. 25.
11. *Ibid.*, p. 26.
12. Sartre, "Materialisme et revolution," *Les Temps Modernes*, Vol. IX.
13. *Economie politique et philosophie*, p. 40.

still be a chimerical realization of the human essence, for once man is defined as consciousness, he becomes cut off from all things, from his body and his effective existence. He must therefore be defined as a relation to instruments and objects—a relation which is not simply one of thought but which involves him in the world in such a way as to give him an external aspect, an outside, to make him "objective" at the same time that he is "subjective." This can be accomplished by defining man as a being who "suffers" or "senses," that is, a being with a natural and social situation but one who is also open, active, and able to establish his autonomy on the very ground of his dependence.[14] *"We see here that consistent naturalism or humanism differs from both idealism and materialism and at the same time constitutes their unifying truth."* [15] It is a matter of understanding that the bond which attaches man to the world is at the same time his way to freedom; of seeing how man, in contact with nature, projects the instruments of his liberation around himself not by destroying necessity but, on the contrary, by utilizing it; of comprehending how he constitutes a cultural world in which "man's *natural* behavior has become *human* . . . , in which human being has become his *natural* being, his *human nature* has become his nature." [16] This environment—not supernatural but transnatural—in which men "daily create their lives anew" is history.[17] "History is the genuine natural history of man." [18] Marxism is not a philosophy of the subject, but it is just as far from a philosophy of the object: it is a philosophy of history.

Marx often called his materialism a "practical materialism," by which he meant that matter enters into human life as the support and body of praxis.[19] Matter plain and simple, exterior to man and in terms of which his behavior could be explained, is simply not at issue. Marx's materialism is the idea that all the ideological formations of a given society are synonymous with or complementary to a certain type of praxis, i.e., the way this society has set up its basic relationship with nature. It is the idea that economy and ideology have interior ties within the totality of history, like matter and form in a work of art or a perceptual thing. The meaning of a picture or a poem cannot be separated from the materiality of the colors or the words; it is neither created nor understood from the idea out. A perceptual thing can be understood only after it has been seen, and no analysis or verbal report

14. *Ibid.*, p. 78.
15. *Ibid.*, p. 76.
16. *Ibid.*, pp. 21–22.
17. *L'Idéologie Allemande*, p. 166.
18. *Economie politique et philosophie*, p. 79.
19. See, for example, *l'Idéologie Allemande*, p. 160.

can take the place of this seeing. Likewise, the "spirit" of a society is already implied in its method of production because this latter is already a particular way in which men—whose scientific, philosophical, and religious concepts are either the simple development or the imaginary counterpart of that method—co-exist. It is therefore understandable that the introduction of the notion of the *human object*, which phenomenology has taken up and developed, was reserved for Marx.[20] Classical philosophies dissociated this notion; for them, streets, fields, houses were complexes of colors in all ways comparable to objects of nature and merely endowed with human significance by a secondary judgment. When Marx speaks of human objects, he means that this significance adheres to the object as it presents itself in our experience. This is carrying the Hegelian conception of a *mind-phenomenon* or an *objective spirit*, which is conveyed by the world and not withdrawn into itself, to its concrete conclusions. The spirit of a society is realized, transmitted, and perceived through the cultural objects which it bestows upon itself and in the midst of which it lives. It is there that the deposit of its practical categories is built up, and these categories in turn suggest a way of being and thinking to men. We therefore understand that logic can be "the currency of the spirit" or that "the fetishism of goods" can introduce a whole mode of "objective" thinking appropriate to bourgeois civilization.[21] As has been justly noted, the frequently celebrated relationship between ideology and economy remains mystical, pre-logical, and unthinkable insofar as ideology remains "subjective," economy is conceived as an objective process, and the two are not made to communicate in the total historical existence and in the human objects which express it.[22] Thus J. Domarchi is one hundred per cent correct in crediting Marx with the phenomenology of the cultural world which Hegel had roughly outlined in his analysis of the 18th century as the century of money and which might well be carried out for each period and each civilization.[23] But Naville would object that, for Marx, "the manifestation—the phenomenological aspect of reality, and especially of 'ideal' reality—is exactly what needs explaining." [24] It is nothing but appearance—the reality being economic. As if a phenomenology could not distinguish "founding" phenomena from "founded" ones, and, above all, as if the relationship of ideology to

20. *Economie politique et philosophie*, p. 30.
21. *Ibid.*, p. 48.
22. Raoul Levi, "Art moderne et realité sociale," *Les Temps Modernes*, VIII, 1499.
23. *Revue Internationale*, No. 2.
24. *Ibid.*, No. 3.

economy which one finds in Marxism is that of appearance to reality. The bourgeois ideologies which contaminate all of bourgeois society, including its proletariat, are not *appearances;* they mystify bourgeois society and present themselves to it in the guise of a stable world. They are exactly as "real" as the structures of capitalist economy, with which they form a single system. Both these ideologies and this economy are appearances with respect to socialist economy and life, which are already taking shape within them; but until these latter have been realized, the bourgeois forms of production and life retain their weight, their effectiveness, and their reality. Lenin, who said that the class struggle would last for years after the Revolution, knew this well. The only rigorous definition and defense of Marxist "materialism" against the counter-offensives of mechanism would be for Marx to have developed his theory of praxis or of social existence as the concrete milieu of history, equally removed from idealism and metaphysical materialism.

This being the case, what can the situation of philosophy be in the Marxist perspective? It is an ideology (in other words, an abstract aspect of total historical life), and, insofar as it desires to "autonomize itself," it is just "another of man's chimerical realizations" playing its part in mystifying the bourgeois world. But, "the farther the domain we are examining gets from economy and the closer it comes to pure and abstract ideology, the more we will discover accidental elements in its evolution and the more its curve will trace a zig-zag." [25] Thus any attempt to give a massive explanation of a philosophy in terms of economic conditions is inadequate: we must see its content; we must discuss its basis. "It is not correct to say that the economic situation is the cause and alone is active, and that all the other phenomena are only a passive effect.[26] Here as everywhere, causal thinking is insufficient. "The ordinary conception of cause and effect as strictly opposed poles" is abstract.[27] A philosophy, like an art or a poetry, belongs to a time, but there is nothing to prevent it from capturing—precisely through that time—truths which are acquired once and for all, just as Greek art discovered the secret of an "eternal charm" (Marx). The economy of a time gives rise to an ideology because it is lived by men who seek their realization in it. In one sense, this economy limits their views; but in another it is their surface of contact with being, their experience, and it can happen, as it happened to Marx himself, that they do not merely submit to this economy but understand it and thus virtually go beyond it. Philosophy would be false only insofar as it remained abstract,

25. Engels to Starkenburg, 1894.
26. *Ibid.*
27. Engels to Mehring.

imprisoning itself in concepts and beings of reason, and masking effective interpersonal relations. Hence Marxism does not mean to turn away from philosophy but rather to decipher it, translate it, *realize* it. . . . "The practical political party in Germany is right in clamoring for the negation of philosophy. Its error is to stop at this demand, which it does not fulfill and cannot fulfill seriously. It fancies itself bringing this negation about by turning its back on philosophy and dedicating a few banal and ill-tempered phrases to it under its breath and with its eyes averted. . . . In a word, you cannot do away with philosophy without fulfilling it." [28] The *cogito* is false only in that it removes itself and shatters our inherence in the world. The only way to do away with it is to fulfill it, that is, to show that it is eminently contained in interpersonal relations. Hegel is not wrong; he is true from one end to the other, but he is abstract. We must simply give their historical names to the mythological combats he describes between consciousness in itself and consciousness for itself. Hegel's logic is, as has been said, "the algebra of the revolution." The "fetishism of goods" is the historical accomplishment of that alienation which Hegel enigmatically describes, and *Das Kapital*—again as has been said—is a concrete Phenomenology of Mind. What the philosopher and the later Hegel must be taken to task for is fancying that through thought they, and they alone, can get at the truth about all other existences, integrate them, go beyond them, and, from the depths of their wisdom, obtain the revelation of the meaning of history to which other men simply submit. To be a philosopher is just one of many ways to exist, and, as Marx said, no one can flatter himself that he has exhausted "religious existence," "political existence," "juridical existence," "artistic existence," or broadly speaking, "true human existence" in a "purely philosophical existence." [29] But if the philosopher knows this, if he assigns himself the task of pursuing the immanent logic of other experiences and other existences instead of putting himself in their place, if he forsakes the illusion of contemplating the totality of completed history and feels caught up in it like all other men and confronted by a future *to be made*, then philosophy fulfills itself by doing away with itself as isolated philosophy. This concrete thinking, which Marx calls "critique" to distinguish it from speculative philosophy, is what others propound under the name "existential philosophy."

As its name suggests, existential philosophy consists of taking as one's theme not only knowledge or consciousness understood as an activity which autonomously posits immanent and transparent objects but also existence, i.e., an activity given to itself in a natural and his-

28. Contribution á la critique de la Philosophie du droit de Hegel, p. 93.
29. *Economie politique et philosophie*, p. 84.

torical situation and as incapable of abstracting itself from that situation as it is of reducing itself to it. Knowledge finds itself put back into the totality of human praxis and, as it were, given ballast by it. The "subject" is no longer just the epistemological subject but is the human subject who, by means of a continual dialectic, thinks in terms of his situation, forms his categories in contact with his experience, and modifies this situation and this experience by the meaning he discovers in them. In particular, this subject is no longer alone, is no longer consciousness in general or pure being for itself. He is in the midst of other consciousnesses which likewise have a situation; he is for others, and because of this he undergoes an objectivation and becomes generic subject. *For the first time since Hegel, militant philosophy is reflecting not on subjectivity but on intersubjectivity.* Transcendental subjectivity, Husserl pointed out, *is* intersubjectivity. Man no longer appears as a product of his environment or an absolute legislator but emerges as a product-producer, the locus where necessity can turn into concrete liberty.

F. Alquié accuses Heidegger of obscurity on this point, and, applying a method of analysis which dissociates what Heidegger would unite, he puts the matter of knowledge (considered as irrational) on one side and Spirit on the other, making Heidegger an irrationalist. Then he is amazed that Heidegger wants to create a philosophy and integrate the values of reflection, science and truth.[30] But the whole point is that Heidegger wants to reflect on the unreflected; that he very deliberately proposes to study the being-in-the-world which is always presupposed by reflection and is anterior to predicative operations; that Heidegger—like Hegel—makes Spirit or Unity a future and a problem; that he wants in any event to see them emerge from experience, not take them for granted. In the same way, when speaking of Sartre, G. Mounin finds a "shameful materialism" and a "shameful idealism" in his philosophy—which is one way of saying that it is an attempt at an integral philosophy.[31] There are just as many—or just as few—reasons for saying that dialectical materialism is a "shameful materialism" and a "shameful dialectic." Any dialectical philosophy will always resist being labeled, since, according to Plato, it sacrifices nothing willingly and always wants "both." And so the philosophical effort to get past abstractions is sometimes challenged in the name of matter and sometimes in the name of Spirit. Everyone keeps the bee in his bonnet.

P. Hervé, wanting in turn to get into the debate, retains nothing of Husserl but his oldest formulas: the philosophy of essences, philosophy as a strict or absolute science, consciousness as a transcendental and

30. Alquié, *Revue Internationale*, Nos. 3–4.
31. Mounin, *Cahiers d'Action*, No. 1.

constituting activity. And it is true that Husserl maintained these formulas to the very end. But he himself, or his collaborator, E. Fink, introduced others as well: the point of departure as a "dialectical situation," philosophy as "infinite meditation or dialogue." What makes Husserl's career interesting is that he never ceased to question his demand for absolute rationality and never stopped interrogating himself about the possibility, for example, of that "phenomenological reduction" which made him famous. He kept getting a clearer and clearer picture of the residue left behind by all reflexive philosophy and of the fundamental fact that we exist before we reflect; so that, precisely to attain complete clarity about our situation, he ended by assigning, as the primary task of phenomenology, the description of the lived world (*Lebenswelt*), where Cartesian distinctions have not yet been made. Thus it was that, just because he began by seeking absolute evidence, he arrived at the program of a philosophy which describes the subject thrown into a natural and historical world, the *horizon* of all his thoughts. Thus it was that, having started with a "static phenomenology," he ended with a "genetic phenomenology" and a theory of "intentional history"—in other words, a logic of history. In this way he, more than anyone else, contributed to describing consciousness incarnate in an environment of human objects and in a linguistic tradition. And so, having perhaps "set obstacles in the way of the Hegel revival" at the beginning of his career, he is now contributing to it. Philosophers take their own good time, and we have no right to hold it against them. One has only to see how Marx treats the young people who are in too much of a hurry to "get beyond Hegel." Demanding that a philosopher go straight to the conclusions of his work on the pretext that action is urgent would be to forget that, as Marx said, the curve of ideologies is even more complicated than that of political history. It would be sacrificing the serious to the spectacular in the name of a political romanticism which Marx took pains to avoid. But, someone will say, existentialism is not just a philosophy but is a fashion, and no fashion can be serious. Of course. But it is easy to reply on this level: although phenomenology and existentialism started in opposite directions, they have in fact awakened more students to the problems of history than they have lulled into the quietism of transcendental consciousness. There is a story that in the last years of his life, when Husserl wanted to go to Belgrade to give the lectures he had been forbidden to give in Germany, the Gestapo was assigned the task of first reading his manuscripts. Are we in our turn going to look at philosophy through the police chief's glasses? Philosopher Husserl, we declare you suspected of anti-Hegelianism, and have consequently placed you under surveillance. . . . So Naville and Hervé, each for his own reasons, have something other to do than master the texts of an untranslated and two-thirds unpublished Husserl? All right. But then why talk about it?

Fortunately, with or without Husserl, the truth is dawning upon those who love philosophy. When Hervé leaves the phenomenologists alone and gives his own definition of his position, he does so in terms that are hardly scientist at all, and in fact are passably phenomenological. Rehabilitation of the sensory or perceived world, truth defined by what we perceive or know—all to the good. Knowledge understood not as the formal operation of the "I" upon "sensations" but as the envelopment of form in matter and matter in form and consequently as putting "the abstract universe of science" and "the fatality of the absolute Logos" back into "a human activity which achieves self-knowledge in the context of the reality it discovers in the course of its labors" and which cannot count on any "net set up by Providence to break its possible falls"—also good. The condemnation of all theories of "consciousness-as-receptacle," whether in the coarse form of "physiological secretion" thinking or in the more refined form of a logical and social accident—yes. These are the theses which Hervé reaches by Hegelo-Marxist paths and which others have reached from the starting point of phenomenology.[32] Whenever Mounin (in the same issue of *Cahiers d'Action*) demands a return from consciousness to "the brain" and maintains that consciousness "reflects the world," he thinks he has dealt a blow to existentialism. What he is really doing is jointly repudiating Marxism and philosophical culture.

32. Hervé, "Conscience et connaissance," *Cahiers d'Action*, No. 1, pp. 5–6.

PART III

Politics

10 / The War Has Taken Place

EVENTS KEPT MAKING it less and less probable that peace could be maintained. How could we have waited so long to decide to go to war? It is no longer comprehensible that certain of us accepted Munich as a chance to test German good will. The reason was that we were not guided by the facts. We had secretly resolved to know nothing of violence and unhappiness as elements of history because we were living in a country too happy and too weak to envisage them. Distrusting the facts had even become a duty for us. We had been taught that wars grow out of misunderstandings which can be cleared up and of accidents which can be averted through patience and courage. We were attending an old school in which generations of socialist professors had been trained. They had experienced World War I, and their names were inscribed by entire classes on the memorials to the dead. But we had learned that memorials to the dead are impious because they make heroes out of victims. We were encouraged to suspend the history which had already been made, to recapture the moment when the Trojan War might still not have taken place and a free act might still, in a single stroke, have exploded all the exterior fatalities. This optimistic philosophy, which reduced human society to a sum of consciousnesses always ready for peace and happiness, was in fact the philosophy of a barely victorious nation, an imagined compensation for the memories of 1914. We knew that concentration camps existed, that the Jews were being persecuted, but these certainties belonged to the world of thought. We were not as yet living face to face with cruelty and death: we had not as yet been given the choice of submitting to them or confronting them. Outside the peaceful garden of our school where the fountain immemorially and everlastingly murmured, there awaited us for our vacation of '39 that other garden which was France, the France of walking trips and youth hostels, which was as self-evident as the earth itself—or so we thought. We lived in a certain area of peace, experience, and freedom, formed by a combination of exceptional circumstances. We did not know that this was a soil to be defended but thought it the natural lot of men. Even those of us who, better informed by their travels or made sensitive to naziism by their birth or already equipped with a more accurate philosophy, no longer separated their personal fate from European history, even they did not know how right they were. Debating with them as we came back together, we justified the objections: the die has not yet been cast; history has not yet been written. And they answered us in conversational tones. From our birth we had been used to handling freedom and to living an individual life. How then could we have known that these were hard to come by? How could we have learned to commit our freedom in order to preserve it? We were consciousnesses naked before the world. How could we have known that this individualism and this universalism had their place on the map? What makes our landscape of 1939 inconceivable to us and puts it once and for all beyond our grasp is precisely the fact that we were not conscious of it as a landscape. In the world in which we lived, Plato was as close to us as Heidegger, the Chinese as close as the French— and in reality one was as far away as the other. We did not know that this was what it was to live in peace, in France, and in a certain world situation.

Whether by chance or by design, the representatives whom Germany sent among us were ambiguous. Bremer, a lecturer at the University of Paris, revered the values of war, consorted with Montherlant, and was to make some of the ties he had formed before the war useful to his government when he came back here in 1940 as cultural attaché. But in 1938 he was fond of saying he was an "old radical." By talking loud enough, one could get him to back down on the principal article of naziism. He showed surprise and injured feelings one day when, as he was speaking of the Spanish government officials and insistently calling them "Reds," we asked him to take his propaganda elsewhere. I witnessed his dismay when, in 1938, he had to leave France to put in a period of military service in Germany. He believed—as much as a man of his sort can believe in anything— Germany's "European" propaganda; or at least he wanted to believe in it, since it allowed him to reconcile his pleasure at living in France with his loyalty to the government of his country. One morning in March, 1939, I entered the room of another Parisian German to tell him of the occupation of Prague. He leaped up, ran to the map of Europe (which he did have on the wall), and said, with every intonation of sincerity, "But that is mad! That is impossible!" Naïveté? Hypocrisy? Probably neither. These fellows said what they thought, but they didn't think anything very clearly, and they kept themselves in the dark to avoid a choice between their humanism and their government, a choice by which they would have lost their respect either for themselves or for their country. There was only one solution to their inner debate: a German victory. When they came back to Paris in 1940, squared away with their country now that they had followed it into war, they were of course prepared to "collaborate" with France (within the limits imposed upon them by the German high command and Nazi policies) and to forget the military interlude. Before 1939 their slackness led them to choose to represent Germany in Paris; this played a part in the propaganda, and their irresolution sustained our unawareness. After 1940 their good feelings were supposed to serve the same ends, and they lent themselves half-consciously to this game until the day total mobilization caught them up, hurling Bremer to the Russian front where he met his death and the other to the African front where, it is said, he was severely burned. So it is that history attracts and seduces individuals. Thus when we look closely at things, we find culprits nowhere but accomplices everywhere; so it is that we all played a part in the events of 1939. The only difference between our Germans and ourselves was that they had had naziism right under their noses, and as yet we had not. They could not have been unaware of how they were being used; we had not yet learned that game.

*   *   *   *

Our being in uniform did not essentially change our way of thinking during the winter of 1939–1940. We still had the leisure to think of others as separate lives, of the war as a personal adventure; and that strange army considered itself a sum of individuals. Even when we worked with a will at the job of war, we did not feel involved, and all our standards were still those of peacetime. Our colonel had a 155 fired to disperse a German patrol near our position, and a captain was detailed to recover the shoulder-straps and papers of two dead Germans: we were as bemused over those stretchers as we would have been over a deathbed. We lingered over that German lieutenant who had lain dying in the barbed wire, a bullet in his stomach, and had cried out, "French soldiers, come get a dying man" (it was night, our position was isolated, and we had been ordered not to go out before daybreak). We looked long and compassionately at the narrow chest which the uniform barely covered in that near-zero cold, at the ash-blond hair, the delicate hands, as his mother or wife might have done.

After June of 1940, however, we really entered the war, for from then on we were no longer permitted to treat the Germans we met in the street, subway, or movies as human beings. If we had done so, if we had wanted to distinguish Nazis from Germans, to look for the student beneath the lieutenant, the peasant or working man beneath the soldier, they would have had only contempt for us and would have considered it a recognition of their government and their victory, and then they would have felt like victors. Magnanimity is a rich man's virtue: it is not hard to be generous with the prisoners one has at one's mercy. But we were the prisoners. We had to relearn all the childish behavior which our education had rid us of; we had to judge men by the clothes they wore, reply rudely to their well-mannered commands, live side by side with them for four years without living with them for one minute, feel ourselves become not men but "Frenchmen" beneath their glance. From then on our universe of individuals contained that compact gray or green mass. Had we looked more sharply, we could already have found masters and slaves in peacetime society, and we could have learned how each consciousness, no matter how free, sovereign, and irreplaceable it may feel, will become immobile and generalized, a "worker" or a "Frenchman," beneath the gaze of a stranger. But no enslavement is more apparent than that of an occupied country. Even those of us who were not disturbed and continued to paint, write, or compose poetry, sensed—when they went back to work—that their former freedom had been sustained by the freedom of others and that one is not free alone. If they had once felt cheerfully in control of their lives, that, too, had been a mode of co-existence, possible only in a certain atmosphere; and they became aware of that general milieu—unmentioned in their past philosophy—where each consciousness communicates with every other.

German anti-Semitism not only horrified but mystified us. With our background we had to ask ourselves every day for four years: how is anti-Semitism possible? There was of course a way to avoid the question, by denying that anyone really lived anti-Semitism. Even the Nazis pardoned certain Jews whom they found serviceable, and a chance connection allowed a Jewish actor to appear on the Paris stage for four years. Maybe there was not a single anti-Semite after all? Maybe anti-Semitism was wholly a propaganda device? Maybe the soldiers, the SS, the newspapermen were only obeying orders in which they did not believe, and maybe the very authors of this propaganda did not believe in it any more than they did? Launched by calculating agitators and borne along by confused elemental forces, anti-Semitism would have been a sinister mystification. So we thought up to 1939; now that we have seen those busloads of children on the Place de la

Contrescarpe, we can no longer think so. Anti-Semitism is not a war machine set up by a few Machiavellis and serviced by the obedience of others. It is not the creation of a few people any more than language is, or music. It was conceived in the depths of history. In the last analysis that cops and con-men conception of history which emphasizes agitators and elemental forces, cynicism and stupidity, is naïve: it attributes too much awareness to the leaders and too little to the masses. It does not see any middle-ground between the voluntary action of the former and the passive obedience of the latter, between history's subject and object. The Germans made us understand, on the contrary, that leaders are mystified by their own myths and that the troops are their half-knowing accomplices, that no one commands or obeys absolutely. An anti-Semite could not stand to see Jews tortured if he really saw them, if he perceived that suffering and agony in an individual life—but this is just the point: he does not see Jews suffering; he is blinded by the myth of *the* Jew. He tortures and murders the Jew through these concrete beings; he struggles with dream figures, and his blows strike living faces. Anti-Semitic passion is not triggered by, nor does it aim at, individuals.

Thus we encountered the Marxist formula, which at any rate has the merit of placing us in a social context, "Anti-Semitism is the socialism of imbeciles." A convulsed society with a foreboding and dread of revolution will transfer the anguish it feels about itself to the Jews and in this way appease it. This might explain the hypocritical anti-Semitism of the Maurrasians, which is always accompanied by reservations or exceptions and which retreats before particular cases. But what about the racism of the SS, what about Drancy, what about the children taken from their mothers? Like all explanations based on a transferred emotion, this too collapses before passion. Transference of passion is not a final explanation, since the question is, precisely, what motivates it and why the anguish and sadism of a decadent society focus on the Jews. Here, as with all passion, we run into an element of chance and pure irrationality without which passion would be grounded in something and would no longer be passion. A certain man loves a certain woman today because his past history has prepared him to love that particular personality and face, but also because he *met* her, and this meeting awakens possibilities in his life which would have remained dormant without her. This love seems like fate once it has become established, but on the day of the first meeting it is absolutely contingent. An obsession may indeed be motivated by an individual's past, but it yields more than it promises: it has, when actualized, its own weight, which is the brute force of the present and of what exists. It is likewise impossible to explain all the whys and wherefores of anti-Semitism. One may point out its motivations, such as the social problem and the role the Jews once played in the development of a certain form of capitalism, but such motivations only sketch the outline of a possible history. The most that rational explanation can do is to say that the anguish in Germany around 1930 went back into the past and chose to find relief in anti-Semitism. Since anguish always turns away from the future, such explanation can go no further. Passion creates itself apart from its motivations and cannot be understood in a universe of consciousnesses. German anti-Semitism makes us face a truth we did not know in 1939. We did not think there were Jews or Germans but only men, or even consciousnesses. It seemed to us that at every moment each of us chose to be and to do what he wished with an ever-new freedom. We had not understood that, just as an actor slips into a role which envelops him and which alters the meaning of all his gestures, just as he carries this great phantom with him, animating it and yet controlled by it, so, in co-existence, each of us is presented to others against a historical background which we did not choose; and our behavior toward others is dictated by our role as "Aryan," Jewish, French, or German. We had not understood that consciousnesses have the strange power to alienate each other and to withdraw from themselves; that they are outwardly threatened and inwardly tempted by absurd hatreds, inconceivable with respect to individuals; and that if men are one day to be human to one another and the relations between consciousnesses are to become transparent, if universality is to become a fact, this will be in a society in which past traumas have been wiped out and the conditions of an effective liberty have from the first been realized. Until that time, the life of society will remain a dialogue and a battle between phantoms—in which real tears and real blood suddenly start to flow.

* * * *

We were no longer permitted to be neutral in this combat. For the first time we were led not only to awareness but to acceptance of the life of society. Before '39 we were not interested in the police: they existed, but we would never have dreamed of joining them. Who among us would have helped arrest a thief, who would have been willing to be a judge, to pass sentence? For our part we did not want to be criminals or thieves, because this is what we had decided. But what right did our freedom have to annul that of another person, even if the murderer had himself decided the outcome of another man's life? We found it intolerable that sanction should wish to parade a moral character, and we reduced it to one of the necessities of police order, which we carefully distinguished from moral rules. It was base work to which we did not want to consent even if we were involved in it. I remember my bewilderment when I learned that, as a second lieutenant in the reserves, I could be required by the police to aid in an arrest and that I was even supposed to offer my services. We certainly had to revise our thinking on this subject, and we saw that it was indeed up to us to judge. If the arrest and conviction of an informer had depended on us, we could not have left this task to others. Before the war, politics seemed unthinkable to us because it treats men as statistics, and we saw no sense in treating these unique beings, each of whom is a world unto himself, according to a set of general rules and as a collection of interchangeable objects. Politics is impossible from the perspective of consciousness. But the moment came when our innermost being felt the impact of these external absurdities.

We have been led to take upon ourselves and consider as our own not only our intentions—what our actions mean for us—but also the external consequences of these actions, what they mean in a historical context. Twenty years ago a historian denounced the Allies' share of responsibility for World War I. During the Occupation we were stupefied that this same historian should publish—with the permission of the censors—a pamphlet denouncing England's role in starting World War II. He did not understand that to implicate England with the Germans occupying Paris was to accept responsibility for propaganda no pacifist had the right to further, since it was the instrument of a martial regime. In the spring of 1944 all professors were asked to sign a petition entreating Pétain to intervene and stop the war. It would be overly simple to assume that the men who composed and signed this petition were agents of the Germans trying to end the war before the German defeat. Treason is rarely committed with such clarity, at least among professors, and they are the type of men who are never swayed by self-interest alone, but also by ideas. Let us then try to imagine one of the authors of this petition. For him, the passions of war *do not exist:* they gain their apparent strength from the consent of men who are *equally free at every moment.* Therefore there is no world at war, with democracies on one side and Fascist states on the other, or with the established empires lined up against the late-comer nations eager to found empires for themselves (the former accidentally allied to a "proletarian" state). There are no empires, no nations, no classes. On every side there are only men who are always ready for freedom and happiness, always able to attain them under any regime, provided they take hold of themselves and recover the only freedom that exists: their free judgment. There is only one evil, war itself, and one duty, refusing to believe in victories of right and civilization and putting an end to war. So this solitary Cartesian thinks—but he does not see his shadow behind him projected onto history as onto a wall, that meaning, that appearance which his actions assume on the outside, that Objective Spirit which *is* himself.

The Cartesian would doubtless reply that if we hold ourselves responsible for the most distant consequences of our thoughts and actions, the only thing left for us to do is refuse all compromise as does the hero. And, he would add, how many heroes are there among the men who today take pride in their having resisted? Some were civil servants and continued to draw their salary, swearing in writing— since they had to—that they were neither Jews nor Masons. Others of them agreed to seek authorization of what they wrote or staged from a censorship which let nothing pass which did not serve its purpose. Each in his own way marked out the frontier of the permissible. "Don't publish anything," said one. "Don't publish anything in the newspapers or magazines," said another. "Just publish your books." And a third said, "I will let this theater have my play if the director is a good man, but if he is a servant of the government, I will withdraw it." The truth is that each of them settled with outward necessity, all except a few who gave their lives. One could either stop living, refusing that corrupted air, that poisoned bread, or one could continue, which meant contriving a little hide-out of private freedom in the midst of the common misery; and this is what most of them did, putting their consciences to rest by means of some carefully weighed sacrifices. Our compromise does not acquit the traitors who called this regime down upon us, aided it more than what was absolutely necessary, and were the self-appointed keepers of the new law. It does, however, prohibit us from judging them in the name of a morality which no one followed to the letter and from basing a new philosophy on the experience of those four years, since we lived according to the old one. Only the heroes really were outwardly what they inwardly wished to be; only they became one with history at the moment when it claimed their lives. Those who survived, even at the greatest risk, did not consummate this cruel marriage, and no one can speak of this silence or recommend it to others. Heroism a thing not of words but of deeds, and any preaching would be presumptuous here, since the man who is still able to speak does not know what he is speaking of.

This line of reasoning is hard, but it leads in the direction we want to go. It is true that we are not innocent and that the situation in which we found ourselves admitted of no irreproachable conduct. By staying here we all became accomplices to some extent, and we must say of the Resistance what the combatants said about the war: no one comes back except the man who at some moment or another reduced the risks he was running, who, in that sense, elected to save his life. Nor can those who left France to pursue the war elsewhere with arms or propaganda lay any more claim to purity, for they escaped a direct compromise only by yielding the ground for a while, and in this sense they too had a part in the ravages of the Occupation. Several of our comrades asked themselves the question and made the best choice, but nothing can turn their decision into a true solution. One compromised oneself whether one stayed or left; no one's hands are clean (which is perhaps why the Germans found the corpses of Martel and several others at Paris). We have unlearned "pure morality" and learned a kind of vulgar immoralism, which is healthy. The moral man does not want to dirty his hands. It is because he usually has enough time, talent, or money to stand back from enterprises of which he disapproves and to prepare a good conscience for himself. The common people do not have that freedom: the garage mechanic had to repair German cars if he wanted to live. One of our comrades used to go to the Rive Gauche Bookstore for the German philosophy books he needed. When the day came, he took part in the uprising and was shot by the Germans. We are in the world, mingled with it, compromised with it. This is no reason to surrender all that is exterior and to confine ourselves to our thoughts, which are always free, even in the mind of a slave. This division of interior and exterior is abstract. We give the world both too little and too much credit. Too much because we bring weight to it when the time comes, and the State, as was evident with the Vichy State, is nothing without our consent. Too little because it arouses our *interest*, because we exist in it, and the wish to be free on the fringe of the world will end in our not being free at all. A judgment without words is incomplete; a word to which there can be no reply is nonsense; my freedom is interwoven with that of others by way of the world. Of course, those of us who were neither Jews nor declared Communists could manage to meditate during those four years: we were not denied Plato or Descartes or rehearsals at the Conservatory on Saturday mornings. We could begin our adolescence all over again, return to our gods and our great writers as if they were vices. This did not bring us any nearer to ourselves or to the spirit of the times. Yet for all that, we did not get out of history. Our finest thoughts, seen from London, New York, or Moscow, had a place in the world, and they had a name—the reveries of captives—and even their value as thoughts was altered as a result. One cannot get beyond history and time; all one can do is manufacture a private eternity in their midst, as artificial as the eternity of the madman who believes he is God. There is no vital spirit in gloomy isolated dreams; spirit only appears in the full light of dialogue. We were no more free, as we meditated on our great men, and no more pure consciousnesses, than the Jew or the deportee who became pure suffering, unable to see and unable to choose. No effective freedom exists without some power. Freedom exists in contact with the world, not outside it.

*　　*　　*　　*

In this we rediscovered one of the truths of Marxism. But even Marxism had to be taken up anew, for it threatened to confirm our prewar prejudices. Under the pretext that history is the history of class struggle and that ideological conflicts are only its superstructure, a certain kind of Marxism detaches us from all situations in which the fate of the classes is not immediately at stake. Marxists of this type classed the Second World War as imperialistic, at least until the intervention of the U.S.S.R., and were not interested in it. True history would recommence for them on the day when the social struggle could again manifest itself. Since fascism was, after all, nothing but a poor relative of capitalism, the Marxist didn't have to take sides in this family quarrel, and whichever faction won made little difference to him. Certain of us thought that capitalism could not allow itself to be liberal in a crisis, that it would become rigid in all things, and that the same necessities which gave birth to fascism would stifle freedom in the pretended democracies. The worldwide war was just an appearance; what remained real beneath that appearance was the common fate of the proletariats of all nations and the profound solidarity of all forms of capitalism through the internal contradictions of the regime. Thus there could be no question of the national proletarians in any way assuming responsibility for the events in which they found themselves involved: no proletarian in uniform can feel *anything but* proletarian. Thus certain among us frowned on their own delight at the news of some German defeat and pretended not to share the general satisfaction. When we presented the situation of an occupied country to them as the prototype of an inhuman situation, they did their best to dissolve this phenomenon in the more general one of capitalistic exploitation and oppression. Entrusted from the start with the secret of history, they understood patriotic rebellion better than it understood itself and absolved it in the name of the class struggle. And yet when liberation came they called it by name, just like everyone else.

They didn't have to give up Marxism in order to do so. The experience of those four years had, in fact, brought a better understanding of the concrete relationship of the class struggle to Marxist ideology. The class struggle is not *more real* than ideological conflicts; they cannot be reduced to it, as appearances to reality. Marx himself pointed out that, once they become established, ideologists have a weight of their own and set history in motion in the same way that the flywheel drives the motor. There must be more, consequently, to a Marxist analysis of Hitlerism than summarily classifying it as "a capitalistic episode." Such an analysis undoubtedly lays bare the combination of economic events without which it would not have existed, but this situation is unique, and to define it fully, to bring it back into contact with actual history, we must take local particularities into account and consider naziism's human function as well as its economic one. The Marxist must not simply keep applying the capital-work formula in some mechanical way but must think each new event through afresh to determine in each case the serpentine route of the proletarian future. He is not obliged to consider oppression in an occupied country as a surface phenomenon, beneath which the truth of history is to be sought. There are not two histories, one true and the other empirical; there is only one, in which everything that happens plays a part, if one only knows how to interpret it. For a Marxist in a French environment, the German Occupation was not a historical accident but an event of the first magnitude. The German and Anglo-Saxon victories are not equivalent from the point of view of the class struggle. No matter how reactionary the Anglo-Saxon governments are and wish to be, they are curbed in their own countries by their liberal ideology, and the social struggle's imminent re-emergence into the spotlight gains in interest for men who do not have a hundred years to live and who would have had to spend perhaps fifty years under Fascist oppression. Marxism does not suppress history's subjective factors in favor of objective ones; it binds the two together. The ideology of nationalism cannot be classed once and for all as bourgeois: its function in shaping the historical conjunction must be newly appreciated at every moment, and this function may at times be progressive and at other times reactionary. Nationalistic feeling (which is not to say chauvinism) is revolutionary in the France of today and was so in 1940. This does not merely mean that national feeling is in fact opposed to the immediate interest of French capitalism and that, by a pious trick, the Marxists can make it serve their own struggle. It means that the historical conjuncture frees the national reality from the reactionary mortgages which encumbered it and authorizes the proletarian consciousness to integrate it. One might try to argue that in Marxist political thinking the nation can only be a means, never an end, that Marxist patriotism can only be tactical, and that for the Marxist a purgation of morals, for example, serves the ends of revolution, whereas the primary concern of the patriot is, on the contrary, the integration of the movement of the masses into the nation. But even this kind of language is not Marxist. It is the particular attribute of Marxism not to distinguish the means from the end, and, in principle, no system of political thought is less hypocritical and less Machiavellian. It is not a question of abusing the patriots' good faith and leading them where they do not wish to go. Not the Marxist but history transforms nationalist feeling into the will to revolution. It is a question of making the patriots see (and events as well as Marxists undertake to do this) that in a weakened country like France which the movement of history has reduced to a second-rate power, a certain political and economic independence is possible only through a dangerous oscillation or within the framework of a Socialist Confederation of States which has no chance of becoming a reality except through revolution. To be a Marxist is not to renounce all differences, to give up one's identity as a Frenchman, a native of Tours or Paris, or to forego individuality in order to blend into the world proletariat. It is indeed to become part of the universal, but without ceasing to be what we are. Even in a Marxist perspective the world proletariat is not a revolutionary factor so long as it only exists objectively, in economic analysis. It will become such a factor when it realizes that it is a world proletariat, and this will only happen through the concerted pressure or a meeting at the crossroads of actual proletarians, such as they exist in the different countries, and not through an ascetic internationalism wherein each of them loses his most compelling reasons for being a Marxist.

* * * *

To sum it all up, we have learned history, and we claim that it must not be forgotten. But are we not here the dupes of our emotions? If, ten years hence, we reread these pages and so many others, what will we think of them? We do not want this year of 1945 to become just another year among many. A man who has lost a son or a woman he loved does not want to live beyond that loss. He leaves the house in the state it was in. The familiar objects upon the table, the clothes in the closet mark an empty place in the world. He converses with the absent person, he changes nothing in his life, and every day his actions, like an incantation, bring this ever more evanescent shadow back to life. The day will come, however, when the meaning of these books and these clothes will change: once the books were new, and now they are yellow with age; once the clothes were wearable, and now they are out of style and shabby. To keep them any longer would not be to make the dead person live on; quite the opposite, they date his death all the more cruelly. In the same way there will come a moment when what we wish to preserve of the friends who were tortured and shot is not our last image of them, what they were in those four years and in that feverish summer, but a timeless memory in which the things they did mingle with what they might have done, given the direction of their lives. We have not of course gotten to this point, but since what concerns us here is writing, not recounting our griefs, should we not go beyond our feelings to find what they may contain of durable truth?

The war was not over before everything had already begun to change—not only because of man's inconstancy but also because of an inner necessity. Unity had been easy during the Resistance, because relationships were almost always man-to-man. Over against the German army or the Vichy government, where social generality ruled, as it does in all machines of State, the Resistance offered the rare phenomenon of historical action which remained personal. The psychological and moral elements of political action were almost the only ones to appear here, which is why intellectuals least inclined to politics were to be seen in the Resistance. The Resistance was a unique experience for them, and they wanted to preserve its spirit in the new French politics because this experience broke away from the famous dilemma of being and doing, which confronts all intellectuals in the face of action. This was the source of that *happiness* through danger which we observed in some of our comrades, usually so tormented. It is only too obvious that this balance between action and personal life was intimately bound up with the conditions of clandestine actions and could not survive it. And in this sense it must be said that the Resistance experience, by making us believe that politics is a relationship between man and man or between consciousnesses, fostered our illusions of 1939 and masked the truth of the incredible power of history which the Occupation taught us in another connection. We have returned to the time of *institutions*. The distance between the laws and those to whom they apply is once more apparent; once again one legislates for X; and once again the good will of some resumes its class features which make it unrecognizable to others. We must again worry about the consequences of what we say, weighing the objective meaning of every word, with no hope of convincing by the sheer force of truth. This is what we did during the Occupation when we had to avoid any public gesture which might have "played into the hands of the occupying forces." But among friends at that time we had a freedom to criticize which we have already lost. Are we now going to subject our words and gestures to that completely exterior rule—which so aroused Péguy's indignation—which enjoins us not to "play into the hands" of the reactionaries, the Communists, or the Government? For four years we witnessed the abrogation of personal life. There is nothing more to *learn* from that, and if politics is definitely hell, we have no choice but to give it up. Indeed, this is why, on the eve of another war, the founders of the N.R.F invited authors and public to abandon the values and the attitudes of the war. They wanted to demobilize consciousness, to return to purely aesthetic problems, to disengage themselves from history. . . .

Assuredly—and this is the point we want to make—those five years have not taught us to think ill of what we once judged to be good, and in the eyes of conscience it is still absurd to hide a truth because it harms one's country, to kill a man because he lives on the other side of the river, to treat another person as a means rather than an end. We were not wrong, in 1939, to want liberty, truth, happiness, and transparent relations among men, and we are not now abandoning humanism. The War and the Occupation only taught us that values remain nominal and indeed have no value without an economic and political infrastructure to make them participate in existence. What is more, in actual history values are only another way of designating human relationships, as these become established according to a man's mode of work, the nature of his loves, and the shape of his hopes; in brief, according to the way he lives with others. It is a question not of giving up our values of 1939 but of realizing them. Imitating the tyrants is not the question, and, insofar as such imitation was necessary, it is precisely for having forced us to it that we cannot forgive them. It is doubtful whether tyranny can ever be eliminated from political life, whether the State could wither away and men's political or social relations could ever be reintegrated into their human relationships. But even if we have no guarantee that these goals will ever be realized, we can at least see very clearly the absurdity of an anachronistic tyranny like anti-Semitism and of a reactionary expedient like fascism. And this is enough to make us want to destroy them roots and branch and to push things forward in the direction of effective liberty. This political task is not incompatible with any cultural value or literary task, if literature and culture are defined as the progressive awareness of our multiple relationships with other people and the world, rather than as extramundane techniques. *If all truths are told, none will have to be hidden.* In man's co-existence with man, of which these years have made us aware, morals, doctrines, thoughts and customs, laws, works and words all express each other; everything signifies everything. And outside this unique fulguration of existence there is nothing.

June 1945

11 / For the Sake of Truth

STENDHAL's republicans were mad for sincerity in the face of the "knaves" and "rascals" who peopled the lawcourts and antechambers. The Dreyfusist professors of 1900 wanted justice at any price. They said that there had to be a retrial—even if reopening the case meant compromising the Army General Staff and the national defense, since an unjust France would be France no longer and would not deserve to be saved. Maurras countered that politics should be regulated not by what we personally feel to be just or unjust but first and foremost by the conditions of existence and by the national interest, without which there would be no civilization and, in the end, no justice. "One occasionally sees tribunals without justice but never justice without tribunals," he declared. Therefore in the name of justice itself the authority of the tribunals had to be preserved and Dreyfus left on Devil's Island. But all these arguments were in vain. Neither Péguy nor the Kantians could accept France's losing her reasons for existence in order to save her life. In its own way, the Surrealist movement assumed the same function of judging and scandalizing, and Surrealist headquarters took on the task of calling attention to all the absurdities of "real" life regardless of the consequences. In the period between the two wars most French intellectuals approached political questions from the point of view of morality. For Gide, for Alain, for Andrée Viollis, for the early Aragon, for Breton, for Bernanos, it was always right to tell the truth, in opposition to the government, the nation, or the party, if necessary. Even when Malraux rediscovered that efficacy is the first rule of politics, his two finest books offer ample evidence that he did not accept this idea without a struggle. No doubt he never did accept it completely, since his "realism" could not meet the test of the Russo-German pact. The French people, like their intellectuals, judged and spoke frankly: much to the surprise of

[153]

other nations, Daladier or Reynaud were treated sometimes with indulgence and sometimes with contempt but, in any case, never with caution or respect.

We certainly have changed. We have seen "where it leads," as the saying goes. Rightly or wrongly, we attribute France's troubles to French cynicism and independence. We are all repentant. We will not be caught in the same trap again. Each of us feels as responsible for his country or party as he does for his family. Before speaking a truth we consider the consequences. We have gained in propriety and gravity, but as the result of weighing our words and hearing only weighed replies, we have acquired the rather base habit of interpreting, hinting, turning phrases. If an intellectual recommends the spirit of synthesis, it means, in the vocabulary of our time, that he wants to "get in good with" the Communists, and the Socialists raise their eyebrows. A sanctimonious, insinuating tone reigns practically everywhere—the tone of Balzac's La Sapinière and of the Congrégation in Stendhal. The game is played underhandedly. The foils are buttoned. Conservatives call themselves "socialists," revolutionaries back the government, everyone replies indirectly, and the result is that discussions become dialogues of the deaf. Everybody is a realist, an opportunist, a tactician—all except Bernanos, whose anger, like Raimu's, is too predictable and impresses no one. Maurras may be in jail, but Maurrasianism is rampant. Stendhal would count us all knaves.

Does our only choice lie between being either a cynic or a knave? We must make sure that this dilemma is unavoidable before we resign ourselves to it. Perhaps commitment only curtails freedom of thought when such commitment is confused, in the absence of political thinking able both to accept all truths and to take a stand in reality. No political party in France consciously thinks out its actions or openly states what it is doing. Each is playing a double game. As for ideas, they are not formed in contact with the present and in order to understand it; they are ideological tatters which we inherited from the 19th century and which poorly clothe the facts. It is not surprising that, with only ambiguities to choose from, we do not feel at ease anywhere, and loyalty to a party has become an arduous task.

* * * *

Two large Marxist parties control the majority in France. That should inject a certain proletarian frankness into our politics. Let us see how much frankness there actually is.

The Communists have invented "dissenting support." They criticized the government last winter, but how could they carry their criticism to its logical conclusion when they are themselves part of the government? They protested against the electoral law, but they began by declaring that their ministers would in no case resign. They recommended voting *oui/non*, but their ministers remained members of a government whose head, in a radio address, counseled a vote of *oui/oui*.[1] They protested the arrest of Indochinese in Paris, but they shared responsibility for these arrests with all members of the government. "Put an end to trusts!" their election leaflets proclaimed. As if the trusts were already half-dead, as if they had only to be finished off. In a sense all the early Communist themes (the class struggle, anticolonialism, antimilitarism) figure in the politics of today's Communist Party. This is why *Action* almost always manages to give the politics of the Party a Marxist accompaniment. But if the themes are still there, they no longer serve as guiding principles, as is evident when *Action* gives its wholehearted approval to the policies of the Big Three.[2] The function of Marxist ideas is no longer so much to determine policy as to comment on it and to give it an *aura* of Marxism. The two things may look the same to an artless observer, but to an old-school Marxist they are as distinct as the dog—a barking animal—is from the Dog, a heavenly constellation. Even if the U.S.S.R. takes a stand against colonialism in connection with the Syrian affair, the fact that it has not set up soviets in any of the countries which it occupies forces one to admit that the liberation of colonized countries has ceased to be an unconditional principle of Russian policy. This does not mean that the U.S.S.R. has become an imperialist power, as people casually say. Imperialism leads to exploiting "backward" nations to the advantage of "advanced" countries, which go there seeking cheap labor, raw materials, a market for their manufactured goods, and investment possibilities, and which as a result usually find it in their interest to keep the colony as backward as they found it. It is certain that, in order to integrate the economies of the countries under its influence into its own, the U.S.S.R. will be led to establish—whether openly or not—a socialistic method of production, with the result that the Russian occupation will, in fact, be "progressive." But it also seems sure that the U.S.S.R. no longer professes the ideology of its economy, or, more exactly, that in today's Russia the revolutionary themes have become

1. During the formation of the Fourth Republic in 1945, a national referendum asked the following two questions, to be answered *oui* or *non*:

(1) Do you authorize the legislators to draft a new Constitution?

(2) Do you approve the proposals of the Provisional Government on the duration and powers of the legislature?—Trans.

2. From a Marxist point of view, the Big Three's political course is of course preferable to Russia's isolation and to the Western bloc. It is not, for all that, any closer to the universalist foreign policy defined by Russia in 1917.

an ideology in the true sense of the word: a collection of *a posteriori* justifications. Since 1917 Marxism has had a homeland and is incarnate in a certain part of the world. From that moment on the Communists have had to defend both the body and the spirit of Marxism, just as Spanish Catholics had to defend both the visible Church, with its clergy and its tabernacles, and the invisible Church which dwells in all human hearts and relationships. The two do not always go together. *Action* defends the body of Marxism by supporting the policy of the Big Three, but one certainly cannot claim that it is simultaneously defending its spirit, since Marxism has always been hostile to secret diplomacy and to "power politics" among the heads of state. It should be clear in what follows that in our opinion it would have been insane, from a Marxist point of view, to sacrifice the U.S.S.R.'s existence to the abstract principles of a Marxist policy and that the new course of Soviet policy is amply explained by the stagnation of revolution throughout the world and by the mortal danger in which this places the U.S.S.R. But before we explain and perhaps justify as inevitable the changes which have occurred in Communist policy, let us first recognize these changes. The Communist Party is playing a double game in that, although it is effectively proletarian and seeks daily agitation on the classical proletarian themes, it does not desire any break with the established governments and at the decisive moment does whatever is necessary to avoid such a rupture.[3]

The Socialist Party's double game consists in continuing to style itself "Marxist" while living under the surveillance of the bourgeoisie. It might be better to base one's reasoning on events which are already over and done with, and whose significance is for that very reason less debatable. We recall the stages of Léon Blum's thinking: he had been "appalled" by the neo-socialist theses favoring participation in the cabinet and the exercise of power under a bourgeois regime. A few years later he accepted these theses as his own. The leader of a party which reaffirms its Marxist nature at each annual congress, he agreed to direct a "Popular Front" experiment aimed at improving the conditions of workers within the capitalist framework. "In all our propaganda," he said in May of 1936, "we have used the analysis of the economic crisis to condemn the present social regime. . . . We have concluded that our efforts should be directed at substituting for this

3. This opinion is in no way belied by the crisis which preceded the formation of the second Gaullist cabinet. Despite all the efforts of the reactionary press to present the Communists as ogres, the fact remains that they agreed to take part in a government of national unity in which, together with the Socialists, they hold only ten out of twenty-two cabinet appointments even though the two Marxist parties won a majority—small, it is true—in the elections.

society another which is fundamentally different and which will establish order and reason where we now see only contradiction and chaos. . . . But—and I want to say this with the same frankness and the same clarity—the task of the Popular Front government . . . is different, different, in any case, at present. There is no Socialist majority; there is no proletarian majority; there is a Popular Front majority. . . . From this it follows that we must work from inside the present regime, the same regime whose contradictions and unfairness were demonstrated in our campaign. . . . In brief, it is a question of knowing whether, in the framework of the present regime, it is possible to guarantee adequate relief of the miseries of those who are suffering." But there is no need to create a new society if capitalism can be amended, and if it cannot, there is no need to initiate a Popular Front experiment in all good faith within the framework of capitalism. There is an evident contradiction between the Marxist premises and the reformist conclusion. Léon Blum tried to diminish it by presenting the Popular Front as a transitional phase. "It is a matter," he went on, "of knowing whether minds and things can be prepared for the inevitable coming of the regime which remains our act and our goal, by the actions we accomplish inside the present regime. . . . The question which our experiment puts to the nation even more urgently than to the party is how the change will come about . . . , whether there is a possibility of its being effected, I repeat, peacefully and amicably." [4]

Thus the Popular Front could be interpreted in two ways. On the one hand, it could be seen as a loyal attempt to bring out all the order and justice still to be found in capitalism, in which respect it called for the cooperation of all men of good will. On the other hand, it was the beginning of socialism, and Léon Blum, as a Socialist, could not view it otherwise. Hence Blum's two ways of talking: the substance of what he said to business leaders and to the Senate was that "strikes and seizures of factories are illegal, but they exist. The choice is up to you. You can either make the necessary concessions and see lawfulness re-established, or you can refuse to make them, and then you will have only yourselves to blame for the revolution." To the proletarian voters, on the contrary, he said: "No one can maintain that we are engaged in saving bourgeois society, since the downfall of that society is in reality an accomplished fact." [5] The reforms of 1936 were ambiguous, presented to business leaders as a guaranty against revolution and to the masses as the beginning of it. This double game was not honest

4. This and the previous statement by Blum are taken from his Address to the Congress of the Socialist Party (SFIO), May 31, 1936, quoted in *L'Exercice du pouvoir*, pp. 52–55.
5. Speech broadcast nationally on December 31, 1936, quoted in *ibid*.

with either side. The business leaders were not fooled; they knew the bulwark they were being offered against revolution was weak. True, they used it in the crisis of June 1936; they even conceived a certain admiration for a statesman of such distinction, who played the game of legality so naturally. But they did not forget his veiled threats— laughable coming from a man who was so determined not to be involved in starting the revolution—and when the country's fever had abated, they unceremoniously dismissed him. Blum in his politics was no more loyal toward the proletariat: a transitional coalition government would be conceivable in a Marxist perspective, but only if it took on the task of proving that reformism was in point of fact impossible, if it drew support from the masses at each new obstacle, opposing Parliament if need be, and if it played the game of bourgeois legality only to make bourgeois inefficacy all the more obvious. A proletarian party cannot be sincere with everyone in a time of bitter class struggle; it can either be sincere with the proletariat and must therefore deceive capitalism, or it can comply with capitalism's accepted commitments and with the formal, universal rules of morality, in which case it deceives the proletariat. Léon Blum's "objectivity" and "intellectual honesty" are praised to the skies. What one fails to see is that this "objective" manner, this habit of treating the revolution as already accomplished or still to come, *never as a present for which we are responsible,* is fraudulent. Such manifestations of "objectivity" are duperies when we are concerned with transforming the world rather than contemplating it. It is dishonest for a Marxist politician to postulate any universal truth or morality, since Marxism is a theory of revolution, which opposes the capitalistic world to its proletarian counterpart and forces us to choose between them. On May 31, 1936, Blum said to the Socialist Party: "Should insurmountable resistance force us to conclude that modern society cannot be amended from the inside . . . , I myself would be the first to come and tell you so." On December 31 of that same year, noting the persistent "panic rumors," the hoarding and the withdrawal of capital, he did not turn to his constituents as he had promised but once again *to the others.* "Must I repeat once more that we are not a Socialist government, that we are not trying—either directly or insidiously—to put the Socialist program into practice, that we are working with complete loyalty within the framework of present institutions, present society, and the present system of private property. . . ." [6] No further mention of the inevitable death of capitalism or the march toward socialism through the Popular Front. Whether the issue is non-intervention or social questions, the

6. *L'Exercice du pouvoir,* pp. 55, 348.

1936 speeches are remarkable for their constant *effort at self-justification in the eyes of the opponent*. It was Hitler and Mussolini—never the Spanish Republicans—whom Blum wanted to convince of France's loyalty. In domestic policy he is "loyal" in the parliamentary world which he chose as a member of a bourgeois Parliament but not in the proletarian world he chose as a Marxist. If some shrewd person now says that Léon Blum no longer believes in Marxism, then let us have no more talk of loyalty.

After this, it is hardly necessary to reread the discussions of this summer's Socialist Congress. As far back as 1936 Blum was governing in the spirit of a class action which respects the national interest—itself understood in a conservative fashion. Nothing is subtracted from Marxism. One simply adds: the national interest. The result of this innocent touching up is that socialism is no longer an unknown future. It is already here; it reigns everywhere. We are in actual contact with it, and it holds no fears for us.[7]

At first the attitude toward the Communist Party would appear clear: if, said *Le Populaire,* the Communists had had any reservations about those Big Three decisions which humiliated France, we would immediately have proposed joining up with them. But one fears lest the Socialists are too delighted at this argument. After all, unity among the workers might entail a transformation of the Communist Party itself, and the Socialists would be free to introduce their habits of criticism and discussion. Their general policy offers adequate proof that what they fear in the Communist Party is not only an overly blind devotion to the U.S.S.R. but the proletarian spirit which the Party continues to represent in spite of its tactical turnings. French politics occasionally looks like a scene from a comedy of errors: the Communist Party which, because of its composition and its propaganda, was originally and has largely remained a class party, reaches the point of extending its hand to the Socialists and even to certain bourgeois parties, whereas the Socialists (who since 1936 have been oriented toward a policy "in the public interest") and the bourgeois parties, which deny the class struggle in principle, pretend not to see the hand which is offered to them and refuse the chance this would give them to secure the neutrality of the proletariat.

In a society in which the proletarian movement called itself the "National Front" at one point and the conservative mentality labels

7. Although the Communist Party helped appease the working class in 1936—to which Thorez' famous phrase, "One must know how to end a strike," bears witness —it never used this tone to solicit the confidence of its opponents. Its turnabouts are motivated by discipline alone; one feels that the Communists do not inwardly submit to those they try to attract, and it is in this that they maintain the proletarian style.

itself "Socialist," political thinking and the analysis of events cannot help being very confused. There are no ideas which have not been mutilated; the political position of each of us is not so much defined by a certain number of theses to which we subscribe as by our adherence to one of the two opposing blocs. To be a Communist or a Socialist *on the level of ideas* no longer means anything definite. We have reached a state of political nominalism of which there is perhaps no other example in French history. The notions of "Socialist" and "Communist," to say nothing of the Christian Democrats, will soon be as impossible to define and to communicate in this country, which once prided itself—to take Thibaudet's word for it—on putting a whole view of life into its politics, as the notions of "Republican" and "Democrat" are in the United States. Last winter a café waiter attributed the riots during the Brussels uprising to the Fifth Column, went on regretfully about the slowness of the purge, and concluded with the remark, "The big fish always get away." This is how "patriotic" and "Marxist" motifs are intertwined in men's minds. In a recent conversation with a political radical, this author said that the Communist Party was no longer really after a rupture and that if the industrialists were more farsighted, they would make the most of this opportunity. A Communist man of letters, by no means poor, was present at this exchange. He warmly approved and added that for the moment it was "unfortunately" not a question of taking up Lenin's politics again.

One might be tempted to explain the decline of our political thinking by that of our country. We are a second-rank power. Our politics and our thoughts are no longer autonomous; they no longer spring from us. Our decisions are limited to a choice between two centers of attraction, the Russians or the Anglo-Saxons. France is now comparable to those Central and South American states where the parties are equally representative of foreign influences and where ideology's only function is to mask these influences. But this explanation does not get us very far. The Big Three are no less confused than we. The same attrition and the same breakdown of ideas is everywhere to be seen. Neither doctrinal Marxism nor doctrinal liberalism any longer exists. True, Marxist or liberal ideas may still be used in speeches by heads of state, but now they are just instruments of diplomatic offense and defense. The Atlantic Charter had been long forgotten when it suddenly reappeared in one of Truman's speeches, which in other respects was threatening. We are still using the political vocabulary of the 19th century ("liberalism," "proletariat"), and this vocabulary inadequately expresses the political forces which actually confront us. The class struggle is masked. We are at an ambiguous moment in history. Neither capitalism nor revolution fights openly any more: because capitalism is unsure of its own future and cannot project itself in terms of a positive theory, and because Marxism—even if it retains a palpable influence on the mode of production and the economic structure of those countries in which it has triumphed—has ceased to animate a proletarian politics. Pierre Hervé once took up the problem of the Communists' double game in *Action*. The difference between the double game of the Communists and that of the new "Socialists" is, he said, that the former can, and the latter cannot, admit what they really are; a Communist will have no trouble acknowledging that putting France back on her feet, reconstruction, purgation, and renovating the army and the judiciary are impossible without a revolution, for this is the truth. The Communist Party wants both revolution and homeland with no ambiguities, because, at this turning point in history, the country cannot revive without revolution. Thus the Communist has nothing to hide: his double game is based on facts. "Socialism," on the contrary, is a mystification because it pays lip service to the opposite of what it actually wants and is preparing for. Hervé forgot only one thing: that the Communist Party has not been able to push national insurrection or the purging of the Underground Army and its incorporation into the regular army to their revolutionary conclusions, that Communist ministers have remained in their offices when the government sabotaged purges and amalgamation, and that, all in all, the policy of patriotic revolution—and this includes Hervé's "sincere" article on the double game—has served patriotism better than revolution. It is perfectly true that patriotism can be integrated into Marxism under certain conditions of time and place. But to retain its true character it would still have to show at each step the revolutionary implications of this integration. When Thorez came back from Moscow last winter, he declared, on the contrary, that purgation has its limits. The audience at the big sports stadium, the Vélodrôme d'Hiver, was evidently surprised. The causes behind the ambiguity of our politics and the ways to dissipate this ambiguity remain to be discovered.

Very simple, the Trotskyite would say: the confusion in which we live comes from the increasing discrepancy between the objective and the subjective situations, between the class struggle which is in fact going on, which is indeed lived in connection with every concrete question, and the ideas which are circulated by the parties and which preclude any thought of this struggle. Isn't the remedy, then, within arm's reach? Would it not be sufficient to make what is latent manifest and to apply the classical Marxist schemas to the present, in order to realign the parties, to make political life once again transparent and political choice and loyalty easy once again? Doesn't a truly Marxist policy get beyond the conflict of morality and political realism, sincerity and commitment from which we started, since such a policy, which prolongs the effective movement of history, is both open to all truths and capable of maximum efficiency? Marxism does not like talking about morality and distrusts values insofar as they are abstract and help mystify men by luring them away from their lives, their conflicts, and their necessary choices. But the dominant idea of Marxism is not, in the last analysis, the sacrifice of values to facts, of morality to realism. It is the idea of replacing the verbal morality which preceded the revolution with an effective morality, creating a society in which morality is truly moral, and destroying the morality that exists, dreamlike, outside the world, by realizing it in effective human relationships. In the Marxist view of history, morality is given in the bargain. Would not the rediscovery of the Marxist inspiration which originally animated Socialists as well as Communists be enough to make all the Machiavellian scheming vanish, and with it all the perplexing difficulty of the scrupulous intellectual's position?

This abstract and naïve solution forgets that compromise and the double game are not arbitrary creations of parties but are the expression, at the political level, of the world's vital situation. It forgets that, after years of equivocation, compromises have molded minds in their own image, that they have acquired a certain weight of their own, and that no purely mental conversion, no attempt at knowledge, explanation, or propaganda will be enough to dissolve them. Men are to a great extent mystified by their own compromises—that is, they stop feeling they are compromises. We said that today the class struggle is masked. This does not mean that it continues unchangingly along the lines laid down in Marxism's classical works and is simply veiled by words. Marx thought the class struggle could not bring about revolution as long as it was unaware of what it was; he also thought that no predetermined process makes such awareness inevitable, and he feared that for want of understanding its own history, the world may rot and dissolve into barbarism. It may be that we have reached this very point. The proletariat is too weakened as a class to remain an autonomous factor of history at present. Today, instead of the proletarians of every country lining up against capitalism, we have a capitalism torn apart by increasingly violent contradictions. Proletariats are divided among themselves and are more or less won over to class collaboration, and, on top of this, a State has socialized production but regulates its relations with other States along the lines of traditional diplomacy and strategy and does not openly seek to unite the scattered proletariats against capitalism. The national, geographical, and psychological factors which intersect the class struggle and which blur the broad Marxist lines of history—in brief, the historical "hazards," to speak like

Engels—have not been reabsorbed by the factors which are considered essential. We are not saying that this fact refutes Marxism, since Marx himself pointed out that chaos and absurdity were one of the possible ways for history to end. He emphasized the role of contingency in history: he forbade one to hope that the path of Marxist action could maintain the beautiful straightness which it had had at certain privileged moments and which it would still have could it rely on a preordained movement of history.

The most rigorous Marxism has never been able, in either theory or practice, to exclude compromise and the accompanying derailment of history which we are now witnessing. The Soviet government of 1917 was forced from the very first to come to terms with factual situations in which it could not absolutely avoid ambiguity or preserve an absolutely rational character in the history it was *making* on its own behalf. As soon as it was organized, it was confronted with the problem of the peace treaty. The Russian Army, utterly exhausted and drained by the operations of 1914–17, could not go on with the war any longer. The Soviet government had to ask for an armistice. Did they have to sign a peace treaty? To continue the war with an exhausted army would be to risk losing all that the October Revolution had gained. Signing a treaty with imperialist Germany would risk giving credence to the rumor being spread by the bourgeois governments that there was a connivance between Berlin and the Russian revolutionaries and so risk disappointing Western and German proletarians. From a Marxist perspective one had to refuse to choose between Germany and the Allies and propose a democratic peace to the workers of all nations. Such a proposition was indeed made, but of course it remained a dead letter in the face of the bourgeois governments with their national proletariats well in hand. Being thus unable to *go beyond* the given situation, the current world conflict, it was necessary to take a stand about it. The party was split. Lenin proposed to drag out the negotiations at Brest-Litovsk and to sign the treaty in the event of a German ultimatum. "If we should have to die for the success of the German revolution," he said, "we would be obliged to do so: the German revolution would be infinitely more important than our own. But when will it come? Impossible to know. For the moment there is nothing in the world more important than our revolution. It must be protected at any cost." Bukharin and the majority of the party refused any agreement with an imperialist power and were for revolutionary war. Trotsky wanted to break off negotiations in the event of a German ultimatum, to declare peace established *de facto,* without a treaty, and, should the Germans launch an offensive, to sign at bayonet point a treaty which would not be ambiguous under these conditions. This solution prevailed. The German offensive took place, and the Soviet delegates had to sign without reading a treaty whose conditions were much harsher than they would have been if the Russians had given in sooner. It was not a *good* solution: the Baltic states had been lost to the Soviet government, and the world proletariat had perhaps not understood. The Soviet government's conduct could have been completely rational only if the strikes which took place in Germany and Austria in October of 1917 had paralyzed the German army and heralded a second revolution. Lenin had given historical Reason its chance, but history had not responded to this solicitation. It had in fact been necessary to treat with German imperialism and to free German troops which might have carried the day on the western front. Their deepest conviction about the meaning of history has never prevented the greatest Marxists from recognizing that the ways of history are unfathomable.

When the Red Army was organized, the committees of soldiers from the imperial regiments sent the old discipline flying. There should henceforth be only volunteers, military authority was to be decentralized, reactionary officers were to be dismissed. A fraction of the party wanted to develop this spontaneous movement into a new theory of war: no more "professionals"; elected leaders; a centralized army—so they thought—is the army of imperialist States. Trench warfare is imperialist warfare; the revolution brings with it movement, maneuvering, a war conducted by small detachments employing all types of weapons and backed by popular support: in a word, guerrilla warfare. These ideas seemed logical enough: how, in a Marxist philosophy of history, could the revolution help but bring about basic changes in army organization and the art of war, as in all other areas? Nevertheless Trotsky, who was then in charge of inspecting the army, wrote: "All of that was extremely abstract and, at bottom, an idealization of our weakness. The sober experience of civil war soon broke down these prejudices." Even if one considers the class struggle as the essence of history and consequently favors proletarian solutions to each particular problem, it remains to be seen *whether the process which will finally shape the broad lines of history directly determines this or that individual episode of history.* The revolution and the proletariat's future in the world might be compromised by wanting to give the army a revolutionary and proletarian structure too soon. The problem is to recognize the proletarian spirit *in each of its momentary guises.* "The chaos of the guerrilla undertakings," Trotsky went on, "was the very expression of the rural underside of the revolution. The struggle against the guerrillas was consequently a battle for the proletarian political spirit against the anarchic *petit-bourgeois* element which was tending to undermine it." Policies which are proletarian in form may be reactionary in fact. Marxist action presupposes a concrete view of particular circumstances and of their *probable* significance, a certain reading of history in terms of what is likely—and with whatever errors such a reading may imply—and it cannot, in any case, be mechanically deduced from theory. It should not proceed continually and simply "to the left"; compromise may be more Marxist than "leftism."

The story of what exhausting discussions took place to establish the party "line" in the first years of the Revolution has often been told. Thus the most conscious fraction of the proletariat, which *was* the revolution in progress, questioned itself as to what it might be and want at that precise moment of history. Indeed there was a problem about the party line, since there is a perpetual ambiguity about history. Lenin tried to set forth a theory of this difficult march and the principles of a true course somewhere between "leftism" and opportunism, in the famous *Maladie infantile du Communisme*.[8] But wasn't it a contradiction to seek objective criteria by which Marxist compromises might be distinguished from opportunistic ones? If such criteria had existed, there would have been no need for the party to discuss them, decisions could in every instance have been deduced, and there would have been no more problem about the line. "I have the right," said Lenin, "to hand over my money to a thief if I do so under threat of death and try to have him arrested as soon as I can. I do not have the right to join a gang of thieves and profit from their thefts." It is obvious that this criterion permits a decisive settlement only in extreme cases and that one passes from valid compromises to "rotten" ones by imperceptible stages. This is why one must, as Lenin said, "put one's own mind to work to find one's bearings in each particular case." To put it another way, some compromises are truly in line and represent the true Marxist intransigence; some intransigences are abstract and *petit-bourgeois* and are actually counter-revolutionary; and, outside of the extreme cases, there is nothing but a set of probabilities to help us decide. To be properly appraised they require a certain Marxist flair or a Marxist perception of the local and world situation which is on the level of talent or genius. But where will one stop if that talent and that exact estimate—sufficiently cautious and sufficiently bold—of what is possible at each moment happens to be lacking? It is possible to slip from Marxist or dialectical contradictions into opportunistic compromises because there is no logical difference between them. That is why Lenin did not want to impose on Trotsky his "opportunistic" solution to the problem of the treaty, although the latter's solution was to cost Russia

8. Translated as *The Infantile Sickness of "Leftism" in Communism* (New York, 1920).—Trans.

the Baltic provinces. The most brilliant Marxist recognizes a possibility of error, deviation, and chaos in his own decisions. The decisive moment comes when a man takes up and carries forward the course of things which he *thinks* he reads in objective history. And in the last analysis at that moment all he has to guide him is *his own* view of events.

Marxism has never excluded from the theoretical plane the ambiguity it encounters in action. The spontaneous development of objective history can give us nothing more than a certain convergence of facts, and only history as it is thought and wished by men can make a univocal meaning emerge from that given arrangement. On another occasion Trotsky wrote, "The whole historical process is the rule of right as seen through the fortuitous. To use the language of biology, one can say that the rational rule of history comes about through a natural selection of accidental facts. Conscious human activity develops on this basis, subjecting the accidental to an artificial selection." Accidental facts—that is, the isolated facts which are not necessary to the total situation—disappear from history of their own accord for want of historical supports, agreements, and complicities, just as mutational monsters disappear by themselves, according to Darwin, because they are incompatible with the general life of the organism. This selection, however, only guarantees the destruction of nonviable systems and irrational societies; it does not guarantee the appearance of a new viable form, which would presuppose a selection guided this time by an idea. Thus it is consciousness which *definitively* puts reason into history by linking the constellation of facts in a particular way. Every historical undertaking is something of an adventure, since it is never guaranteed by any *absolutely* rational structure of things. It always involves a certain utilization of chances, and one must always use cunning with things (and people) to the extent that an order must be extracted from them which was not given with them. There is always the possibility of an immense compromise, of a historical decay where the class struggle, although strong enough to destroy, would not be sufficiently powerful to construct and where the dominant lines of history, as indicated in the *Communist Manifesto,* would be erased.

Are we not, to all appearances, at this point now? When, instead of continuing in a series of revolutions throughout Europe the Russian Revolution remained isolated in the face of a bourgeois world (and, even more clearly, when the war threatened the U.S.S.R.'s very existence), Russia had to come to terms with bourgeois governments and could no longer openly remain the moving spirit behind class struggles throughout the world. Before it was a theory, "Socialism in one country" was a factual situation to which the U.S.S.R. had to adapt.

It matters little whether the U.S.S.R. might or might not have given another direction to history at a particular moment, whether the theory was imposed by the facts, or whether, on the contrary, it set them in motion. The Third International might perhaps have weakened the bourgeois governments from within by leading the world proletariat in another way. But it is more likely that it would have led Russia to her doom by leaving her alone before German aggression. Whatever the reason, the stagnation of revolutions in the world and "Popular Front" tactics have modified the proletariats and the recruitment and theoretical formation of Communist parties too profoundly to allow one to hope for a renewal of open class struggle in the near future or even to propose to the militants revolutionary orders which they would not *feel*. Thus, instead of two clearly defined factors, the history of our time consists of *composites:* a Soviet Union which is obliged to deal with bourgeois States; Communist parties which rally to the politics of Popular Fronts or, as in the case of Italy, are arrested in their proletarian development by the impact of Soviet power politics; bourgeois parties incapable of defining a coherent economic policy but, in the weakened nations, conscious of their powerlessness and vaguely won over to a "revolutionism" which may lead them to temporary understandings with the Left. Even if Marxism remains "true" in that a *clear statement* of the problem of the modes of production would separate the regressive forces from the progressive ones, since neither of these forces is very conscious, the old-Marxist perspective does not reveal the particular features of our time. Instead it skims over factual details, and to that extent one can grant the skeptical historian that its interpretation of history is abstract and arbitrary.

*   *   *   *

If, after gaining control in Russia and being accepted by one-third of the French people, Marxism today seems incapable of giving a detailed explanation of the history we are living, if the essential threads of history which it separated out are today entangled, in the tissue of events, with the national and psychological factors which it considered secondary but which now overlay it, doesn't this prove that nothing in history is essential, that everything counts equally, that no perspective is preferable to any other, and doesn't this then lead us to skepticism? Shouldn't politics abandon the idea of basing itself on a philosophy of history and, taking the world as it is no matter what our wishes, dreams, or judgments may be, define its ends and its means by what the facts authorize? But one cannot do without a perspective, and, whether we like it or not, we are condemned to wishes, value

judgments, and even a philosophy of history. It has not been sufficiently noted that, after demonstrating the irrationality of history, the
skeptic will abruptly abandon his methodological scruples when it
comes to drawing practical conclusions. If one wishes to regulate
action, certain facts must indeed be considered dominant and others
secondary. No matter how realistic it wishes to be, no matter how
strictly based on facts, a skeptical politics is obliged to treat (at least
implicitly) certain facts as more important than others and to that
extent it harbors an embarrassing philosophy of history—one which is
lived rather than thought but which is no less effective. For example, it
will calculate the future of France as a function of the British Empire,
the United States, or the U.S.S.R., defining these once and for all by
their geographical characteristics, natural resources, and unalterable
psychological traits. In point of fact, historical skepticism is always
conservative, although it cannot, in all strictness, exclude anything
from its expectations—not even a revolutionary phase of history.
Under the pretext of objectivity it freezes the future and eliminates
change and the will of men from history. When it believes it is simply
facing facts by admitting the necessity of an "elite" in every society or
acknowledging the omnipotence of natural riches and geographical
conditions, it is really making a bet, expressing a preference and a
wish, and assuming a responsibility. If we wanted to be truly sub-
missive to the facts and completely realistic, we would have to
reject all assumptions, all *a priori* philosophy of history, and especially
that skeptical premise that men always act foolishly, being dominated
by the past and exterior causes or else led by a few rogues, who
thoroughly understand them, toward goals of which they know
nothing. There would be no history if everything made sense and if the
world's development was nothing but the visible realization of a
rational plan; but neither would there be any history—or action, or
humanity—if everything was absurd or if the course of events was
dominated by a few massive and unalterable facts like the British
Empire or the psychology of the "leader" or the "crowd," which are,
after all, merely products of the past and do not necessarily engage our
future.

To sum up, we can no longer have a Kantian system of politics,
because such a system is not concerned with consequences, whereas
when we act it is indeed to produce external results, not just to make
a gesture and ease our conscience. We cannot have "skeptical" politics
because, appearances to the contrary, it chooses its goals and makes a
selection of facts (which it then asks us to recognize) according to
values it does not acknowledge, proposing to guide us to a definition of
the "possible" on the basis of these facts. Nor can we any longer have a

proletarian Marxist politics along classical lines, because this politics has lost its grip on the facts. Our only recourse is a reading of the present which is as full and as faithful as possible, which does not prejudice its meaning, which even recognizes chaos and non-sense where they exist, but which does not refuse to discern a direction and an idea in events where they appear. Take, for example, the result of the French elections and, in particular, the progress the Communist Party has made since 1936. It would be absurd to believe that what is at stake is *simply* the proletariat's progress toward class consciousness and revolution. But it is equally impossible to declare that the fact is insignificant. We know what the skeptic would say here: the Socialist Party pulled off its maneuver and duped voters; its patriotic tactics won back the formerly Socialist voters, and illusory nationalizations were thrown as a sop to the proletarian voters. During this time the Socialists, having rallied to the *oui/oui* attitude and the Western bloc, filled positions formerly held by the Radicals. In short, nothing has changed but the names. Nothing has happened in this country. The shift to the Left—or, as Thibaudet put it, the "immanent *sinistrisme*" —of French politics is only an appearance, for the parties are slipping to the right while the country slides to the left.

But one would be very wrong to believe that names can change without things changing too. Something is happening all the same the day a French peasant votes Communist for the first time in his life; something is happening to the party, which is modified by its new recruit, but something is also happening to the peasant. And that is what we would like to know. What is today's French Communist like? What does he think of small farms, religion, morality, homeland, society? What, finally, does he want—not only with his deliberate will but with the tacit will visible in his family relationships, his mode of work or entertainment? Can we pretend to be unaware of those five million Frenchmen, probably the most resolute and the most alive among us, who have just voted for the Communist Party? And likewise, what is today's Soviet Russian like? What are his views on life, on death, the West, Germany, family, morality, and love? Russian armies occupy part of Europe, and a few newspapermen have penetrated into their zone—but when they described the Russian officers in Prague with their fine manners and their kissing of hands, it was either with a conservative's ill-natured delight or a convert's zeal, both all too eager to prove that the Soviets are just like everybody else. The fact is that we have not known anything about the U.S.S.R. for at least six years, and our information from 1939 has been proved worthless by the way Russia conducted and won its war. One can see a state socialism developing in Europe under Russia's influence; it has now reached

Czechoslovakia and Yugoslavia and tomorrow may reach France. We know almost nothing about nationalizations: their modalities, their probable impact on production, or their yield. Nor do we know anything about the real situation in the United States or Great Britain. What is an English worker? What is the Truman Administration like? What are the tendencies of capitalist circles in the United States? How do they envisage their future? What perspectives would be opened up by the ever possible American depression? What assistance might the United States and Russia give tomorrow to the reconstruction of Europe? We are called upon to choose between the United States and Russia, and we choose according to whether we prefer liberty or the dictatorship of the proletariat, whether our first thought is of reconstruction or of the class struggle, without asking ourselves whether the United States (which only emerged from the Depression because of the war and which is threatened by another crisis, perhaps even more serious than that of 1929) will be able to guarantee its citizens real liberty for any length of time and assuming that Russia profoundly changed after 20 years, can be defined simply as a proletarian dictatorship—without asking ourselves whether the United States will want to undertake the reconstruction of Europe and assuming that Russia will always be absorbed in the task of its own reconstruction and will never be able to participate in ours. The job of French intellectuals is not to maintain the devotionary, hysterical atmosphere or the vague fervors and terrors which impart a mythical and almost puerile character to French politics but is rather to take stock of this century and the ambiguous forms which it offers us. If, thanks to information and facts, this ambiguity came to be no longer merely endured but understood, then our political life might cease to be haunted by phantoms and might recover a little reality.

Such is the task for the years ahead. But what are we to do at present? Here we should reach a precise understanding with the reader. Enough authors in the past 15 years have falsely "gone beyond" Marxism to make us careful to distinguish ourselves from them. To go beyond a doctrine, one must first reach its level and give a better explanation of whatever it explains. If we put a question mark next to Marxism, it is not because we prefer some conservative philosophy of history which would be even more abstract. We are not saying that the class struggle will never play an essential role in world history. We simply don't know. Events—for example, a depression in America— may bring it rapidly into the foreground. We are only saying that at present it is masked and latent and that a proletarian revolution in France, if it were to take place, would provoke Anglo-Saxon intervention. But we should be careful that nothing we do helps to check the proletarian movement if it revives throughout the world. If there is a strike, be for the strikers. If there is civil war, be for the proletariat. Do whatever is in our power to avoid a conflict between the United States and Russia. In short, pursue what is, in effect, the policy of the Communist Party. Reconstruct with the proletariat: for the moment, there is nothing else to do. Only, we will play this waiting game without illusions about the results to be hoped from it and without honoring it with the name of dialectic. Do we know whether a dialectic still exists and whether history will in the end be rational? If Marxism is still true, then we will rediscover it on the path of prevailing truth and in the analysis of our time.[9]

November 1945

9. When these lines were written, Russian pressure on Yugoslavia, which Tito's dissidence has since made evident, was less domineering or less known in France. As for the other countries in her circle of influence, Russia was following an optimistic line and allowing them a fairly broad autonomy—to judge by appearances, her adversaries would say, but who would deny that the Beneš regime was not Gottwald's. It was possible to imagine—and necessary to accelerate by a friendly discussion with the Communists—the formation of free, new social structures in the countries of Western Europe which would spare Europe the alternative of "people's democracy" or reactionary policies, Stalinist communism or the anti-Soviet crusade. Since then, while the West was shaping up a war machine, the U.S.S.R.—having returned to pessimism, pure authority, and ultimatums, made it necessary for the non-Communist left to state clearly, under pain of mystification, why it was not Communist, and would not in any case put up a liberal front for the system. This does not mean that when this was written and within the framework of what was then possible, the attitude expressed here was not justified as one which had a chance of saving both socialism and liberty.

12 / Faith and Good Faith

PIERRE HERVÉ was right in his recent reply to Father Daniélou.[1] To give Catholicism its due, it is easy to cite Christian and pontifical texts or individual acts which promote freedom and oppose the interests of established regimes. But it is even easier to find texts in the Catholic tradition which are hostile to freedom. Above all, historical Catholicism is not merely a certain number of texts nor a sum of individuals; it is a machine, an institution or a movement with an over-all logic, which is unquestionably operating in a reactionary direction despite certain texts and individual sentiments, or even with the help of the ambiguity which these create. There was once a young Catholic who was led "to the Left" by the demands of his faith. This was the time when Dollfuss inaugurated Europe's first Christian Socialist government by shelling the working-class sections of Vienna. A magazine inspired by Christians protested to President Miklas, and the protest was said to be supported by the most progressive of our great religious orders. The young man was welcomed at the table of some monks belonging to this order. In the middle of lunch he was astonished to hear that, after all, the Dollfuss government was the established power, that it had the right to a police force since it was the proper government, and that the Catholics, as Catholics, had nothing against it, although as citizens they were free to censure it. In later life the young man never forgot this moment. He turned to the Father (a bold and generous man, as was seen later) who had first voiced these opinions and told him simply that this justified the workers' opinion of the Catholics: in social questions they can never fully be counted on.

Hervé's criticism is, however, incomplete. It puts the sentiments of

1. *Action*, Dec. 14, 1945.

the Catholics back into the context of institutional Catholicism and pontifical diplomacy. It shifts the discussion from the plane of ideas to that of facts. But this is the very reason it will never convince Father Daniélou. One can imagine him reading Hervé's conclusive text but remaining unconvinced. How could he separate Catholicism from what he himself thinks and wants? In his own eyes the Catholic is progressive, although for others the Catholic is reactionary. Reverend Father Daniélou feels that he is free, just, and bold in his political thinking, and as a matter of fact he is. But we see him only through the social body which he inhabits, just as we see an alien consciousness only through that unchanging physical body, that frozen past, which carries so little weight for the consciousness itself. Father Daniélou will agree that the past gives him the lie—but he will add that the problem is constantly to recall Christianity to itself, to reawaken its hunger and thirst for justice. He will plead guilty for the past and innocent for the future. He will appeal from the outside to the inside, from historical Catholicism to its conscience, from a history which today's Catholics never made to the one they want to create from now on. He will always have the right to think that bad luck was behind any reactionary manifestations of the Catholic religion and that the institution and the luck may change.

The question could be settled only by illuminating the relationship of the religion itself to the conservative spirit and the revolutionary spirit. We must understand why organized Christianity has assumed a certain guise throughout history, why the Christian is not the same for others as for himself. In the last analysis, our bodies bear witness to what we are; body and spirit express each other and cannot be separated. The Catholic's social conduct cannot be criticized without touching on his inner life. We cannot rest content with blaming the political and social infrastructure of Catholicism; along with the critique of the underlying structure there must go a critique which would grasp Catholicism in its totality and define it globally as a certain stand about the world and men which yields both generous sentiments and conservative conduct. There must be an ambiguity in Catholicism as a spiritual way of life to correspond to its ambiguity as a social phenomenon.

*　　*　　*　　*

Catholicism posits a belief in both an interior and an exterior God. This is the religious formulation of its contradictions.

"Turn inward," said St. Augustine. "Truth dwells within the inner man." One finds God by turning away from things. Whether God is the model according to which my spirit was created or whether I experience and, so to speak, touch God when I become conscious of myself as spirit, God is in any case on the side of the subject rather than on the side of the world. He is "within me more myself than I," *intimior intimo meo,* to quote St. Augustine once again. He is fully that clarity, that light which I am at my best moments. What is evident for me cannot be less so for Him, since it is precisely upon my inner experience of the truth that I base my affirmation of an absolute Truth and of an absolute Spirit which thinks it. Since God is truth, I always serve Him in saying what I think, on the sole condition that I have done my utmost to clarify my ideas. To be faithful is to be sincere. Faith is good faith.

Obedience to God does not, therefore, consist in yielding to an alien and obscure will but consists in doing what we really want, since God is more ourselves than we. To confess God in words is nothing: "The letter kills, but the spirit quickens." All that is valuable is the evidence which the spirit within us gives to itself. It exists in men who do not call God by name but who recognize Him in spirit and truth. As for the others, force is powerless to save them. Force may impose gestures but not an inner conviction. Canon Law states: "No one can be constrained by force to embrace the Catholic faith." Religion can be neither attacked nor defended by arms. "Who lives by the sword shall die by the sword." Here religion is placed in a dimension of eternity where it is invulnerable. God, unlike things, does not need time and space in order to exist: He is everywhere, and nowhere in particular. He is not diminished when men turn away from Him. In this sense, sin is unreal. If my actions go against my conscience, I cease to be spirit, I cease to be myself, I do nothing positive; and evil is only the absence of good. The expression "to *do* good" loses its sense because good resides only in the spirit and finally in God, who is eternal. There is always an element of Stoicism in the idea of God: if God exists, then perfection has already been achieved outside this world; since perfection cannot be increased, there is, strictly speaking, nothing to do. "My kingdom is not of this world." Good works are the by-products of religion. They do not add to the total Good, just as infinity is not increased by the addition of another unit. Our fate here matters little in the other world because God is worthy of our adoration no matter what. Let us find our rest in Him. Quietism. Our fate here below is unimportant in any case; we have only to take it as it comes, for better or for worse. After all, we do not have any claim on life. "Thy will be done." Man renounces his claim on his life. He lives in the will of God as children live in the will of their parents. As Hegel said, it is the reign of the Father.

The Incarnation changes everything. Since the Incarnation, God has been externalized. He was seen at a certain moment and in a certain place, and He left behind Him words and memories which were then passed on. Henceforth man's road toward God was no longer contemplation but the commentary and interpretation of that ambiguous message whose energy is never exhausted. In this sense Christianity is diametrically opposed to "spiritualism." It reopens the question of the distinction between body and spirit, between interior and exterior. Catholicism does not like reflexive proofs of God and only grudgingly does it make room for them. One can prove the existence of God with the human spirit as a starting point, but only by taking it as one part of Creation with the same standing as the heavens and the earth which "declare the glory of God." The human soul can signal God's place at the origin of the world, but it can neither see nor understand Him and cannot therefore be centered in Him. The world ceases to be like a flaw in the great eternal diamond. It is no longer a matter of rediscovering the transparence of God outside the world but a matter of entering body and soul into an enigmatic life, the obscurities of which cannot be dissipated but can only be concentrated in a few mysteries where man contemplates the enlarged image of his own condition. Pascal said, and Jacques Rivière says now, that the dogmas of the Incarnation and Original Sin are not clear but are valuable because they reflect man's contradictions of body and soul, nobility and wretchedness. The parables of the Gospel are not a way of presenting pure ideas in images; they are the only language capable of conveying the relations of religious life, as paradoxical as those of the world of sensation. Sacramental words and gestures are not simply the embodiment of some thought. Like tangible things, they are themselves the carriers of their meaning, which is inseparable from its material form. They do not evoke the idea of God: they are the vehicle of His presence and action. In the last analysis the soul is so little to be separated from the body that it will carry a radiant double of its temporal body into eternity.

Hegel said that the Incarnation is "the hinge of universal history" and that all history thereafter has only developed its consequences. And the God-Man and the Death of God do, in effect, transform spirit and religion. As if the infinite God were no longer sufficient, as if something moved in Him, as if the world and man became the necessary moments of a greater perfection instead of being a useless decline from the originating perfection. God can no longer be fully God, and Creation cannot be completed unless man freely recognizes God and returns Creation to Him through Faith. Something is happening; the world is not futile; there is something to be done. Man could not return to God unless he had been separated from Him. "Fortunate the fault which merited such a Redeemer." One should not regret paradise lost: in it man lived like an animal under the natural law of God. It is through sin that he acquired the knowledge of good and evil, that he became consciousness and became man. *Omnia cooperantur in bonum, etiam peccata.* Sin is real. It serves the glory of God. It is no longer a question of man's withdrawing from the world like the Stoics or regaining purity and sincerity in the Socratic manner, by the exercise of his understanding. His relation to God is ambiguous because it does not exist without separation. Kierkegaard thought it impossible to say "I am a Christian" in the way one says "I am tall" or "I am short," because being a Christian means living the contradiction of good and evil, and so it also means not being a Christian. Never absolutely good or absolutely bad, man cannot be sincere, for sincerity supposes a definite nature which one can assess without ambiguity. It is a matter not of contemplating oneself but of constructing and going beyond oneself. "Faith is in things unseen." It is an adherence that goes beyond the guarantees which one is given and therefore excludes an ever-present sincerity. The Christian should not "deny in darkness what he has seen in light." He will not challenge his God and his Church even if he does not at first understand their decrees; he will not doubt the sacraments even though they afford him no happiness.

The paradox of Christianity and Catholicism is that they are never satisfied with either an interior or an exterior God but are always *between* one and the other. We must go beyond ourselves; we must "lose our life," but in its loss is its salvation. Faith is reliance, but the Christian knows whom he is relying on: *scio cui credidi.* Catholicism does not want to give everything over to Christian faith. The Syllabus states that no one is a Catholic who doubts reason's ability to prove the existence of God, and modernists have been censured for wanting to *replace* the God of philosophers and scholars with the God perceived by the heart. Catholicism finds distasteful a philosophy which is merely a transcription of Christian experience, doubtless because such a philosophy, when carried to its logical extreme, would be a philosophy of man instead of a theology. *Tu es vere Deus absconditus.* There is nothing one can say about this hidden God inaccessible to speculation, whose affirmation lies in the shadowy regions of faith, and in the end He would appear to be a postulate of human life rather than the most certain of beings. One does not of course challenge Christian experience and Pascal's description of it: one just maintains it on the indistinct plane of existence, the essences of which are still judged by speculative philosophy and Thomism.

The Incarnation is not followed out in all its consequences. The first Christians felt abandoned after the death of Christ and looked everywhere for a trace of Him. Centuries later the Crusaders plunged into the search for an empty tomb. And this was because they worshiped the Son in the spirit of the religion of the Father. They had not yet understood that God was with them now and forever. The meaning of the Pentecost is that the religion of both the Father and the Son are to be fulfilled in the religion of the Spirit, that God is no longer in Heaven but in human society and communication, wherever men come together in His name. Christ's stay on earth was only the beginning of his presence, which is continued by the Church. Christians should not remain polarized by an historical episode, no matter how decisive it might have been, but should live out the marriage of the Spirit and human history which began with the Incarnation. Catholicism arrests and freezes this development of religion: the Trinity is not a dialectical movement; the Three Persons are co-eternal. The Father is not surpassed by the Spirit; the religion of the Father lives on in the religion of the Spirit, for Love does not eliminate the Law or the fear of God. God is not completely with us. Behind the incarnate Spirit there remains that infinite gaze which strips us of all secrets, but also of our liberty, our desire, and our future, reducing us to *visible objects*. Likewise, the Church is not rooted in human society but is crystallized on the margin of the State. The Spirit is everywhere, but its privileged dwelling place is the Church. For a second time men are alienated by this second gaze which weighs upon them and which has more than once found a *secular arm* to serve it. What is surprising about this? Not only is it tempting, it is urgent to hold men in check when one *knows* that they are wasting their time in an idle search while on the reverse side of things an infinite Knowledge has already settled everything. And so love changes to cruelty, the reconciliation of men with each other and with the world will come to naught, the Incarnation turns into suffering because it is incomplete, and Christianity becomes a new form of guilty conscience.

The ambiguity of Christianity on the political plane is perfectly comprehensible: when it remains true to the Incarnation, it can be revolutionary, but the religion of the Father is conservative. Hindsight may reveal that sin helps create the general good and that man's trespass had fortunate results. But one cannot say this at the moment of decision, for at that moment sin is still forbidden. Adam would therefore have done better to avoid sin. Perfection is behind rather than before us. The Christian always has the right to accept existing evil but may never purchase progress with a crime. He can rally to a revolution that is already over, he can absolve it of its crimes, but he cannot start it. Even if a revolution makes just use of power, it remains seditious as long as it is unsuccessful. The Catholic as Catholic has no sense of the future: he must wait for that future to become part of the past before he can cast his lot with it. Fortunately, the will of God is not always clear, and the only way to know it, as Coûfontaine says in *l'Otage*, is to try to oppose it.[2] And, fortunately again, the Catholic as citizen is always free to join a revolution—but he will keep the best part of himself separate from it, and as a Catholic he will be indifferent to it. Claudel and Jacques Rivière were right in saying that the Christian is a nuisance to the Establishment because he is always somewhere else and one can never be sure of him. But the Christian makes revolutionaries uneasy for the very same reason: they feel he is never completely with them. He is a poor conservative and an unsafe bet as a revolutionary. There is just one case where the Church itself calls for insurrection: when a legal power violates divine law. But one has never in fact seen the Church take a stand against a legal government for the simple reason that it was unjust or back a revolution simply because it was just. On the contrary, it has been seen to favor rebels because they protected its tabernacles, its ministers, and its property. God will not fully have come to the earth until the Church feels the same obligation toward other men as it does toward its own ministers, toward the houses of Guernica as toward its own temples. There is such a thing as A Christian revolt, but it is very localized, appearing only when the Church is threatened. The Church is conservative insofar as it demands the boldness and heroism of the faithful for itself alone and makes them live on two different levels. This, in short, is what the Hegelian and Marxist theories of alienation say; and this is what Christianity itself says with complete awareness: "No man can serve two masters." No one loves well what he does not love best of all. But since Christians also believe in the Incarnation, since it is supposed to animate their lives, they can come as close to the revolutionaries as they wish—at least for a while—as shown by the example of Bergamin and several others. There is no doubt that they then have that second-class sincerity which consists of saying what one thinks. One does not see how they could have that sincerity of the first order which consists of purging oneself of the equivocal.

* * * *

Are we therefore to take up Gide's phrase, "Simple faith exempts one from good faith," once again? Gide himself made all the comment necessary: "It is not freedom which brings man happiness but rather the acceptance of a duty."[3] If sincerity is one's highest value, one will

2. English translation of Claudel's play by P. Chavannes, *The Hostage* (New Haven, 1917).—Trans.

3. Preface to *Vol de nuit*. [English translation by Stuart Gilbert, *Night Flight* (New York and London, 1932).]

never become fully committed to anything, not to a Church or to a party, not to a love or a friendship, not even to a particular task; for commitment always assumes that one's affirmation surpasses one's knowledge, that one believes by hearsay, that one gives up the rule of sincerity for that of responsibility. The intellectual who refuses his commitments on the pretext that his function is to see all sides is in fact contriving to live a pleasant life under the guise of obeying a vocation. He resolves to avoid all resolutions and to supply strong reasons to those weak in conviction. He who is not with me is against me. Not being a Communist is being anti-Communist. Sincerity itself is deceitful and turns into propaganda. From the moment we do something, we turn toward the world, stop self-questioning, and go beyond ourselves in our action. Faith—in the sense of an unreserved commitment which is never completely justified—enters the picture as soon as we leave the realm of pure geometrical ideas and have to deal with the existing world. Each of our perceptions is an act of faith in that it affirms more than we strictly know, since objects are inexhaustible and our information limited. Descartes even said that believing two and two makes four demands an act of will. How can the Catholic be blamed for living equivocally if everybody dwells in the same state and if bad faith is the very essence of consciousness?

In reality there is no such dilemma as faith versus good faith. There can be no question of *sacrificing* good faith to faith, and only a dead or sectarian faith demands such a sacrifice. Completely devoid of sincerity, faith becomes sheer obedience or madness. "The party is no place for robots! Let no lips be sealed!" exclaimed Thorez one day.[4] Today's overly docile neophyte is the turncoat of tomorrow. Sincerity is not enough in a creature such as man, who is at every instant thrown beyond himself by knowledge as well as action and therefore is unable to give an exact account of his motives at every instant. "When a man is sincere, he doesn't think about it or put it on display. The very act of calling oneself sincere implies a double point of view, a reflection which corrupts one's vaunted sincerity and reduces it to an attitude. . . . Making a value of sincerity is precisely characteristic of an insincere society, which turns inward upon itself instead of acting upon the world." [5] Sincerity is not a goal, but, for exactly the same reasons, insincerity must never be a system, a rule, or a habit. If commitment goes beyond reasons, it should never run contrary to reason itself. Man's value does not consist in either an explosive, maniac sincerity or an unquestioned faith. Instead, it consists of a higher awareness which enables him to determine the moment when it

4. Louis Aragon, "Maurice Thorez et la France," *Labyrinthe* (Dec. 15, 1945).
5. P. Hervé, *La libération trahie*, p. 96.

is reasonable to take things on trust and the moment when questioning is in order, to combine faith and good faith within himself, and to accept his party or his group with open eyes, seeing them for what they are.

Lenin intimated something of this sort in his formula "democratic centralism." The party must welcome discussion but must also maintain discipline. The decisions must express the will of the active members, and at the same time the members must consider themselves committed to party decisions even if these run contrary to their personal views. The revolution is *both* a reality which the spontaneous course of events is preparing and an idea being worked out in the minds of those individuals who are most aware of what is happening. If the Communist attracts no followers after defending his view of the truth before the party, it means that his proposed solutions are premature or historically false, since they do not reflect the wishes of the party and the masses, who are the revolution in action. This has nothing to do with asceticism or fideism or an anti-individualist point of view. Rather, it is the idea that political action is more than an intellectual exercise and presupposes an effective contact with history as it takes shape; the idea that one's commitment to the party does not depend solely on an intellectual consent but also upon involvement in effective history, which counterbalances and regulates theory. Lenin was fully aware of the tension which sometimes exists between the individual and the party, between judgment and loyalty. Although it is impossible and would be unhealthy to ignore this conflict, he thinks it is transcended by the individual's life in the party which is *his* party. If the individual goes along with the party and against his own private opinion, it is because the party has proven its worth, because it has a mission in history, and because it represents the proletariat. There is no such thing as unmotivated commitment. What makes the Marxist notion of the party different from all others, what makes it a new cultural phenomenon and explains its place in modern literature and thought, is precisely this conception of an exchange, a vital communication between individual judgment and historical reality through the intermediary of the party.

"In any political structure the directors are necessarily granted a certain measure of trust, indeed, of orthodoxy, even if one doesn't like to admit it. This orthodoxy is undoubtedly relative, based on reason and constantly re-examined, but it is nevertheless beyond the competence of any citizen to analyze, unravel, and judge everything by himself in the complexity of world politics. Where one places one's trust is determined by a direct personal examination of those facts one is in a position to judge and, for the rest, by just plunging in, which in no way means blindly swearing allegiance, nor does it exclude the effort to understand. Let us frankly admit that a certain bias is involved, but a bias which is much closer to the spirit of free questioning and honest objectivity than the false objectivity of the intellectuals detached from ordinary custom. . . . ." [6] I repeat that it involves an exchange between private judgment and party decisions, a give-and-take, living actively *with* the party, not just passively obeying it. In speaking of a bias which can be carefully scrutinized, an objective subjectivity, a vigilant trust, faith which is good faith and freedom which is commitment, Hervé is describing that communication between opposites which a frivolous author recently attributed to "reactionary philosophy." One can well believe that it is difficult to maintain an equilibrium between these opposites, since Communist criticisms of existentialism—of which there have recently been many—certainly give off more heat than light and reveal more faith than good faith.

6. *Ibid.,* pp. 32–35.

13 / Man, the Hero

THERE ARE several indications, at least in the world of letters, of a return to peace. Heroes are fading away, and protests, which are cautious today but tomorrow will be bold, are being raised against "heroic" morality. A man of letters who fought in the First World War and who has been silent since the beginning of the Second, writes to a friend, "I was already scandalized to hear Gide in his *Entretiens imaginaires* humming, to a melody by Offenbach: 'We need heroes even if there are none left in the world.' [1] For my part I would much prefer a grain of wisdom, intelligence, and reason. Having myself been a hero in my youth either of necessity or unnecessarily, I distrust heroes just as Mme Cardinal distrusted women."

When he has to judge a novel or play with a heroic ending, a Catholic like Gabriel Marcel implies that there is heroism and heroism; he is perfectly willing that nature be surpassed, but only if this is done according to the rules and by following certain paths. "Artistic" writers claim a separate domain for literature, one which is safe from politics and history.

This kind of debate raises embarrassing questions. How can a hero praise heroism? And how can anyone do so who is not a hero? It would be better to know exactly what there is behind this grand word.

There has always been a cult of the hero. However, insofar as a civilization believes that beyond this world lies another eternal world where good wins out over evil, the great man does not stand by himself but is the agent of a Providence. The cult of the hero does not take on its tragic cast until the end of transcendent beliefs, or at all events until the emergence of the idea of a world in process. The turning point

1. English translation by Malcolm Cowley, *Imaginary Interviews* (New York, 1949).—Trans.

[182]

comes with Hegel. For him, "the individuals of world history" are those who, although born on a certain date, under certain laws, and into certain moral structures just like everyone else, are the first to understand that this system has no future; they forsake happiness and by their deeds and their example create a law and a moral system in which their time will later recognize its truth. At first they stand alone, since they stand against custom; they have a presentiment of the future although, of course, no knowledge of it: they sense it in their tastes, their passions, and their very being rather than see it clearly before them. Their heroism resides in their having worked out and won for others, with nothing certain to go on and in the loneliness of subjectivity, what will afterwards seem the only possible future, the very meaning of history: this is the unexpected junction of reason and unreason. "They should be called heroes in that they have drawn their goals and their vocation not only from the calmly ordered course of events which the reigning system has consecrated but also from an underground source in the inner spirit whose content is hidden and which has not yet broken through the surface of actual existence but which strikes against the outer world as against a shell and cracks it because such a shell is unsuited to such a kernel. . . . They were people who thought, who knew what was needed, for whom the moment came to know the truth about their time and their world; one might say they were the new race which already existed within the old. . . . That is why the heroes of an era should be recognized as wise men."

If one ceases to believe not only in a benign governor of this world but also in a reasonable course of things, then there no longer is any external support for heroic action; it cannot gather strength from any divine law or even from a visible meaning in history. This heroism which lacks both rules and content is that of the Nietzschean "superman." If the Hegelian hero sacrificed his personal happiness and introduced chaos into his life, it was to save history from chaos; if he questioned the established order, it was to bring another order into the world. The Nietzschean superman is beyond everything that *has been or is to be done;* he is interested only in power itself, and since he refuses to devote it to any particular task, it can only assert itself *against* something or someone. Pure power can only consist in conquering other holders of power and the most powerful opponent of all, death. Hegel had already described this undertaking and this impasse, for all power overcome, just because it is overcome, ceases to have value as power: the death through which the hero has passed was not really death since it could not hold him; the other men whom he has reduced to slavery cannot bear adequate witness to his strength since he was able to conquer them. Therefore, unless he grows old and has himself made an honorary hero, he will always be looking for other risks to run and other men to subdue, knowing in advance that he will never find what he is seeking because he is hoping for the impossible: a life which really integrates death into itself and whose free recognition by others is assured once and for all. For Hegel the true hero is not the master but the slave who has chosen life and who works to transform the world in such a way that in the end there is no more room for the master.

The hero of our contemporaries does not fit either Hegel's or Nietzsche's mold. He is not what Hegel called "the steward of the World Spirit," nor does he believe in any World Spirit which arranges everything for his success and points him clearly on his way. In *For Whom the Bell Tolls* Robert Jordan, on the verge of risking his life, asks himself quite frankly whether he is doing so for the materialistic society which is to come. Then part of him says: "Since when did you ever have any such conception? Never. And you never could have. You're not a real Marxist and you know it. You believe in Liberty, Equality, and Fraternity. You believe in Life, Liberty, and the Pursuit of Happiness. Don't ever kid yourself with too much dialectics. They are for some but not for you." [2] It is not that at the moment of risk he is looking for excuses and pretexts. The mission has been accepted and will be accomplished. It is simply a question of his motives, and no matter what he does, Jordan cannot manage to make the society of the future the sole motive for his sacrifice. The society is desirable to him only as the probable guaranty, for himself and for others, of the freedom he is exercising at that very moment.

A Marxist like Kyo in *La Condition humaine* confronts the question at the *very core of Marxism*.[3] In Marxism, he says, there is both a will and a fatality: when, then, is one to follow the course of events, and when should one force them into a certain channel? If one sticks to the facts, it seems that the Chinese Communists are probably doomed and that the Kuomintang will carry the day. But one can be sure of facts only after giving up the attempt to change them: is it not the moment to bring decisive aid to the Communists, thereby forcing history's hand? No philosophy of history can eliminate this hesitation. "For isn't it true that the essence of life, the basic cause of our anguish, can be defined as freedom of choice? But the Communist gives up a certain

---

2. *For Whom the Bell Tolls*, p. 305.

3. English translation of the Malraux novel by Haakon A. Chevalier, *Man's Fate* (New York, 1934).—Trans.

degree of free choice and submits to a discipline only because this is necessary for action to be effective. . . ." [4]

The hero of *Pilote de guerre* has a different idea of the world but asks himself the same questions.[5] In previous generations the bourgeoisie had its absolute values: one carried out orders; one died for one's country—but perhaps this was because the bourgeoisie had never been face to face with chaos. What sense did it make in June of 1940 to carry out a mission over Arras, at a moment when we could no longer have the slightest effect against the German tanks assembling there, when the announcement could no longer even be broadcast? It is easier to *serve* in a powerful army, at a time when history is clearly heading toward a certain goal. But how can a man help thinking of himself and his own death when the very world goes out of joint and reels before his eyes? How is he to serve if service is useless?

The motto of the contemporary hero is not, however, that of Barrès or Montherlant: he does not serve in order to "blow his own horn" or to prove his mastery in the face of death by means of some "useless service." Saint-Exupéry plunges into his mission because it is an intimate part of himself, the consequence of his thoughts, wishes and decisions, because he would be nothing if he were to back out. He recovers his own being to the extent to which he runs into danger. Over Arras, in the fire of the anti-aircraft guns, when every second of continuing life is as miraculous as a birth, he feels invulnerable because he is *in* things at last; he has left his inner nothingness behind, and death, if it comes, will reach him right in the thick of the world.

But perhaps he will be wounded, perhaps he will have to lie long hours on the ground dying. The same cruel consolation will still be offered him: to be and think like a living person for as long as he does live, to remain poised in the direction of his chosen ends. Wounded behind Fascist lines where he has just blown up a bridge, Robert Jordan has to part from his comrades and even from his beloved Maria.

> Then she started to cry.
> "No, *guapa*, don't," he said. "Listen. We will not go to Madrid now but I go always with thee wherever thou goest. Understand? . . . Thou wilt go now, rabbit. But I go with thee. As long as there is one of us there is both of us. Do you understand? . . . What I do now I do alone.

4. Roger Vailland, *Drôle de jeu*, p. 163. [English translation by Gerard Hopkins, *Playing for Keeps* (Boston, 1948).]

5. English translation by Lewis Galantière, *Flight to Arras* (New York, 1942).— Trans.

I could not do it well with thee. Do you not see how it is? Whichever one there is, is both." [6]

Later, when he is alone:

It does no good to think about Maria. Try to believe what you told her. That is the best. And who says it is not true? Not you.[7]

The man who is still alive has only one resource but a sovereign one: he must keep on acting like a living man. We die alone, but we live with other people; we are the image which they have of us; where they are, we are too. Once more and until the very end Jordan submits to that activity which binds him to others and to things and which is beyond judgment because it is the condition of all unhappiness and all happiness. Left alone, he will not commit suicide.

And if you wait and hold them up even a little while or just get the officer that may make all the difference. One thing well done can make——[8]

It is not fascination with death, as in Nietzsche, which allows the hero to sacrifice himself, nor is it the certainty, as in Hegel, that he is carrying out the wishes of history; rather, it is loyalty to the natural movement which flings us toward things and toward others. It is not death that I love, said Saint-Exupéry, but life.

Today's hero is not skeptical, dilettantish, or decadent; he has simply experienced chance, disorder, and failure—in 1936, during the Spanish Civil War, and in June of 1940. He lives at a time when duties and tasks are unclear. He has a sharper sense of human liberty and of the contingency of the future than anyone has ever had before. Taking everything into account, nothing is certain—not victory, which is still so far away, and not other people. Never before have men had such good evidence that the course of events is full of twists and turns, that much is asked of daring and that they are alone in the world and before one another. But sometimes—in love, in action—a harmony is created among them and events respond to their will. Sometimes there is that flash of fire, that streak of lightning, that moment of victory, or, as Hemingway's Maria says, that *gloria* which in its brilliance blots out everything else.

Except in times of faith when man thinks he finds in things the design of a ready-made destiny, *who can avoid these questions and who can give a different answer?* Or rather, is not faith, stripped of its illusions, itself that very movement which unites us with others, our

6. *For Whom the Bell Tolls*, p. 463.
7. *Ibid.*, p. 466.
8. *Ibid.*, p. 470. [Hemingway's italics.]

present with our past, and by means of which we make everything have meaning, bringing the world's confused talk to an end with a precise word? This is just what the Christian saints and the heroes of past revolutions have always done—although they tried to believe that their fight had already been won in heaven or in History. This resource is not available to the men of today. The contemporary hero is not Lucifer; he is not even Prometheus; he is man.

Bibliographic Note

In their original form, the essays that constitute this volume—with the exception of *Man, the Hero,* which was especially written for *Sens et Non-Sens*—appeared in the following publications:

Cézanne's Doubt (Le Doute de Cézanne), *Fontaine,* No. 47 (December 1945).

Metaphysics and the Novel (Le Roman et la Métaphysique), *Cahiers du Sud,* No. 270 (March 1945).

A Scandalous Author (Un Auteur scandaleux), *Figaro littéraire* (December 6, 1947).

The Film and the New Psychology (Le Cinéma et la Nouvelle Psychologie), *Les Temps modernes,* No. 26 (November 1947).

Hegel's Existentialism (L'Existentialisme chez Hegel), *Les Temps modernes,* No. 7 (April 1946).

The Battle over Existentialism (La Querelle de l'Existentialisme), *Les Temps modernes,* No. 2 (November 1945).

The Metaphysical in Man (Le Métaphysique dans l'Homme), *Revue de métaphysique et de morale,* Nos. 3–4 (July 1947).

Concerning Marxism (Autour de Marxisme), *Fontaine,* Nos. 48–9 (February 1946).

Marxism and Philosophy (Marxisme et Philosophie), *Revue internationale,* Vol. I, No. 6 (June–July 1946).

The War Has Taken Place (La Guerre a eu lieu), *Les Temps modernes,* No. 1 (October 1945).

For the Sake of Truth (Pour la Vérité), *Les Temps modernes,* No. 4 (January 1946).

Faith and Good Faith (Foi et bonne Foi), *Les Temps modernes,* No. 5 (February 1946).

Index